Yerba Buena

Land Grab and Community Resistance in San Francisco

by Chester Hartman, with:

Alvin Averbach
Marsha Berzon
Roger Crawford
Stephen Dutton
Jeffrey Freed
Robert Goodman
Amanda Hawes
Dennis Keating

Robert Kessler
Richard LeGates
Sandra Marks
Michael Narvid
James Reed
Lee Rosenthal
Les Shipnuck
Charles Turner

D1707691

Library of Congress Cataloging in Publication Data

Hartman, Chester W.
    Yerba Buena: land grab and community resistance in San Francisco.
    "A publication of the National Housing and Economic Development Law Project, Earl Warren Legal Institute, University of California, Berkeley."
    1. Urban renewal—San Francisco—Case studies.
2. San Francisco. Yerba Buena Center. I. Title.
HT177.S38H37   309.2′62′0979461   74-6049
ISBN 0-912078-36-7 (case). 0-912078-37-5 (paper).

Copyright © 1974 by the National Housing and Economic
Development Law Project (Earl Warren Legal Institute,
University of California, Berkeley).
Published by Glide Publications, 330 Ellis Street,
San Francisco, California 94102.

Manufactured in the USA
Production: Douglas Mount And Others/David Charlsen
Book design: Jon Goodchild

The research reported herein was performed pursuant to a grant from the Office of Economic Opportunity, Washington, D.C. The opinions expressed herein are those of the authors and should not be construed as representing the opinion or policy of any agency of the United States Government or of the University of California or any institute or project thereof.

A preliminary version of Chapter VI appeared in the November, 1973 *Land Economics*, pp. 440-453, under the title "The Illusion and the Reality of Urban Renewal: A Case Study of San Francisco's Yerba Buena Center", by Robert P. Kessler and Chester W. Hartman.

Contents

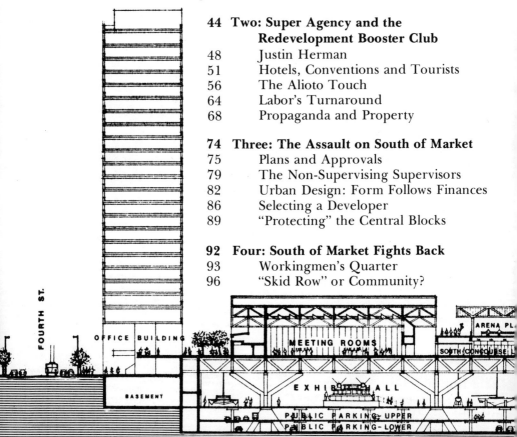

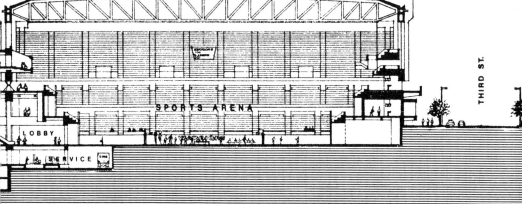

Downtown San Francisco showing current YBC project area

Acknowledgements

As Director of the Third World Fund, I was approached by Glide, a non-profit publishing house, for funding to support their publication of *Yerba Buena*. Since we support only community organizing projects, my initial response was rather negative. After reading the draft by Chester Hartman however, I became fascinated by his research and infuriated at the audacity of the San Francisco Redevelopment Agency and the city's political establishment. While I do not consider myself naive, I was shocked at how easily these so-called leaders and spokespeople of the community at large will sell out the interests of their constituents. At the same time, I was filled with admiration for Tenants and Owners in Opposition to Redevelopment (TOOR) for its unrelenting determination to fight and win under tremendous pressures. Neither TOOR nor its predecessors in the Western Addition renewal area won total victories, but both struggles demonstrated the effectiveness of organizing people to determine their own lives.

Glide Publications, Chester Hartman, Regional Young Adult Project, the Housing Law Center and I have agreed that, subject to OEO approval, royalties from sales of this book will be contributed to TOOR and other organizing groups to support their struggles for decent housing and human dignity. I am pleased to have the opportunity to help bring this story to the general public.

—Ida Strickland, Director
Third World Fund

Since its inception in 1949, at a cost of more than ten billion dollars, the urban renewal program has demolished some 300,000 more housing units than it has produced, most of them the homes of minority people and the poor. Federal relocation housing requirements, although repeatedly strengthened and increased over the years, have been largely evaded through statistical manipulations by local redevelopment agencies and ineffective enforcement by the federal government. Until 1968, jurisdictional technicalities were invoked against displaced persons to deny them even access to the courts. Reluctantly and belatedly their standing to be heard has come to be judicially recognized, and urban renewal relocation plans have now been challenged in cities across the country: Philadelphia, Chicago, New York, Minneapolis, Nashville, Tucson, Seaside (California), Norwalk (Connecticut), Hamtramck (Michigan), Huntington (New York), Keyport (New Jersey) and elsewhere.

The story of Yerba Buena in San Francisco provides a microcosm of these struggles and in a larger sense, a basis for examining both the utility of the downtown renewal approach and the effects of power and powerlessness in urban America.

Acknowledgements

Several considerations underlay the Housing Law Center's† decisions to participate in the Yerba Buena residents' struggle and subsequently to undertake the extensive research that led to this book.

The first and most important purpose in undertaking litigation was to assist the people of that area in asserting their statutory rights to decent, safe and sanitary relocation housing at rents they could afford. In this regard, the litigation was a law enforcement action; it was not law reform. The law was and is simple and clear: redevelopment agencies must demonstrate to the U.S. Department of Housing and Urban Development, as a prior condition to receiving federal funds, that adequate housing meeting federal statutory standards exists for the people who will be uprooted by the project, or that it will be provided. In order to avoid the costs and burdens of providing relocation housing, the San Francisco Redevelopment Agency cynically insisted that sufficient adequate housing already existed. In fact, it did not.

The second purpose of the litigation was to directly challenge the time-honored practice by redevelopment agencies across the country of juggling relocation statistics in order to obtain required HUD approvals. In this context, the Yerba Buena law suit was intended to make clear that a continuation of this pattern and practice would be imprudent. An injunction against further proceeding with a renewal project, issued in the course of redevelopment, and the delays incident thereto, can be expensive.

The third purpose was to document and expose to the public and to Congress and state legislative bodies the destructive effects of urban renewal when, as in San Francisco, statutory replacement housing requirements are evaded. Testimony on the Yerba Buena litigation and similar controversies in other cities was presented to the House Committee on Public Works in 1970 and was instrumental in obtaining

---

†The Housing Law Center, the full name of which is the National Housing and Economic Development Law Project of the Earl Warren Legal Institute, is one of several national "backup centers" established by the Legal Services Program of the Office of Economic Opportunity (OEO). The function of its housing law component, directed by Alvin Hirshen, is to provide specialized information, advice and support, including co-counsel relationships in important ligitation such as Yerba Buena, to legal services lawyers, in the general areas of housing law. Other backup centers perform similar functions in such fields as education, consumer law, health problems, welfare, juvenile law and migrant problems; and a second component of the Housing Law Center serves similar functions in the area of community based economic development. The OEO legal services program provides financial support for approximately 2,000 legal services attorneys who work in neighborhood law offices throughout the country representing low-income people and community organizations in civil matters. Their clients must meet "poverty" eligibility standards established by the individual programs within guidelines issued by OEO.

Acknowledgements

important relocation protections in the Uniform Relocation Assistance and Land Policies Acquisitions Act of 1970. On the other hand, the public at large has yet to fully recognize the social costs imposed by mass destruction of low-income housing to make way for urban renewal, highways and other projects or to become aware of the actions taken by public agencies to subvert relocation laws. San Francisco's two major newspapers, the *Chronicle* and the *Examiner*, portrayed the litigation and TOOR's activities as mindless disruption or worse. Their failure to report and explain the proven facts, together with the importance of documenting the Yerba Buena story, both for its own sake and as a prototype, led to our decision to undertake research for this book.

While the Yerba Buena litigation centered on the narrow factual issue of whether there was or was not adequate relocation housing for displacees, the controversy that arose around the litigation raises broader questions of urban planning, social policy, economics, power relationships and community organizing strategy. This case study attempts a frank and critical examination both of those broader elements and the administrative-political processes by and through which the key decisions are made.

—Kenneth F. Phillips, Director
*National Housing and Economic
Development Law Project*

Regional Young Adult Project, a San Francisco based organization, is dedicated to improving the quality of people's lives by providing information and support for groups such as Tenants and Owners in Opposition to Redevelopment. Our strong commitment to community empowerment and citizen participation in the decision-making process made it logical for us to contribute toward the joint publication of this important book. We feel *Yerba Buena* provides lessons to be learned and significant information to be shared that will help persons in other communities who are confronted with similar redevelopment struggles.

—Herbert N. Allen, Director
Regional Young Adult Project

Preface

> **Finding blight merely means**
> **defining a neighborhood that**
> **cannot effectively fight back,**
> **but which is either an eyesore**
> **or is well-located for some**
> **particular construction that**
> **important interests wish to build . . . .**
> **Urban renewal takes sides;**
> **it uproots and evicts some**
> **for the benefit of others.**
> Lawrence M. Friedman, Professor of Law,
> Stanford University,
> *Government and Slum Housing*, 1968

The idea of writing a book on the Yerba Buena Center urban renewal project took root in March of 1971, on the day a copy of the *American Institute of Planners Newsletter* arrived in my mailbox. The *Newsletter's* lead item was an announcement of the planners' 1971 annual convention the coming October in San Francisco. A photograph accompanying the article depicted an architects' model of YBC, with a typical public relations blurb about this "center city redevelopment to include a sports arena, 800-room hotel, office buildings, and parking for 4,000 cars . . . going up only a few blocks from the San Francisco Hilton." I had just returned from a session of the Yerba Buena Relocation Appeals Board, established by federal court order, on which I was serving as the member selected by Tenants and Owners in Opposition to Redevelopment (TOOR), plaintiff community organization in the neighborhood being bulldozed away for the Center. Throughout these sessions I was seeing vividly the effects of this redevelopment project on the elderly people living in the area, the poor relocation housing they were being offered, and the tactics being used by the San Francisco Redevelopment Agency to clear the area of "undesirables" so that this shiny new downtown could be constructed.

The chamber-of-commerce rhetoric of the *Newsletter* was, I realized, the only image of YBC being presented to the planners and to the outside world; no notice was being taken of the costs the city's poor were being forced to pay for such "progress." The Northern California chapter of the planners' organization had even given Yerba Buena Center an award for its contribution to "urban environmental design." I sat down and wrote an angry letter to the *Newsletter*, describing the project as I saw it, and suggested that when the planners came to San Francisco in October perhaps I could arrange to give them a fuller picture of the project and its impact on the city.

Having made this vague threat, it occurred to me that what I was talking about really had not been done before. Although there are nearly 2,100 urban renewal projects in the country, not a single case-study existed which attempted to cover the myriad economic, social, political and planning/design causes and effects which go to make up a redevelopment project. The process of urban redevelopment, whether undertaken by private developers, the urban renewal program, or federal revenue-sharing and bloc grants, exhibits certain similarities, with respect to origins, goals and implementation. A detailed study of a single large project could provide insights of more general applicability.

Within a few weeks, I gathered a group of knowledgeable and talented people, many of whom were personally involved with the Yerba Buena Center project—particularly the legal, community organizing, and planning/design elements. We agreed to undertake a collaborative research and writing effort to produce a book on YBC and a presentation at the planners' convention. (Our research-in-progress was presented to the October convention as a Citizens' Board of Inquiry on the Yerba Buena Urban Renewal Project.) Despite diverse backgrounds, we shared a common perspective: that Yerba Buena was not a good project in terms of its goals, the political processes that produced and continued to propel it, and the way it was distributing costs and benefits among different elements of the city's population. The University of California's Housing Law Center gave full support to our work by making available the major part of my time, as well as a portion of the time of two other staff members, and by furnishing the funds to hire a small research staff.

Research on the political history of the Yerba Buena project was undertaken by Dennis Keating, an attorney and urban planner on the Housing Law Center staff, and by Marsha Berzon, Michael Narvid and Lee Rosenthal, all law students at the University of California, Berkeley. Rob Kessler, a researcher with the Housing Law Center, analyzed the economics of the project, with the assistance of Rob McBride of the San Jose State University Department of Economics. Amanda Hawes, an attorney with the San Francisco Neighborhood Legal Assistance Foundation, drafted the material on litigation; and Sandra Marks and Steve Dutton, organizers for TOOR, drafted the material on the community's other efforts to oppose the project. Planning and design critiques were the responsibility of Charles Turner and James Reed of the Community Design Center, University of California Extension, and Les Shipnuck, a member of the People's Architecture Collective in Berkeley, assisted by Ron Jonash. Richard LeGates, an attorney and urban planner on the Housing Law Center staff, researched HUD's involvement in the YBC project. The experience of businesses displaced by YBC was studied by Roger Crawford of the San Francisco

Preface

State University Departments of Urban Studies and Geography. The early history of the South of Market area was written by Alvin Averbach. Bob Goodman helped to draft the introduction and concluding chapter. Jeffrey Freed helped organize and formulate our second draft. And finally Frank Shipe worked with me in editing the final draft; the four exhausting but immensely enjoyable and productive weeks we worked together show what a good editor can do to improve an author's manuscript. Overall responsibility for the first and final drafts of the book is, however, exclusively mine.

The Yerba Buena saga spans two decades and is immensely complex. We have provided a Chronology, which precedes the text, to give the reader an overview of the major events. Our primary source of information was personal interviews with virtually every major figure connected with Yerba Buena, in local and federal government and in the private sector. We also examined all relevant reports of official agencies, private organizations, and their consultants; reviewed the minutes of key public agency meetings; and attended dozens of public hearings. Our second most important source of information was the newspapers, and we acknowledge with gratitude the extensive clipping files on San Francisco redevelopment made available to us by John Dykstra of the San Francisco Redevelopment Agency and Edith Witt of the San Francisco Human Rights Commission. Several key participants in the Yerba Buena story were part of our research group and were able to draw on their first-hand experience. Citations to all written sources appear in numbered footnotes at the end of the text; the few uncited quotes are from our interviews or from statements made at public meetings and hearings.

We are grateful to all persons who gave of their time in interviews, phone calls and correspondence relating to our research. In addition, John Kriken provided useful insights into alternative plans for Yerba Buena Center in the course of a studio he and I jointly ran in the Department of Architecture at the University of California, Berkeley, in 1971, and the Richard and Rhoda Goldman Fund provided us with a small grant for exploring such alternatives. James Dombroski undertook research on M. Justin Herman, executive director of the San Francisco Redevelopment Agency from 1959 to 1971. Melvin Mitnick supervised interviews with YBC relocatees during the summer of 1971, and the First Congregational Church of San Francisco kindly provided us with office space for meetings and management of our relocation surveys. Mary Logan, Kathy Jamison and Willa Crowell ably typed the several drafts of the book. The index was prepared by Suzanne Lipsett.

I would also like to thank the following persons for giving us the benefit of their comments and criticisms on earlier drafts: Harry Brill, George V. Denny III, Leonard Duhl, Debbie Dupee, Dan Feshbach,

Preface

Amy Fine, David Gurin, Al Hirshen, Tony Kline, Roger Montgomery, Harriet Older, Dan Pearlman, Ken Phillips, Jon Pynoos, Fred Wirt, Sid Wolinsky.

Finally, it is important to note that the Yerba Buena story is not ended. The outlines of its likely denouement seem clear, but given its long and rocky history, other scenarios are still possible. The uncertainty of the local political situation; the retreat of the federal government from urban renewal funding; the rapid inflation of construction and financing costs; and the possibility of continuing litigation over the project—any or all of these factors could modify Yerba Buena Center radically, or end it altogether. Should this happen, we will be back with "Son of Yerba Buena," to describe and analyze why this occurred and what gives when irresistible forces clash in the city.

Chester Hartman
San Francisco, California
March, 1974

Ira Nowinski

Introduction

**This land is too valuable
to permit poor people to park on it.**
Justin Herman, Executive Director,
San Francisco Redevelopment Agency, 1970

You live it 24 hours a day," Peter Mendelsohn told the
man sitting next to him at the hearing. He was watching a
redevelopment official testifying before a committee of San
Francisco's governing Board of Supervisors. The official was
arguing against a proposal that might rehabilitate a few old
hotels in the South of Market area, downtown, where
Mendelsohn and his friends lived. "You can't help it," Mendelsohn
continued as he listened to the official complaining about the prospect
of having poor people living near his agency's new project, "you can't
help it because that's your life they're playing with."

For Peter Mendelsohn, chairman of Tenants and Owners in Opposition to Redevelopment (TOOR), it was one more meeting in a long,
difficult battle which had begun some six years earlier when the government first approved plans to tear down his neighborhood and replace it with one of the largest urban renewal projects in the country.
Four thousand residents—mostly poor, elderly men—and over 700
small businesses were to be uprooted and their land cleared for what
planners term a "higher and better use": an 87-acre, half-billion dollar
complex of convention and sports facilities, office buildings and parking garages, to be called Yerba Buena Center.

This government-sponsored invasion of San Francisco's South of
Market area was to capture public attention in large part because of its
David and Goliath aspect: the attempt by a small group of seemingly
powerless people and their "poverty lawyers" to bring to a halt, because
of its illegal indiscriminate displacement activities, a massive redevelopment project backed by the city's financial and political power
structure.

For years, redevelopment of the South of Market area has been
aggressively pushed by the city's larger corporations, City Hall, hotel
owners and others in the convention and tourist industry, building and
construction trade unions, and the newspapers and other media. For
these powerful interests, the fight for Yerba Buena Center has been a

Introduction

fight to bring "progress" to San Francisco—more business, more jobs, more conventions, a larger tax base, slum clearance and a revival of the downtown.

Those opposed to Yerba Buena Center see it as the ultimate example of the horrors of urban redevelopment: the conscious destruction of an entire community and the attempt to remove its population from the downtown area and possibly from the city altogether—to make room for bigger business. They claim that the Yerba Buena Center project, together with other downtown and nearby redevelopment undertaken by the city of San Francisco, has systematically destroyed the homes, jobs, and neighborhoods of thousands upon thousands of working-class and poor people, especially racial minorities and the elderly. Their resistance arose out of a realization that in the eyes of official San Francisco, they were no longer welcome or needed.

A detailed anatomy of the Yerba Buena Center project provides important answers about who gains and who loses in the urban redevelopment process, and why. More generally, it reveals who has power in the city, and how and for what purposes this power is wielded. It also analyzes the forms and results of resistance and struggle on the part of those who do not have power. Yerba Buena is really the backdrop for a broader struggle over people's rights to decent housing, over "turf" rights to the city's land, over priorities in urban redevelopment and the ways in which political and economic decisions are made in our cities. In this sense the battle over Yerba Buena Center raises critical issues that have affected or will affect every urban area in the United States.

The South of Market residents and their advocates did manage to stall Yerba Buena Center and gain significant concessions from the power structure. Their achievement has given them the image of victors, and they are justifiably proud of their struggle; but at the same time they see themselves also as losers. A drive through their former community—which now resembles a bombed-out city, pockmarked with parking lots and a few remaining structures—raises questions about such victories: What does "winning" mean? To what extent and at what price did South of Market residents win? And, finally, what lessons are there for other communities faced with similar threats?

Commonly Used Abbreviations

BAC. Bay Area Council
BART. Bay Area Rapid Transit
BCTC. Building and Construction Trades Council
CAO. (San Francisco) Chief Administrative Officer
CDC. (University of California) Community Design Center
CVB. Convention and Visitors Bureau
HEA. Hotel Employers Association
HHFA. (United States) Housing and Home Finance Agency
HUD. (United States) Department of Housing and Urban Development
ILWU. International Longshoremen's and Warehousemen's Union
MAPA. Mexican-American Political Association
NAACP. National Association for the Advancement of Colored People
OEO. (United States) Office of Economic Opportunity
SFNLAF. San Francisco Neighborhood Legal Assistance Foundation
SFRA. San Francisco Redevelopment Agency
SPUR. San Francisco Planning and Urban Renewal Association
TODCo. Tenants and Owners Development Corporation
TOOR. Tenants and Owners in Opposition to Redevelopment
WACO. Western Addition Community Organization
WAPAC. Western Addition Project Area Committee
YBC. Yerba Buena Center

A YBC Chronology

Redevelopment Area D, 1953

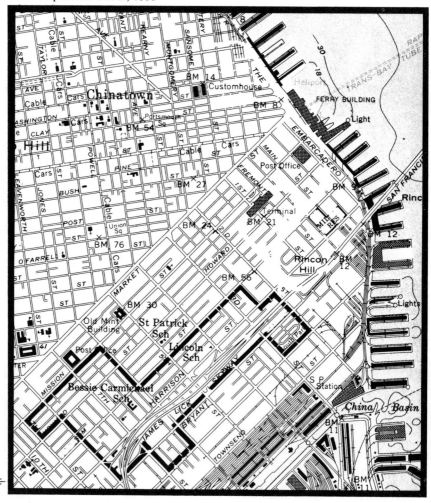

1953

San Francisco Board of Supervisors approves large area South of Market (Area D) as possible redevelopment project under federal urban renewal program.

1954: Ben Swig unveils his "San Francisco Prosperity Plan" for South of Market convention center, sports stadium, high-rise office buildings and 7,000-car parking garage.

1955: City Planning Director Paul Oppermann studies Swig area, finds little blight, and opposes plan as contrary to intent of federal urban renewal program.

Late 1956: Swig plan temporarily dropped due to combined opposition of Oppermann, Mayor George Christopher and federal urban renewal agency.

1959: Blyth-Zellerbach Committee of corporate leaders forms San Francisco Planning and Urban Renewal Association, which immediately begins planning for South of Market slum clearance.

April 1959: Mayor Christopher appoints M. Justin Herman Executive Director of the San Francisco Redevelopment Agency (SFRA).

February 1961: Mayor Christopher asks SFRA to plan for South of Market urban renewal.

1961: SFRA applies for federal urban renewal survey and planning grant for area including but slightly larger than Swig plan area and nearer central business district.

October 1962: U. S. Housing and Home Finance Agency (HHFA) approves $600,000 planning grant for YBC.

February 1964: SFRA unveils Yerba Buena Center plans and applies to HHFA for urban renewal grant reservation.

June 1965: HHFA announces it is setting aside $19.6 million grant for Yerba Buena Center.

Chronology

January 1966: Planning Commission unanimously approves YBC plan.

April 1966: Board of Supervisors approves YBC plan, 9-2.

December 1966: SFRA signs loan and grant contract with Department of Housing and Urban Development (HUD—successor to HHFA).

July 1967: SFRA, in preparation for YBC, begins displacing residents and demolishing buildings.

September 1967: Mayor John Shelley abruptly abandons re-election campaign. One and a half hours later former Redevelopment Agency Chairman Joseph Alioto announces candidacy.

November 1967: Alioto elected through campaign financed by Ben Swig and other downtown interests.

Late 1968: Acting on Milner Hotel residents' complaints of poor quality relocation offerings and maltreatment by Agency relocation workers, San Francisco Neighborhood Legal Assistance Foundation (SFNLAF) attorneys petition HUD for administrative hearing on SFRA's YBC relocation plan. HUD denies the petition.

Spring 1969: YBC residents and attorneys again petition HUD for hearing on relocation plan, warning that unless hearing is granted they will file suit to enjoin the project. HUD contends it has no mechanism for hearing relocatees' complaints.

June 1969: SFRA unveils design for YBC Central Blocks: 350,000 square-foot convention center-exhibition hall, 14,000 seat sports arena, 800 room hotel, 2,200 seat theater, 4,000 car parking garage, Italian Cultural and Trade Center, airlines terminal, office buildings, shops, pedestrian mall.

Summer 1969: YBC residents meet at Milner Hotel and form Tenants and Owners in Opposition to Redevelopment (TOOR).

November 1969: TOOR, alleging displacees are being deprived of decent relocation housing guaranteed under 1949 Housing Act, files complaint and motion for federal injunction against HUD and SFRA.

December 1969: Federal Judge Stanley A. Weigel issues restraining order against SFRA, temporarily halting relocation and demolition.

April 1970: Judge Weigel issues injunction against Yerba Buena Center cutting off all federal funding by July 1 if SFRA does not satisfactorily revise its relocation plan.

September 1970: SFRA moves to end injunction on grounds it has prepared and HUD has approved a revised relocation plan based on Agency-commissioned vacancy survey and the Housing Authority's offer to give YBC relocatees "superpriority" for public housing.

November 1970: Justin Herman signs consent decree committing SFRA to build or rehabilitate 1,500-1,800 units of low-rent housing anywhere in the city by November, 1973, and to retain several

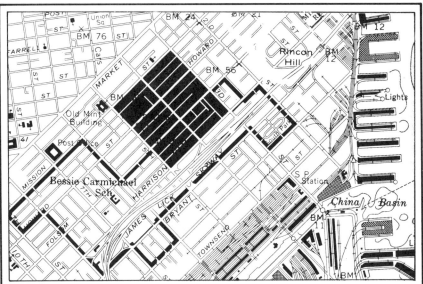

Ben Swig's revised "San Francisco Prosperity Plan," 1955

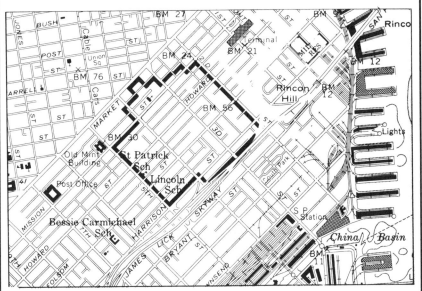

SFRA project area outlined in application for Federal
Survey and Planning Grant, 1961

Chronology

project area hotels as temporary "hostages." Judge Weigel lifts injunction but retains jurisdiction over implementation of consent decree.

June 1971:   TOOR files for second preliminary injunction, citing both SFRA's lack of progress in producing the 1,500-1,800 units and Housing Authority's withdrawal of "superpriority" policy for YBC relocatees.

June 1971:   HUD advises court it wishes to review YBC relocation plan. Judge Weigel orders HUD to report the results of its review within 60 days and for the interim reimposes the April, 1970 restrictions on displacement and demolition.

August 1971:   HUD files report with the court, concluding "there are not now nor will there be sufficient rehousing resources to allow the relocation of Yerba Buena Center residents to continue unabated." HUD orders SFRA to file within 120 days a refined, updated relocation plan and forbids relocation or demolition during this period without HUD permission.

August 1971:   Justin Herman dies.

January 1972:   HUD rejects SFRA's revised relocation plan.

January 1972:   Alvin Duskin brings suit against YBC in state court for failure to comply with the California Environmental Quality Act and other alleged defects.

January 1972: Sierra Club and other conservation groups bring federal suits against YBC for failure to comply with the National Environmental Policy Act.

March 1972:   Board of Supervisors passes SFRA financing plan for YBC public facilities, which calls for up to $225 million in Agency lease revenue bonds.

April 1972:   Gerald Wright files taxpayers' suit in state court, challenging SFRA financing plan as illegal circumvention of constitutional requirements governing general obligation bond issues.

June 1972:   Supreme Court Justice William Douglas enjoins YBC pending full hearing by Ninth Circuit Court on Sierra Club lawsuit.

July 1972:   HUD rejects SFRA's re-revised relocation plan as "lacking clarity."

July 1972:   Judge Weigel denies TOOR's move for a renewed injunction, citing in part the injunction Justice Douglas has issued. Weigel expresses doubts SFRA will produce the 1,500-1,800 units, citing its own admission that only eleven have been completed to date, and orders the Agency to submit detailed quarterly progress reports.

August 1972:   In its first progress report SFRA proposes using city hotel tax to subsidize YBC relocation housing, since federal rent supplement funds will not cover the city's full obligation.

October 1972: HUD approves SFRA's new and final YBC relocation plan.

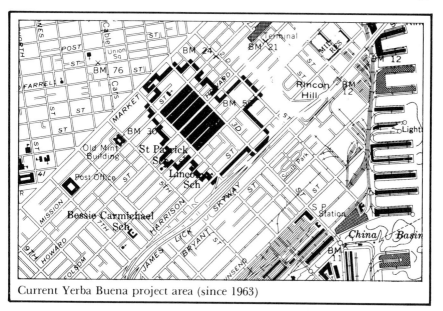

Current Yerba Buena project area (since 1963)

October 1972:   Board of Supervisors approves half percent increase in hotel tax to subsidize YBC replacement housing.

January 1973: Ninth Circuit Court dismisses Sierra Club suit, ruling the National Environmental Policy Act not applicable to YBC since federal funds contracted prior to enactment of the statute.

January 1973:   Alioto advisor William Coblentz convenes settlement discussions with TOOR and SFRA to fashion settlement that will induce TOOR to drop its suit, since suit could with appeals delay project at least two additional years.

May 1973:   TOOR and SFRA sign agreement whereby, in exchange for dropping its suit, TOOR will be assured that SFRA will develop 400 low-rent housing units on four YBC sites, in addition to the 1,500-1,800 units (in other parts of the city) already promised. TOOR will form housing development corporation to sponsor the 400 units, and deadline for the 1,500-1,800 units extended to November, 1974.

July 1973:   Judge Weigel approves TOOR-SFRA agreement and dismisses TOOR suit. Any breach in stipulations can be brought before Judge Weigel once again.

November 1973:   SFRA files in Superior Court,for dismissal of the Duskin and Wright suits on financing and environmental aspects of YBC. As of March, 1974, no progress made toward removing these roadblocks.

19??:   The two thousand units of low-rent replacement housing, and Yerba Buena Center, are completed.

1. The Master Planners

Downtown San Francisco, facing southeast

SFRA

**Our notions of what is wrong and what is right ·
in urban life are so misdirected that a reasonable man
could not be faulted for believing the Devil himself
has been called in as planning director . . .
I've only been a resident since 1955; but I've watched
a real city turn plastic in that time.**
Charles McCabe, *San Francisco Chronicle* columnist, 1974

Yerba Buena Center has its origins and *raison d'etre* in the evolving role of San Francisco and the Bay Area in the nation's corporate economy—a growth spurred by World War II and accelerated in the 1950s and 1960s.

Once celebrated as a quaint city of relaxed and sophisticated attitude, San Francisco has now emerged as a financial launching pad of significant proportions. Corporate giants have consolidated and grown there, and have constructed monumental office towers to house their developing concerns. Oriental trade and Western American business have boomed, and banking and insurance expansion has paralleled the progressions in California's population growth.[1]

The city is now headquarters for such corporate giants as Standard Oil of California, Southern Pacific, Transamerica Corporation, Crown Zellerbach, Utah International, Del Monte, Foremost-McKesson, Potlatch Forests, Levi Strauss, the Bechtel Corporation, Pacific Telephone and Telegraph, and Pacific Gas and Electric. Among the major financial institutions headquartered in San Francisco are Bank of America (the nation's largest bank), Wells Fargo, Crocker National Bank, Bank of California, and Fireman's Fund American Insurance. The increasing importance of Bay Area national and multinational corporations in the domestic economy and in international trade and military relations has created a need to enlarge substantially the administrative and service functions carried out within the city; and hence, the amount of land needed for office buildings. The planning and implementation of YBC is tied to the broader goals and strategems of the region's economic powers and their political counterparts. Recognition of this broader context is necessary to an understanding of the YBC saga.

West Coast cities have always been the launching points for United States advances into the Pacific region, and since the mid-nineteenth century Pacific wars and conquest have provided a powerful stimulus to their economic growth. The Pacific Coast has not only profited by

The Master Planners

serving as a base for the shipment of war-related personnel and goods, but has also reaped the larger corollary spoils of war: United States conquests in the War of 1898 led to a new flow of goods between the western states and new markets in Central and South America, the Philippines, and China. The increasing number of U.S. allies and neo-colonies through World War II and the Korean War furnished additional markets for North American corporations and financial institutions. And most recently, the high level of technology used in the Vietnam War led to an influx of billions of federal dollars annually into the West Coast and stimulated a boom in electronics, aerospace and related industries. As described in a report from the Wells Fargo Bank:

> *Geographically, San Francisco is a natural gateway for this country's ocean-going and air-borne commerce with the Pacific area nations. Trade with Asian nations is gaining in importance especially relative to Europe . . . . The most important stimulus to San Francisco's economic base has been the increasing U.S. involvement in this century in Asian geopolitics with the concurrent buildup in armament production . . . and large gains in foreign trade.*[2]

The lure of the Pacific Rim for West Coast corporations and financial institutions was clearly expressed in 1968 by Rudolph Peterson, President of the Bank of America and a director of the Dillingham Corporation (which, fittingly, was scheduled to be named developer of Yerba Buena Center before bowing out for internal reasons):

> *When I speak of the Pacific Rim, I am putting the broadest possible construction on the term—the western coasts of South America, Central America, and our own continent, and extending beyond Australia and the Far East to India. There is no more vast or rich area for resource development or trade growth in the world today than this immense region, and it is virtually our own front yard . . . . Were we California businessmen to play a more dynamic role in helping trade development in the Pacific Rim, we would have giant, hungry new markets for our products and vast new profit potentials for our firms.*[3]

In the effort to exploit these hungry new markets and vast new profit potentials, the Bay Area is now being developed and organized into specialized, coordinated functions. The Peninsula and South Bay area is the concentration for light manufacturing, electronics, and the aerospace industry; the East Bay is the locus for heavier industry, chemicals and petroleum, and also serves as the regional transportation hub; and San Francisco itself is the center for administration, finance, consulting, and entertainment. Linking the administrative heart of this regional economic unit with its industrial and residential satellites are a network of high-speed freeways and the new Bay Area Rapid Transit system (BART). (The function of the $1.5 billion BART system is to bring suburban workers into the downtown center; within San Francisco BART has only four stations outside the downtown area, and

The Master Planners

whole areas of the city, including most of its lower income population, are not served by it.) *Know* ↓

The consequences of such regional organization for downtown San Francisco are clear. With respect to employment, service industry replaces manufacturing. The number of San Franciscans employed in the professional-technical categories rose 13% in the 1950s, 38% in the 1960s, and in the clerical category the 1950s increase was 9%, the 1960s increase 16%. On the other hand, the number of San Franciscans employed as craftsmen and foremen dropped 20% in the 1950s, 18% in the 1960s, and those employed as laborers decreased 18% in the 1950s and 19% in the 1960s.[4] This in turn produces the changes now in evidence throughout the city—a tremendous increase in high-rise office buildings and hotels, the destruction of low- and moderate-rent housing, and a continuing exodus of blue-collar workers and lower-middle class families. These changes have also been accompanied by a general deterioration in the city's public services, such as transit, education, public housing, health, and welfare.

During the 1960s a vast amount of new office construction in San Francisco's financial center literally changed the city's skyline. From 1960 to 1972, 23 high-rises totaling 598 floors and 9.6 million square feet were built in this relatively small area by such corporate and financial giants as Bethlehem Steel, Pacific Telephone and Telegraph, John Hancock, Wells Fargo, Hartford Insurance, Foremost-McKesson, Alcoa, Bank of California, Great Western Savings, Bank of America, Crocker Bank, Aetna Life, Transamerica, Mutual Benefit Life, Pacific Insurance, and Union Bank.[5] The decade has aptly been described as the "Manhattanization" of San Francisco.[6]

In the context of this development the role of Yerba Buena Center is obvious. If San Francisco is to be increasingly a regional, national, and international service center, its central business district must expand in area. As one executive put it, "The people who run these [financial and corporate] centers want all their services, the people they work with —advertisers, attorneys, accountants around them. It's a complete part of the way we do business in this country."[7]

It was correctly foreseen as far back as the 1950s that the city's relatively small office district could not accommodate the amount of building required in the coming decades. Expansion westward was impossible, since in that direction lay the city's prime retail and hotel area, plus difficult, hilly topography. To the north lay the internally strong residential communities of Chinatown and North Beach, and more hills. A moderate expansion eastward toward the Bay was possible in the area then occupied by the city's wholesale produce market. But if there was to be a substantial increase in the central office district, it would have to expand to the south, across 120-foot wide Market Street, traditionally

The Master Planners

San Francisco skyline photographed from the same position on the bay

the city's "Great Divide."† The South of Market area offered flat land with low-intensity usage, low land prices, and to the corporate eye, economically expendable people and businesses.

A land-use transformation of this magnitude, however—taking over an entire section of the downtown, evicting its occupants, demolishing the existing structures, and converting the land to a different use —requires careful preparation, specialized skills, and most important, a legal and political base of operations. The federal-local urban renewal program, with its powers of eminent domain, land-cost and clearance subsidies, and battery of planners and other technicians, proved the ideal vehicle for downtown expansion. The easier eastward move was accomplished first via the Golden Gateway renewal project, which replaced the produce market with an office headquarters and prestige residential complex (see pages 36-37). Yerba Buena Center represented the "blockbusting" wedge for the more substantial and critical expansion southward.

Corporate Collectivity

All the details of the early planning leading to massive downtown redevelopment projects such as Yerba Buena Center may never be known, but in San Francisco the basic outline is clear. It began during World War II, with the city already thriving as a major trade and financial center. Throughout the war Bay Area business leaders had learned the value of concentration and regional planning for efficient economic organization. Their efforts in this direction were coordinated by the wartime Metropolitan Defense Committee. MDC was the Bay Area's first regional planning agency and held responsibility for fire prevention, law enforcement, health and safety, and transportation. Composed of political appointees and influential citizens (mainly businessmen), it made many region-wide decisions affecting transportation systems, workers' housing, and the location of industrial facilities.

MDC's main drawback was bickering among competing local interests, which by 1944 paralyzed operations and led to a cut-off in federal funding.[8] Regionalism, if it was to work, had to be based on forces more substantial than petty politics. Nonetheless, this wartime

---

† One of the key steps in the planning of the YBC project, in fact, was creation of the so-called "Market Street Breakthrough," extending the project area slightly northward to create an entry to YBC from the North of Market area. The November 28, 1962 *Examiner* quotes a Board of Supervisors committee as calling Market Street "a physical and psychological barrier to the orderly development of South of Market." The story continues, "The South of Market Advisory Committee thus outlined yesterday one of the biggest problems it faces in trying to restore economic life South of Market."

The Master Planners

economic activity established a working model and paved the way for subsequent and more sophisticated modes of regional coordination and planning.

Out of the MDC and the State Reconstruction and Reemployment Commission came the establishment in 1944 of the Bay Regional Council (in 1945 to undergo a permanent name change to the Bay Area Council). The Bay Area Council is essentially the organized muscle of the region's corporate power structure, established to coordinate and plan over the entire Bay Area those functions especially important to the efficient conduct of business.† It is a form of private regional government providing direction in areas where the maze of local governments might prevent efficient government action. In the words of one Council representative: "From a business point of view it makes the greatest common sense to organize the Bay Area on a political basis that corresponds to economic reality."[9]

To insure that economic reality would prevail, the BAC was organized around the corporations and financial institutions which dominate the West's economy and are increasingly oriented toward the Pacific Basin. Six of them—Bank of America, American Trust Company, Standard Oil of California, Pacific Gas and Electric, U.S. Steel and the Bechtel Corporation—each pledged $10,000 annually to provide the Council with some operating funds. The BAC's initial board of directors consisted of: Frank N. Belgrano, president, Central Bank of Oakland; R. E. Fisher, vice president, Pacific Gas and Electric; Stephen D. Bechtel, president and senior director, Bechtel Corporation;[10] Adrien Falk, vice president, S & W Foods, president of BART; Paul Davies, chairman of the board, Foremost-McKesson Corporation; J. B. Dupau, vice president, U. S. Steel; and C. D. Lafferty, industrial agent, Southern Pacific Railroad.

The Council's work focused primarily on transportation and industrial location. Through sponsoring studies, issuing reports, and holding occasional conferences, the BAC pushed for development of airports, freeways and bridges in the area, all laid out in master plans the Council published and lobbied for. BAC was also the primary planner and lobbyist for the BART system. BAC-published industrial location surveys and directories helped to distribute the various economic functions "rationally" throughout the region. It has also involved itself in the issue of air pollution, fostering the notion of voluntary industry cooperation rather than legal regulation.

† "The Council has served as an influencial [sic] 'private chamber of commerce' since that time [1945], and has been an important force in creating an environment amenable to big business in the Bay Area." (BART Impact Studies Final Report Series, *op. cit.*, p. 27.)

Bay area council = corp comm'y fdn. comm'y

The BAC has been a strong supporter of urban redevelopment in the Bay Area. It is of course vitally interested in nourishing the role of San Francisco as the brains and heart of this regional economic unit, for as one of the few studies of its operations notes, "the policy-makers of the Council are primarily officers of large corporations located in San Francisco."[11] Since urban redevelopment must be carried out on the local level by local bodies, the regional structure and image of the Bay Area Council are inappropriate, and local committees involving Council members are more effective.

In San Francisco such a local group was the Blyth-Zellerbach Committee, formed in 1956 by Charles Blyth, a prominent stockbroker and director of the Hewlett-Packard electronics firm, Crown-Zellerbach Corporation, and the Stanford Research Institute. Joining Blyth was J. D. Zellerbach, the pulp and paper magnate.

The immediate impetus to form the Blyth-Zellerbach Committee was the redevelopment potential of the city's wholesale produce market just east of the financial district. The colorful market area, with its stalls, narrow passageways and early morning shouting and human bustle, was run-down and congested to the point of inefficiency. Business and political figures were placing enormous pressure on the wholesalers to move to a more outlying location.

Among those interested in undertaking a massive redevelopment plan for the area was William Zeckendorf of Webb and Knapp, the mammoth New York development firm. In late 1955 Zeckendorf offered to put up $250,000 in planning funds, with the proviso that if the city adopted his plan he would be given the right to purchase 75 percent of the land in the area (and that if the city and Zeckendorf could not agree on a price and the land was awarded to another developer, the successful bidder would have to reimburse Webb and Knapp for its planning costs). In an attempt to forestall this move by eastern money and insure development of the area in accord with local corporate interests, the Blyth-Zellerbach Committee was formed and immediately made a gift of $25,000 to the City Planning Department for an "objective" evaluation of the situation in the produce market area. Several months later a second gift for a similar amount was made. According to Blyth, no personal interest was involved: "We're just a group of fellows devoted to San Francisco."[12] Virtually every one of the fellows, however, was also a member of the Bay Area Council Executive Board.†

---

† Aside from Blyth and Zellerbach, the original members were: Ralph Gwin Follis, former chairman of the board, Standard Oil of California; S. Clark Beise, president, Bank of America; Stephen Bechtel, president and senior director, Bechtel Corporation; Donald J. Russel, president, Southern

The Master Planners

A key element of the Blyth-Zellerbach Committee's operation has
been its low profile. According to a *San Francisco Examiner* account:

*Big financial interests are waiting in the wings, impatient for the city to cut
red tape and begin redevelopment of the old wholesale produce district, it was
revealed yesterday.*

*The disclosure came from Roger Lapham Jr., president of the city planning
commission.*

*Lapham said private financiers have been attracted by members of the Blyth-
Zellerbach committee of prominent San Francisco businessmen, which contributed nearly $50,000 to prepare a redevelopment plan for the 28-block produce
district.* [13]

A subsequent article in *Business Week* stated: "Zellerbach and his col-
laborators have no bylaws, no written policy, no executive director, and
keep no minutes. They regard the absence of such organizational trap-
pings as prerequisite to their operations."[14] The explanation for this,
according to the same article, is to avoid "the epithetical label of 'big
business control'." Insofar as possible, this group representing powerful corporate interests adopted a style and posture that would avoid
publicity and enable achievement of their common goals without facing
public exposure and criticism. And as *Business Week* also noted, "It is
the corporations, really, rather than the executives that comprise the
B-Z Committee." Thus, when Charles Blyth died and Mark Sullivan
retired, they were replaced by Roy L. Shurtleff of Blyth and Company,
and Carl O. Lindeman, Sullivan's successor as president of Pacific
Telephone and Telegraph.

The intervention of the Blyth-Zellerbach Committee in the produce
market question served to force Zeckendorf out of the picture and
resulted in a plan which ultimately became the Golden Gateway, a
51-acre luxury residential and corporate headquarters zone. The project, begun in 1959 and not yet completed, includes the Embarcadero
Center (a five-block high-rise office and hotel complex), the Alcoa
Building, assorted shops, and a mass of pedestrian platforms and out-
door sculpture, all built through urban renewal subsidies. At this writing over 1,200 luxury apartment and town-house units have been built,
with 1,300 more scheduled for development. (Rents range from $200

Pacific Railroad; Ransom M. Cook, president, Levi Strauss; Mark Sullivan,
former president, Pacific Telephone and Telegraph; James K. Lochead, pres-
ident, American Trust Company; Emmett Solomon, vice president, Provident
Security (later president, Crocker-Citizens National Bank); George Granville
Montgomery, chairman of the board, Kern County Land Company, director,
Wells Fargo-American Trust Company; James B. Black, president, Pacific Gas
and Electric; Atholl Bean, president, Gladding-McBean and Company; Jerd F.
Sullivan, chairman of the board, Crocker-Citizens National Bank.

Corporate Collectivity

for studio apartments to $700 for town houses, and a private swimming and tennis club for residents occupies a key site near the waterfront.) The work of the Blyth-Zellerbach Committee thus paid off handsomely in terms of developing a plan for the produce market consistent with corporate interests and at the same time benefiting local investors.

While the Blyth-Zellerbach Committee did serve its purpose as a stimulator of plans for San Francisco redevelopment, its somewhat covert character had limitations. Corporate interests needed a group which could more openly take definitive and active stands; this would be particularly important as drawing-board proposals came up for public approval and the search for funds began. To fill this need, the Committee in 1959 fathered the San Francisco Planning and Urban Renewal Association (SPUR).

SPUR was devised to generate more "citizen" (read business) support for urban renewal. The first step toward its creation came in early 1959 when the Blyth-Zellerbach Committee sponsored and paid for a report on the city's redevelopment program by Philadelphia city planning consultant Aaron Levine. The commissioning and release of the report were widely publicized and praised in the newspapers. Levine's conclusions were not surprising: San Francisco was way behind other large cities in redevelopment, was badly in need of leadership and improved staff for its Redevelopment Agency, and required substantial support from the business community for its redevelopment program. In Levine's own words, "The Blyth-Zellerbach Committee is the logical group in San Francisco to assume this role."[15] Out of the Levine report came SPUR.

In its first three years, SPUR's financing came completely from the Blyth-Zellerbach Committee and related business interests. The committee originally pledged $30,000 a year, and after three years committed itself to funding one-half the SPUR budget, the other half to come from membership dues and private institutions. (The committee has maintained its central support of SPUR; in 1972 it contributed $66,000, nearly two-thirds of the organization's annual budget.†)

Several directors of SPUR were, of course, from either the Blyth-Zellerbach Committee or the Bay Area Council. For example, SPUR's first board chairman was Jerd Sullivan, a trustee of BAC, director of both Crocker-Citizens Bank and Del Monte Properties, and also vice president of the Fairmont Hotel Company. SPUR's 1960-1961 chair-

---

† In 1972 the Blyth-Zellerbach Committee consisted of the following corporate giants: Bank of America, the Bechtel Corporation, Blyth & Co., Crocker Bank, Crown Zellerbach, Del Monte, Fireman's Fund Insurance Co., Pacific Telephone and Telegraph, Joseph Magnin Co., Levi Strauss, Pacific Gas & Electric Co., Roth Properties, Standard Oil of California, Stauffer Chemical Co., Southern Pacific, and the Wells Fargo Bank.

The Master Planners

man was John Merrill, a board member of the San Francisco Redevelopment Agency from 1957-1959, a director of the Blyth-Zellerbach Committee and the Chamber of Commerce, president of an engineering research firm, and a director of both the Arthur D. Little Company and Pacific Telephone and Telegraph. John Hirten, SPUR's first executive director, was a trustee of BAC. Another SPUR director was William Zellerbach.

SPUR immediately focused on redevelopment south of Market Street. According to the February 13, 1960 *Examiner*:

The Planning and Urban Renewal Association took dead aim on the "most blighted area in San Francisco" yesterday with a project for co-ordinated private-public redevelopment of the South of Market St. district.

Calling together civic and business leaders as a "steering committee," association chairman Jerd F. Sullivan Jr. announced a preliminary plan would be worked up for clearing the slums out of an area roughly bounded by Fourth, Minna, Hawthorne, and Harrison Sts. [similar to the eventual boundaries of Yerba Buena Center].

Throughout 1960, SPUR cooperated closely with the San Francisco Redevelopment Agency in holding a series of meetings involving businessmen and influential citizens who favored downtown commercial redevelopment. In December of that year, Mayor George Christopher designated SPUR as the city's official "citizens' group" for urban renewal, a body required under federal urban renewal laws. This "citizen" support shortly thereafter led the mayor to request formally that the Redevelopment Agency involve itself in South of Market urban renewal. According to the February 6, 1961, *San Francisco News*:

Mayor George Christopher yesterday asked the Redevelopment Agency to take another look at the South of Market area . . . . The recommendation to restudy South of Market redevelopment came from John L. Merrill, president of the San Francisco Planning and Urban Renewal Association. This is a citizens group that promotes redevelopment activity.

Ben Swig's Dream

SPUR's entry into planning for South of Market redevelopment in reality took the form of reviving a proposal put forward six years earlier by one of the city's more fabulous proposers and disposers, Ben Swig. This man's dream was the specific starting point for Yerba Buena Center.

Benjamin Harrison Swig is a Bostonian who emigrated to San Francisco in the 1940s, arriving already wealthy from dealings in hotels and real estate.[16] His rise to wealth had been a model story of the self-made man, as he amassed a fortune through real estate and land speculation in the 1920s and 1930s. Although hit hard by the Depression, Swig had

Ben Swig's Dream

kept on wheeling and dealing, concentrating on land brokerage for such chain-store developments as Kress, Woolworth, and J. C. Penney. He emerged a partner in a large New York real estate firm, and with a reputation as a "super-broker" who often conducted 20 to 30 deals simultaneously. By the end of World War II Swig and his partner, J. D. Weiler, were considered the biggest individual real estate dealers in the country.

Within a short time after his arrival in San Francisco, Swig had acquired the prestigious Fairmont Hotel atop Nob Hill, the St. Francis and Bellevue hotels, and other valuable downtown properties. Swig was also a man who cultivated powerful friends and soon became a major Democratic Party fund-raiser and contributor. Besides his wealth and power, he was also a philanthropist *par excellence*, and by 1954 was in a position to assume that San Franciscans would listen when he spoke.†

What Swig was speaking about in 1954 was his vision of massive clearance and commercial redevelopment South of Market. The original Swig plan, soon dubbed the "San Francisco Prosperity Plan," was prepared by local architect John Carl Warnecke. It covered four blocks and called for the construction thereon of a convention center, baseball and football stadium, high-rise office buildings, and parking for 7,000 cars. Swig enlarged the grand scheme in 1955 by adding two adjacent blocks and inserting a transportation terminal, a large luxury hotel with convention facilities, an auditorium and theater, moving sidewalks, a shopping center complete with a network of malls and fountains like Manhattan's Rockefeller Center, and increased parking—for 16,000 cars.

With characteristic energy, Swig moved into action mobilizing resources behind his development scheme. He found some support within the city's political apparatus and then embarked upon winning over businessmen by speaking before numerous civic and business organizations like the Chamber of Commerce and the prestigious Commonwealth Club.

Yet even with substantial support from political and business figures, as well as from the newspapers, Swig's plans ran into trouble. The

---

† A recent study of political influence notes about Ben Swig: " 'You can't be elected dogcatcher here without his blessing,' claims one San Francisco political observer." G. William Domhoff, *Fat Cats and Democrats* (Englewood Cliffs, N. J.: Prentice-Hall, 1972), p. 72. Another study of San Francisco politics notes: "A close observer and business official thought Swig 'practically never fails to get what he wants. I can't remember when he failed.' " See Frederick M. Wirt, *Politics In the City: Decision-Making in San Francisco* (Berkeley and Los Angeles: University of California Press, forthcoming), p. 306 (page reference to draft copy.)

Ben Swig and admirers

Ben Swig and Pres. L.B. Johnson

Governor Brown, Ben Swig and
Pres. J.F. Kennedy

By courtesy of Benjamin Swig

Melvin M. Swig, Betty Swig Dinner, Benjamin H. Swig, Dr. A.L. Sachar, Pres.
of Brandeis University, and Richard L. Swig

major flaw in the "San Francisco Prosperity Plan" was that neither Swig nor any of his friends controlled the site of the proposed development. Without the land, the scheme was just so much paper. Here, as in so many similar situations, the ideal solution seemed to be the urban renewal program with its land acquisition subsidies and powers of eminent domain. But the renewal program was available only for "blighted" areas, and according to the City Planning Department Swig's original four blocks did not qualify for such designation.

The city's Board of Supervisors earlier, in 1953, had approved a large area South of Market, known as Area D, as a possible urban renewal project; however, this area was farther from Market Street and the central business district (see maps, pages 22, 25) and thus less attractive from a private developer's point of view than the blocks Swig proposed for clearance. Paul Oppermann, the city's Planning Director, had made two studies of the Swig area and reported that two of the four original blocks were only ten percent blighted (the two blocks Swig added to his original four in 1955 presented no problem, as they were part of the approved Area D). It was Oppermann's opinion that to use the redevelopment process to erect the center in Swig's area would be a perversion of the purpose of urban renewal, and he recommended that redevelopment of that area be left to the private market. Mayor George Christopher—a Republican, whereas Swig and his allies were mostly Democrats—tended to agree with Oppermann, thus compounding Swig's obstacles. A small businessman, Christopher was not, at least during his first term (1956-1959†), an enthusiastic supporter of urban renewal on a large scale.

Swig, however, was persistent. To encourage the city to designate his six blocks eligible for urban renewal, he even made one of his many charitable donations, this one to the San Francisco Redevelopment Agency to finance preliminary planning studies (a donation which the Agency accepted but later turned back to Swig). According to the new board chairman of the Redevelopment Agency, a young, dynamic downtown lawyer named Joseph Alioto, the purpose of the study was "to find the most expeditious way of declaring the area of Mr. Swig's interest a blighted area."[17] Swig's claims about the public benefits of his "San Francisco Prosperity Plan" and the justification for using government aids were somewhat weakened by his statement that "This is a straight business proposition . . . . I think I'm going to make a lot of

---

† Mayoral elections in San Francisco are held in the year preceding Presidential election years; the mayor takes office on the first or second Monday of the following January. In this book, the designated mayoral terms begin with the inauguration year and end with the year in which the new election takes place.

The Master Planners

money out of it, or I wouldn't be spending all this time on it."[18]

Swig also had been instrumental in bringing William Zeckendorf to San Francisco, to stimulate grand thoughts about South of Market development. (Zeckendorf, however, proved far more interested in the produce market area North of Market, as previously noted, and began to operate independent of Swig.) In December, 1955, Swig, Zeckendorf, and Alioto were able to convince the Board of Supervisors to redraw the boundaries of Area D to include Swig's original four blocks, thereby approving the Agency's similar action the previous October. ("I don't care what Oppermann's conclusions are," said Alioto.)[19] Swig even went so far as to offer to loan the Redevelopment Agency the $12 million he estimated it would need for land acquisition costs, thereby substituting himself for the federal urban renewal agency should the latter prove uncooperative about approving his plans.[20] Oppermann, however, based on his planning studies and his understanding of the urban renewal program, maintained his strong opposition to the Swig plan. Swig was incensed by the planner's attitude and told a Kiwanis Club luncheon, "Private capital knows a great deal better than city planners. I say to our city fathers, 'stop planning, stop thinking, but go out and do something right away'."[21]

In the end, however, Swig had to capitulate to the combined opposition of the Christopher administration, Oppermann, and the federal urban renewal agency, which was unenthusiastic about the plan and at the time did not have an abundance of grant money to hand out. By late 1956 Ben Swig's dream was for all immediate purposes dead.

The Planning Commission and Board of Supervisors subsequently removed the blight designation from half of Area D in order to allow a group of landowners within the area to try to put together a plan of their own; and Oppermann, with the unenthusiastic concurrence of the Redevelopment Agency, prepared an industrial spot clearance renewal plan for that part of Area D which was most blighted, south of Swig's area and farther from the central business district. But there was little dynamism behind this plan, and although the Supervisors adopted it in mid-1957, it was rejected a few months later by the federal urban renewal agency—effectively freezing redevelopment South of Market for several years.

In the long run, although Swig's specific plan was not adopted, it did set the course for succeeding plans for South of Market redevelopment: to begin renewal in the area closest to the central business district, irrespective of "blight" conditions; to rely primarily on the bulldozer approach to renewal; and to construct in the area a massive convention-sports-office center.

In the mid-1950s the corporate powers of the Bay Area had not yet mobilized themselves to plan fully for their future needs and establish the necessary apparatus to carry out their plans. In terms of operating style, background and economic position, Ben Swig was not an integral part of the region's corporate power structure. As powerful and dynamic an individual as he was, he could not unite the forces necessary to pull off his scheme for South of Market redevelopment. Ben Swig failed to realize his original dream, but once the need for expansion of the financial district South of Market was embraced by the broader group, his plan was revived, this time with the necessary government and private support and intervention to make it a reality. Swig and his sons continued to play a role in some aspects of the project, but the driving force passed to other hands. The impetus for redevelopment South of Market was to be resurrected in the early 1960s, through the efforts of the Blyth-Zellerbach Committee, SPUR, and a revitalized urban renewal agency.

If San Francisco decides to compete effectively with other cities for new "clean" industries and new corporate power, its population will move closer to "standard White Anglo-Saxon Protestant" characteristics. As automation increases the need of unskilled labor will decrease. Economically and socially, the population will tend to range from lower middle-class through lower upper-class . . . .

Selection of a population's composition might be undemocratic. Influence on it, however, is legal and desirable for the health of the city. A workable though changing balance of economic levels, social types, age levels, and other factors must be maintained. Influence on these factors should be exerted in many ways—for example, changing the quality of housing, schools, and job opportunities.

Prologue for Action (1966), S. F. Planning and Urban Renewal Association, official Citizens Action Committee, City of San Francisco

2. Super Agency and the Redevelopment Booster Club

Four San Francisco Mayors
Plans for the Port
YBC: Occasion for Optimism

San Francisco business

March 1973

Sixty Cents

Tom Vano, by permission of San Francisco *Business*

From left to right: Mayors Elmer Robinson, George Christopher, John Shelley, Joseph Alioto

There is a benefit of being in redevelopment . . .
You can go to bed each night knowing
you have helped people in the slums.
Justin Herman, Executive Director,
San Francisco Redevelopment Agency, 1970

He [Justin Herman] was one of the men responsible for
getting urban renewal named "the federal bulldozer" and
"Negro removal" . . . . [A HUD official said] "Herman
could move rapidly on renewal—demolition or
construction—because he was absolutely confident that he
was doing what the power structure wanted insofar as the
poor and the minorities were concerned . . . . That's why
San Francisco has mostly luxury housing and business dis-
trict projects—that's what white, middle-class planners and
businessmen envision as ideal urban renewal . . . Also, with
Herman in control, San Francisco renewal never got slowed
down by all this citizen participation business that tor-
mented other cities."
National Journal, September 18, 1971

Ben Swig's dream and corporate San Francisco's plans needed the official backing of the city, assisted by the federal government. Leaving redevelopment, particularly projects the size of Yerba Buena Center, in the hands of private parties was problematic and risky. Financing and assembling land for a massive downtown redevelopment project is an enormous task; and individual developers, unguided in their efforts, might create a patchwork of small developments more a hindrance than a help in changing the face of the city. Such difficulties required that government step in, take land by eminent domain, furnish central direction and guidelines, and provide the financial incentives to guarantee investment by private developers.

As the body shaped to achieve these ends, the San Francisco Redevelopment Agency (SFRA) is far more than just another government department or regulatory body; it is a "super-agency," with broad-ranging political and economic powers reflecting the full authority of the state apparatus. As Frederick Wirt notes:

Like its counterparts in other cities, SFRA is a compound of public and private powers that provide a touch of the corporate state to local government in America. It can make and implement its own plans, move people from one section of town to another, arrange massive sums for financing, condemn property, and promote all its wonders. Traditional controls of public power, so endemic in American governance, run a little thin with these agencies.[1]

SFRA and the Redevelopment Booster Club

Redevelopment agencies are semi-autonomous bodies with vast amounts of independent legal, financial and technical powers and resources. They are in many ways independent from general municipal government, and in California cities are generally ruled by a five-person board of commissioners appointed by the mayor (or chairman of the board of supervisors) for staggered four-year terms. They have access to massive sums of federal funds (during Justin Herman's tenure, the San Francisco Redevelopment Agency secured $128 million in federal urban renewal funds) and develop direct relationships with federal funding agencies, which often bypass mayors and local legislatures. They can issue their own bonds. They have and freely use the power of eminent domain. Indeed a key element in the urban redevelopment process is the power to assemble large sites by taking land—with compensation—from individual owners, or by purchasing the land, with the taking power lurking in the background to create "willing" sellers. Their large technical staffs develop an exclusive familiarity with the complex arcana of urban renewal statutes and administrative regulations and handbooks. In sum, redevelopment agencies have in two short decades become powerful and largely independent forces in our cities.

During most of the 1950s the SFRA's operations were limited, and its relative lack of importance was evident in a small and not very talented staff, generally uninspired appointments to its governing board, and frequent squabbles both internally and with federal urban renewal officials. The urban renewal program had just been introduced in the 1949 Housing Act, and in the early 1950s direction and support from Washington were less than optimal. According to one account, the Agency staff even in the late fifties was "riddled with political hacks."[2]

The tone of the Agency's early operations had been set during the term of Mayor Elmer Robinson (1952-1955). The Agency Secretary at that time was a man who had threatened to oppose Robinson in the 1951 election but withdrew on promise of an Agency position. The chairman was a local optometrist, and another board member was a private detective known as Robinson's "hatchet man" on the Agency. Internal dissension ran high and culminated in the summary firing of Agency executive director James Lash in 1953. The dismissal of Lash (who later became executive vice-president of the American Council to Improve Our Neighborhoods, a national "public interest" lobbying group of big business and developers) brought anguished cries from the city's "good government" advocates, as well as from the newspapers. His successor (following a short-term appointment of the chief assistant clerk of the Board of Supervisors) was Eugene Riordan, the city's retiring Director of City Property, "a gentleman of the old school but with no evident qualifications for so demanding a post."[3] Riordan remained in the position until 1959, when the wheels were set in motion to overhaul the SFRA.

Throughout the 1950s, the federal urban renewal agency was highly critical of the SFRA, its staff and leadership. For example, the August 28, 1957 *Examiner* reported that "M. Justin Herman, regional administrator of the Housing and Home Finance Agency, which controls Federal funds for redevelopment projects, accused the agency of 'the most cumbersome and costly' handling of funds of any city in the U.S."

Within the city, the Agency was criticized from several quarters. In mid-1956, Mayor George Christopher specifically asked the Agency chairman, Joseph Alioto, to resign, calling him an "obstructionist," referring to controversy over the Agency's difficulties in putting together a plan to relocate the downtown wholesale produce market.[4] The mutual acrimony between the Agency and the City Planning Department was well known.

Resurrection for the Redevelopment Agency came at the end of Mayor Christopher's first term (1956-1959). Christopher, who entered office wary of massive renewal schemes, had resisted Ben Swig's Supervisors-approved plan for South of Market and other such redevelopment plans. However, in the closing years of the 1950s the efforts of the Blyth-Zellerbach Committee and its powerful offspring, the San Francisco Planning and Urban Renewal Association, turned Christopher into an enthusiastic supporter of redevelopment. Christopher just could not ignore the urging of the city's corporate representatives, especially at election time. And there was the changing face of San Francisco into a "city of color," with an increasing Black, Asian, Mexican-American and Latino population. This was not lost on Christopher, who reflected the attitudes of the city's Anglo-European (Italian, Irish, Greek) politicians and small businessmen. (It is significant that in the mayoral campaign of 1963, Christopher's friend, fellow Republican and local businessman Harold Dobbs, ran on a straightforward "law'and'order", anti-Black platform.)

The stage was set for renewal of the SFRA when Agency chairman Alioto announced in August, 1958, that he was resigning for business reasons and two months later executive director Riordan, nearing 70, announced his forthcoming retirement. The Blyth-Zellerbach Committee's Levine report (see page 37) and its formation of SPUR in early 1959 provided the necessary impetus for reshaping the Redevelopment Agency. In January, 1959, Mayor Christopher appointed as Alioto's successor Everett Griffin, a retired chemical company president and former director of the Chamber of Commerce. The source of Griffin's support was made clear in the January 13, 1959 *Examiner*: "Christopher said he had never met Griffin . . . . But he said the executive was highly recommended to him by members of the Blyth-

SFRA and the Redevelopment Booster Club

Zellerbach committee of financiers . . . ."

The appointment of commissioners to the San Francisco Redevelopment Agency reveals a good deal about the overlapping roles played by these powerful men, in the city's economy and as public figures ostensibly devoted to serving the general welfare. Christopher's original nominee for the Agency chairmanship had been an up-and-coming State Assemblyman named Caspar Weinberger. Weinberger's nomination was withdrawn when the city attorney ruled that a conflict of interest might be involved, since Weinberger's law firm was representing several wholesale produce firms being relocated for the Agency's Golden Gateway project. Weinberger thereupon was named chairman of SPUR's small executive committee. Three months later Christopher added another appointee to the Redevelopment Agency board, naming Walter Kaplan, secretary-treasurer of the Emporium, a large downtown department store. He succeeded John Merrill, who had asked to be replaced, as he owned property in the Agency's Golden Gateway area which he did not want to sell. Merrill, as previously noted, became chairman of SPUR in 1960.

But by far the most significant step taken by Mayor Christopher in his new-found commitment to redevelopment was his announcement in April, 1959, that M. Justin Herman would become executive director of the San Francisco Redevelopment Agency.

Justin Herman

Until his death in 1971, Justin Herman was official and corporate San Francisco's chief architect, major spokesman, and operations commander for the transformation of whole sections of the city. From these roles, two distinct opinions developed about him. In the downtown high-rise office buildings, banks, and City Hall he was Saint Justin, while in prison-like housing projects of Western Addition and the rat- and roach-infested homes of the Mission *barrio* he was the "white devil."† These opinions mirror the work of SFRA while Herman was its boss.

Herman was a talented and experienced administrator, well ac-

---

† "Negroes and the other victims of a low income generally regard him

quainted with the problems of urban renewal, and with useful connections inside the federal government. From 1951 until appointed to head SFRA, he had served as administrator of the San Francisco Regional Office of the Housing and Home Finance Agency (predecessor to the U.S. Department of Housing and Urban Development), responsible for activities in the western states. Following replacement by a Republican as the Administration strengthened its patronage hold, he had spent several months in 1959 as special assistant to the HHFA Administrator in Washington. Herman's appointment as SFRA chief was based on his familiarity with and strong criticism of the city's redevelopment program during the 1950s, his knowledge of and ability to circumvent federal red-tape, and above all his commitment to the kind of downtown urban renewal that the Bay Area Council, the Blyth-Zellerbach Committee, and SPUR† were pressing for.

As a condition to accepting the SFRA directorship, Herman wanted complete discretion to reconstitute the Agency by appointing new staff and developing new methods of operation. In addition, he made it clear that he would tolerate no interference from other city agencies. Mayor Christopher granted these conditions, and Herman set to work establishing the super-agency.

His command brought rapid results. The Agency soon became a powerful force with a staff of several hundred (compared with 60 in the pre-Herman era), a battery of consultants, close working relations with the mayor's office, and control over eight renewal projects and tens of millions of dollars in federal subsidies. The Agency's professional and political competence under Herman was well reflected in its staff composition, which consisted of expert planning, design, and financing specialists on the one hand, and a raft of political appointees on the other. Particularly during Mayor Alioto's tenure (1968-   ) staff appointments at all levels were frequently known to be political in nature.• (This resulted in an extremely large staff and excessive administrative costs. A 1972 HUD report showed that the San Francisco Redevelopment Agency, with 462 employees, had a

[Herman] as the arch villain in the black depopulation of the city." Thomas C. Fleming, "San Francisco's Land Development Program" *Sun-Reporter,* November 27, 1965.

† SPUR's executive director, John Hirten, was the former redevelopment director for Stockton, California, and "a protege . . . of Herman." (*San Francisco Examiner*, November 15, 1962.)

• "Some of [Mayor] Alioto's labor supporters have received such favors . . . as jobs on his staff or elsewhere in city government, most notably with the Redevelopment Agency." Dick Meister, "Labor Power," *San Francisco Bay Guardian*, December 23, 1970. Mayor Alioto's campaign manager and press secretary were among those receiving key Redevelopment Agency posts.

SFRA and the Redevelopment Booster Club

staff nearly three times as large as Pittsburgh's agency and nearly twice as large as Boston's, even though each of these cities had more redevelopment projects and disbursed far larger sums of grant money than did San Francisco.†)

The role and character of the Agency's board also changed markedly with Herman. The SFRA commissioners, appointed by the mayor but generally acceptable to Herman, were in effect representatives of the Agency's organized constituency. Substantial businessmen such as Walter Kaplan and Everett Griffin were later joined by James Folger, president of Folger Coffee Company (and Bay Area Council founder) and James B. Black, Jr., son of the president of Pacific Gas and Electric and himself a U. S. Steel executive. Within a few years, representatives of organized labor were also appointed to the Agency board. As expected, these business and labor leaders warmly supported Herman's SFRA policies, including the Yerba Buena Center project. This firm backing assured Herman's success in steering his programs through San Francisco's political and bureaucratic structure.

The Agency's initial projects under Herman's guidance exemplified its role as collaborator with and servant to the large corporate and financial elements of the business community. The Golden Gateway (which was initiated prior to Herman's appointment) and Yerba Buena Center were Herman's favorite projects. The Western Addition A-1 Project was part of a longer range development scheme for removing the city's central Black and Japanese ghettos. It involved widening Geary Boulevard—the main thoroughfare connecting central San Francisco with the northwestern part of the city, the Richmond district—into an eight-lane highway and surrounding it with new construction. Some 4,000 families were moved out, virtually none of whom was able to move back.[5] The area now consists of high-rise apartments and condominiums, new office buildings and churches, a Japanese Cultural and Trade Center, and some middle-income housing—all where low-income Black and Japanese families once made their homes. Symbolically, the Agency's new fortress-like headquarters building occupies a site adjacent to the new Geary Expressway.

Under Justin Herman's leadership the San Francisco Redevelopment Agency became a powerful and aggressive army out to capture as much downtown land as it could: not only Yerba Buena and the

---

† The ratio of annual administrative budget to total grant was 1:77 for Pittsburgh and 1:55 for Boston, while San Francisco had only a 1:22 ratio. Department of Housing and Urban Development, San Francisco Area Office, "Task Force Report on HUD Assisted Programs in San Francisco, California, 1972," p. III-14.

Golden Gateway, but Chinatown, the Tenderloin, the Port, and the rest of the South of Market area. Under the rubric of "slum clearance" and "blight removal," the Agency was systematically sweeping out the poor, with the full support of the city's power structure.

Beyond his qualifications as administrator, planner, and knowledgeable navigator of federal channels, Herman was a monument-builder who approached his job like a classical entrepreneur. In many ways he was Ben Swig's counterpart in the public sector, and it is not surprising that the two men were close associates and friends. Herman was more than a redevelopment administrator; he was an enthusiastic proponent of plans to remake San Francisco. Toward this end he used every trick, technique and legal loophole that could be mustered, and when established procedures did not work, he devised new methods, stretching the laws when necessary.[6] He was a man of incredible energy, tenacity, and political talent. Those who knew Herman well regarded him as tough, a perfectionist, someone who relished controversy, a man who wanted to leave his mark on the world through physical monuments. With respect to Yerba Buena Center he was able—despite labor's early qualms about the project —to weld together the necessary coalition of downtown business and labor by appealing to their common interest in higher sales and more jobs, which he promised would result from increased downtown land values.

Hotels, Conventions and Tourists

Perhaps the most active organization behind Yerba Buena Center and its quasi-public facilities is the San Francisco Convention and Visitors Bureau (CVB). Its promotional expertise has been crucial in marshalling support for both the Redevelopment Agency and the Center.

The Bureau plays the dual role of representing the city's private tourism industry, while acting also as a quasi-official agent for the city. It was formed in 1963 on the recommendation of an advisory committee appointed by Mayor George Christopher and headed by J. D. Zellerbach of Blyth-Zellerbach Committee fame. The committee's task was to reorganize and enlarge the city's tourism and convention promotional functions. Once a recommended reorganization plan was submitted, Zellerbach appointed a subcommittee to carry it out consisting of Richard Swig, Ben's son, and Albert E. Schlesinger, who during the 1950s had been president of the Downtown Association and later chaired the Mayor's Tourism and Commerce Committee. On Schlesinger's recommendation the Board of Supervisors enacted a three percent hotel room occupancy tax in 1961 to support an aggressive and centralized tourism promotion agency, and when the Convention and Visitors Bureau finally was formed as a result of the work of

SFRA and the Redevelopment Booster Club

Zellerbach, the younger Swig, and Schlesinger, Schlesinger was named to head it. He was later to become a central figure in the private development group named to build Yerba Buena Center.

The "tourist industry" which the Convention and Visitors Bureau represents are the hotels, retail stores, media, transportation and tour interests, banks, restaurants, athletic teams, hotel and exhibit suppliers, entertainment functions, and certain labor unions. On their behalf, the Bureau's staff of 40 undertake a variety of promotional activities and services: hotel booking for conventions; billboard, magazine, and newspaper advertising; brochures; informational services; sales offices in the East and Midwest; staff assistance to conventions and trade shows; group tour promotion; liaison with travel agencies; and publicity for such annual events as the Chinese New Year celebration, the Japanese Cherry Blossom Festival, Columbus Day and St. Patrick's Day observances.

Under the theory that "what's good for business is good for the city," the CVB receives about 80 percent of its $1.1 million annual budget (1972) from the city's hotel tax. The revenue from the 3% hotel tax introduced in 1961 goes into the city's "publicity and advertising fund"; the CVB in 1967 convinced its membership to accept an increase in the tax from 3% to 5% to create a special fund to help pay for Yerba Buena Center, and later agreed to a further 1/2% increase to provide housing subsidies for YBC relocatees; another 1/2% increase was passed in 1971 to pay for the renovation of Candlestick Park, the city's professional football and baseball stadium. Distribution of the "publicity and advertising fund" is under the sole discretion of the city's appointed Chief Administrative Officer. A certain amount is used to subsidize the opera, symphony, art museum and other cultural activities, as well as to provide a slush fund for bankrolling the entertainment and hosting activities of various private groups. The CVB's tax-supported activities have also led to some questionable behavior, as a recent article in the *Bay Area Guardian* notes:

> . . . [*I*]*n large part they're* [*the CVB*] *using this tax windfall as a cheap way to advertise and promote their private members.*
>
> *For example: their brochures, maps, and free information on where to eat, drink, sleep, shop, and sight-see in the city's vacationland "recommend" the very same restaurants, hotels, stores, and galleries of their member businesses, who pay dues for the privilege of being listed in the S.F. tourist guides . . .*
>
> *Smaller eating or entertainment spots, many with the real flavor of San Francisco, don't get plugs because they can't afford the membership dues* [minimum: $150 per year].
>
> . . . [*T*]*he bureau releases dates and information on upcoming conventions only to its private members. Says General Manager Robert Sullivan, "No one would pay to join if we gave advance information free to anyone."*[7]

Hotels, Conventions and Tourists

The Convention and Visitors Bureau has supported all of Justin Herman's redevelopment projects for San Francisco. Not surprisingly, the tourism industry would like to see removed certain sections of San Francisco and certain elements in the population, thus creating more genial surroundings for tourists and conventions. Yerba Buena Center represented an urban renewal project ideally suited to the needs of the Convention and Visitors Bureau: not only did it remove from the downtown people who in the Bureau's eyes ought not be seen by conventioneers and tourists, but it also provided modern and enlarged convention facilties.

The CVB's interest in South of Market redevelopment is also somewhat more personal, since its founder, Albert Schlesinger, was part owner (with Melvin Swig, another of Ben's sons) of the franchises for both the San Francisco Seals hockey team and the Warriors basketball team. In addition, Schlesinger was a member of the art museum and symphony boards and viewed the proposed center as a perfect spot for a complex combining both sports and culture. With the creation of the CVB in 1963, Schlesinger and the Swigs mobilized the resources of the tourist industry behind YBC.

One of the Bureau's principal promotional activities for YBC was a national tour of convention centers in other cities. Included in the touring party were important city officials, businessmen, union representatives, architects and contractors, who predictably concluded: that San Francisco was no longer competitive in the field of convention and sports facilities, and that the development of Yerba Buena Center was critical to the city's future economic health. If something was not done, San Francisco would face a loss of conventions and meetings to other cities such as Las Vegas, Anaheim, Los Angeles, New Orleans, Chicago, and Dallas, where convention facilities were newer, larger, and more comfortable.

There were indeed certain limitations to the city's facilities for large conventions, trade shows and sporting events. Existing facilities consisted of the city-owned Civic Auditorium and Brooks Hall complex in the (downtown) Civic Center, the state-owned Cow Palace, and the meeting rooms in major hotels. The Civic Auditorium contains an arena with seating for 8,000—sufficient for most large conventions, but too small for many professional sporting events. Brooks Hall is a medium-sized (167,000 square foot) exhibition area, but its 14-foot ceilings are low by trade show standards, and the floor space is broken up by supporting pillars. The Cow Palace (site of the 1964 Republican National Convention) is a much larger hall containing approximately 315,000 square feet of exhibition space (roughly the same size as the YBC convention hall) usable as a 14,000 seat arena and with parking for 6,500 cars. Its major drawbacks are an insufficient number of meeting rooms, its distance from downtown San Francisco (15-20 minutes),

SFRA and the Redevelopment Booster Club

and location in an area with few restaurant or hotel facilities. From the downtown businessmen's point of view, the central objection to the Cow Palace was well expressed by a former president of the Convention and Visitors Bureau, when he stated: "The trouble with the Cow Palace is . . . [i]t doesn't bring any business downtown."[8] Yerba Buena Center is designed to provide a large, modern exhibit space with adequate meeting facilities in the center of the city, located to bring business downtown.

The argument that without new facilities the city will lose existing conventions and shows and be unable to attract events from other cities has been a persuasive line presented before the business community, city agencies, and other interested parties. But there is little hard evidence to prove the point. Most major conventions and trade shows continue to include San Francisco on their rotation lists. The CVB's dual position as both private and public agent makes objective evaluation of this argument difficult, however, as evidence and statistics are guarded by the Bureau's staff as "confidential" and are used strictly to support the need for YBC.†

The Hotel Employers Association (HEA) represents the largest hotels in San Francisco—the Fairmont, Mark Hopkins, St. Francis, Hilton, etc.—and although it is a separate organization, there is substantial overlap between it and the Convention and Visitors Bureau. Virtually every large hotel is represented on the CVB's board of directors, and as a group the hotelmen make up the largest bloc of votes on the board. The CVB's president for 1973-75 is Henri J. Lewin, senior vice-president of the Hilton Hotel Corporation, in charge of its Western Division, and secretary-treasurer is Richard Swig, president of the Fairmont Hotel.

The HEA's interests in Yerba Buena Center are direct and specific: increasing hotel occupancy through added convention business. (About two-fifths of all convention delegate expenditures go to hotels-motels and hotel-motel restaurants.[9]) During the late 1960s and early 1970s there was a rash of hotel building related in part to the city's expanded economic functions. And as *Business Week* noted, "In large measure, the hotel building boom was keyed to the 1972 completion of San Francisco's Yerba Buena Center. . . ."[10] In 1959 the city had fewer than 3,300 first-class hotel rooms; by 1970 the number had risen to 9,000, with another 2,700 being added. But this rapid spurt of construction led to a vacancy rate in the city's hotels of 30 percent by 1971,[11] and expectations were that as more rooms were completed vacancies would rise to 40 percent by 1973. Having built partly in

†The economic pro's and con's of YBC are discussed in detail in Chapter 6.

anticipation of YBC, the hotel owners were adamant that development be hurried, since they had to fill vacant rooms. The hotel owners' plight was expressed, if somewhat hyperbolically, by the Hilton's Henri Lewin: "If that convention center gets killed, we get killed. At least 50 percent of the hotels in this city will go out of business."[12]

Yet the detailed plans for YBC caused the hotel owners mixed feelings, since one element in the central blocks is a 700-800 room luxury hotel designed to serve the exhibit hall and sports arena. Given its proximity to these facilities, the hotel would be a highly profitable operation and could compete successfully with the North of Market luxury hotels. Despite HEA objections, Justin Herman adamantly insisted that this hotel be retained in the design, in order to provide a lucrative enterprise that would insure the Redevelopment Agency's ability to attract a private developer for the Center. Caught in the squeeze between the need to bail themselves out from their overbuilding spree and their desire to forestall additional competition, the hotel owners were forced to compromise and accept the luxury hotel in YBC as part of the price of moving the entire convention development along.†

---

† The entire saga of the YBC luxury hotel is a fascinating vignette of Justin Herman's ability to manipulate and maneuver around the local and federal bureaucracies and act as a broker between power groups. The luxury hotel dates back to Ben Swig's original 1954 plan and was included in the Redevelopment Agency's land-use plan for YBC submitted to the U. S. Housing and Home Finance Agency in 1964. Because the Agency had not undertaken an independent feasibility study on inclusion of hotels (required under a 1959 amendment to the federal urban renewal statutes lobbied through by national hotel owners' groups), the HHFA indicated it would not approve the submitted plan unless all references to hotels were deleted. Herman made the necessary deletions and requested the Agency's planning consultant to disguise the hotel as an office building in his drawings. Nonetheless, a 1,500-room luxury hotel continued to appear in future renderings and models produced by the Agency's consultants.

The Agency realized that inclusion of the hotel was critical in attracting developers, a judgment confirmed by the fact that the developers' agreement it signed in November, 1970, with Schlesinger-Arcon/Pacific provided that the whole agreement was contingent upon the Board of Supervisors approving an amendment to the YBC plan to include a luxury hotel (which it did in the spring of 1971). When the Agency's agreement with the developer was revealed, the Hotel Employers Association, working through Richard Swig, attempted to have the Agency eliminate the hotel altogether. Herman argued this was impossible. The HEA then suggested the hotel be reduced in size to 400 rooms, which Herman also refused.

Richard Swig next took the unusual step of threatening to intervene on the side of the South of Market residents in their relocation lawsuit against the SFRA, on the grounds that the inclusion of the hotel in the YBC plan was

SFRA and the Redevelopment Booster Club

The Alioto Touch

The nature of urban renewal and political timetables is such that a redevelopment scheme and administrator will usually have a lifespan considerably greater than an elected official. Justin Herman's career and his planning for Yerba Buena Center spanned the political life of three mayors—George Christopher, John Shelley, and Joseph Alioto. Following the resurgence of urban redevelopment during Christopher's second term (1960-1963), there came the rocky times—for the city and for redevelopment—during John Shelley's tenure (1964-1967). The advent of the Alioto era was built largely around the push by the city's movers and shakers to get redevelopment rolling again.

Joseph L. Alioto did not fall from the sky, but in the closing months of the 1967 mayoral campaign it looked that way to many San Franciscans. In 1963 Congressman John Shelley, a former state legislator and AFL-CIO leader, had been elected mayor over conservative businessman Harold Dobbs, owner of the Mel's Drive-In restaurant chain, which had received considerable notoriety earlier that year as the target of militant civil rights demonstrations against the restaurants' lily-white hiring policies. John Shelley's term as mayor was not a time of brotherhood and goodwill. As in many large cities, the mid-60s were a period of racial confrontation in San Francisco. Militant civil rights campaigns achieving nationwide publicity were launched against luxury hotels, automobile dealers, and other discriminatory employers. Many of the "riots" of the mid-60s were related to people-removing redevelopment activity in the city's Mission, Bayview-Hunters Point, and Western Addition-Fillmore ghettos. The Western Addition A-2 urban renewal project in particular was singled out for neighborhood opposition. Civil rights groups issued strong statements opposing the project; the Redevelopment Agency and Board of Supervisors were vilified at their hearings regarding the project; people sat in at the mayor's office and in front of bulldozers. John Shelley's background and instincts produced in him a concern and sympathy with the protestors, but in action he vacillated. At first he opposed the project, asked for delays, and raised questions about relocation. In mid-1966, over Justin Herman's opposition, he appointed to the Redevelopment Agency board the militant president of the NAACP, Dr. Joseph Wel-

illegal. This threatened coalition between his most successful opponents and a group he had counted on as loyal, though self-interested, supporters greatly upset Justin Herman and finally moved him to realize that some compromise was necessary. The negotiations that ensued resulted in an agreement to limit the size of the hotel to 700 rooms and assure that it would not be directly connected with the convention center; in return the HEA agreed not to oppose inclusion of the hotel in the final plans.

South of Market in the early fifties

lington, a vocal opponent of the Western Addition A-2 project. But eventually he backed the project.

Shelley also vacillated on Yerba Buena Center. He questioned the expenses and priorities involved, but announced support of the project and stated he would make no changes in the composition of the Agency board until the Agency took its final vote on YBC. He expressed unhappiness with the growing strength and independence of the Redevelopment Agency, a denunciation triggered by Justin Herman's unilateral abolition of the job of Secretary to the Agency, a post that traditionally had been the mayor's appointment in order to place his own "watchdog" in the Agency.[13] In an effort to undercut Herman, Shelley announced he was not reappointing Herman's Agency board chairman, Everett Griffin. The October 27, 1966 *Examiner* labeled this "...a public slap on the wrist [to] the agency's real power, Executive Director M. Justin Herman...." In his stead, Shelley appointed a close personal friend and political neophyte, Francis J. Solvin, a Coast Guard hearing officer. Shelley's off-and-on opposition to redevelopment, combined with serious community protests, resulted in a 6-5 Board of Supervisors vote upholding the Mission district's opposition to a neighborhood renewal program and an unprecedented 6-2 vote asking

SFRA and the Redevelopment Booster Club

the Redevelopment Agency to halt its Western Addition A-2 project (a vote Shelley then vetoed). Justin Herman and his renewal program were on the ropes. The article in the October 27, 1966 *Examiner*, entitled "City Hall and the Slum Dragon," began:

> *The San Francisco Redevelopment Agency is in trouble. In the Mission they call it a plague. In City Hall they charge it with a power grab. Citizen groups have banded together to curb its powers. Young priests and ministers are charging the redevelopers with utter disregard for the fate of the poor. . . .*

Mayor Shelley's ambivalence on the redevelopment issue was one of the principal factors underlying the "dump Shelley" movement initiated by the city's ruling elite. Shelley had begun to organize his reelection effort. Harold Dobbs was once again running his law-and-order campaign, this time with considerably greater chance of success in the dominant white community as a result of backlash from the Hunters Point uprising earlier in the year and other Black rebellions. (State Senator Eugene McAteer, who had been building powerful support for his own mayoral campaign, had died of a heart attack in May. Liberal Supervisor Jack Morrison wanted to run but would not oppose his friend Shelley.) The early public opinion polls indicated Dobbs would make a very strong showing against Shelley.

On September 8, 1967, just two months before Election Day, Shelley held a dramatic press conference to announce he was dropping out of the race, citing as his reasons poor health and exhaustion. Exactly one and a half hours later Joseph Alioto held a press conference (at Ben Swig's Fairmont Hotel) announcing his candidacy. Charges and rumors of dirty politics understandably flew thick and fast. Congressman Phillip Burton, leader of the liberal wing of the city's Democratic party, declared, "Truthfully, it smacks to me like a deal." Noting the extraordinary timing of the two announcements, Burton expressed what most San Franciscans also must have thought: "I can't believe this just happened."[14] A few days later, Jack Morrison announced his own candidacy. A political ally of Burton and clearly the replacement for Shelley whom the liberal Democrats would have preferred, Morrison stated (a trifle optimistically, as events turned out):

> *The events of the past four days indicate to me that the few downtown financial tycoons are making a last desperate grasp for political power in San Francisco . . . I think . . . there was a conviction in the minds of a few fat cats . . . that Shelley could not win. I think there were discussions and arrangements made. I think this would have occurred whether or not Mayor Shelley had a crisis in health.*[15]

In breaking the story of Shelley's withdrawal, the September 8, 1967 *Examiner* confirmed reports that "Alioto, Shelley and former Mayor

Robinson met in the back room of Shelley's office on Tuesday night [three days before the announcement]. One source said when Shelley and Alioto emerged, 'they were smiling.' " The September 9, 1967 *Chronicle* noted that "Alioto, a highly successful lawyer, who represents California's ricegrowers and some other important business accounts, is considered a much stronger 'downtown' candidate than Shelley."

Indeed, the downtown interests had apparently pulled the necessary strings and provided the necessary grease. In late August of 1967 a meeting had been arranged at the Fairmont Hotel by Vernon Kaufman, a San Francisco realtor and later Alioto's campaign manager. Present were representatives of downtown interests, including Ben Swig and Cyril Magnin, department store owner and financier, a prime mover behind the massive Embarcadero City project on the waterfront† and head of the Port Commission. Also present were such political influentials as William Coblentz, a University of California Regent (who six years later, at Mayor Alioto's request, was to put together the negotiations that finally ended the Yerba Buena relocation lawsuit), and former Mayor Elmer Robinson. According to some accounts, at least one important labor representative (from the ILWU) was also present.[16] It was out of this meeting that the decision was made to "dump" Shelley and back Alioto as his successor, and to provide the necessary financial and labor support to get him elected.

Immediately following Alioto's announcement, Vernon Kaufman announced, "we will have all the money we need to elect Joseph Alioto."[17] A scant four days later a group of Alioto backers, including "big financial interests" which previously had supported Mayor Shelley and the late Senator McAteer, were brought together at the Fairmont Hotel at a meeting hosted by Ben Swig (who also had been McAteer's finance chairman) "that raised a cool $203,500 for Joseph Alioto's war chest in exactly 45 minutes."• As for Shelley, several reliable sources

---

† Embarcadero City was a colossal but abortive project (which still may be revived) to develop the city's entire north waterfront, from Fisherman's Wharf to the Ferry Building—an 80-block area—with offices, hotels and recreation facilities; a principal element was to be the 550-foot U. S. Steel tower, which was blocked in 1970 by action of conservationists in a bitter political battle. For a detailed account of this project and the issues and controversy raised, see Richard Reinhardt, "On the Waterfront: The Great Wall of Magnin," in Bruce B. Brugmann and Greggar Sletteland (eds.), *The Ultimate Highrise: San Francisco's Mad Rush Toward the Sky* (San Francisco: San Francisco Bay Guardian Books, 1971), pp. 92-137.

• Walter Blum, *Benjamin H. Swig: The Measure of a Man* (San Francisco: 1968), p. 50; see also *San Francisco Examiner*, September 13, 1967, and *San Francisco Chronicle*, September 17, 1967. Swig's role, as usual, was critical in this series of events. Later that same month Harold Dobbs charged that a close associate of Swig, hotel real estate man Donald Werby, had earlier tried to talk

SFRA and the Redevelopment Booster Club

indicated a "payoff" was involved. According to the September 7, 1967 *Examiner*: "There were reports from City Hall sources that members of the San Francisco 'establishment' were planning to get together a 'retirement fund' for Shelley, who is not personally wealthy." According to the October 31, 1967 *Bay Guardian*, the deal to have Shelley step down had originally been made with McAteer:

> *The package at that time, a key McAteer source said, was $125,000 to be paid to a future employer over a five year period to employ Shelley in a comfy post until his government pension came due. Shelley in return would throw his support to McAteer. Employers under discussion: Stanford Research Institute, Arthur D. Little Co. and friendly unions like laborers local 261.*

To no one's surprise, Shelley endorsed Alioto rather than Morrison. And following an extended recuperation period, he in fact was appointed by Mayor Alioto as the city's lobbyist in Sacramento, a job paying $25,000 a year, plus a healthy expense account.

Joe Alioto comes from a well-established Bay Area family, having many branches involved in Fisherman's Wharf restaurants, real estate, finance and law. Alioto was a highly successful multi-millionaire plaintiffs' anti-trust lawyer, very active in politics on a behind-the-scenes basis until his dramatic emergence on center stage in September, 1967. He had previously held only non-elective public office in the city, first (1948-54) as a member of the Board of Education and its president in 1952-53, later (1955-58) as chairman of the Redevelopment Agency. In the latter capacity, however, he had shown himself a firm supporter of downtown renewal and the Agency, even though the Agency had not been very productive during his tenure. As *Examiner* columnist Dick Nolan wrote of the Agency chairman at the time of the swirl over Ben Swig's "San Francisco Prosperity Plan": "Alioto is dreaming the dream even more ardently—or at least more eloquently—than B. Swig hisself."[18] Labeled "a conservative Democrat" (September 12, 1967 *Chronicle*), Alioto had been co-chairman of Eugene McAteer's mayoral drive until the senator's untimely death and earlier had been a major figure in John Shelley's 1963 campaign. Not adverse to helping Republicans, particularly in San Francisco's nominally non-partisan elections, Alioto also had previously handled George Christopher's mayoral campaign and was one of the key backers of Republican U.S. Senator Thomas Kuchel. His close relationship with the Shelley and McAteer organizations paid off in 1967. According to the September 9, 1967 *Chronicle*: "Alioto. . . has found himself in a position to collect some

Dobbs out of running so that Swig himself could make the race. Although Werby acknowledged having made this approach to Dobbs, he maintained it had been done without Swig's knowledge. See *San Francisco Examiner*, September 27, 1967.

major political IOU's. He withdrew from the Mayor's race in 1963 in Shelley's favor, with at least a tacit understanding that some day he would like to have Shelley reciprocate." And he had no trouble picking up McAteer's organization and financial support.

But Alioto had two major problems to overcome in the two months between his announcement and Election Day: first, as the *Examiner* put it, "to the man on the street he is probably largely unknown";[19] second, as the candidate of the downtown establishment he needed working-class appeal in a town where labor is extremely powerful and in an election where Jack Morrison, a man who had received labor's endorsement in his three previous Supervisorial races, was running against him. As Daniel Del Carlo, head of the Building Trades Council, understated it, "After all, Alioto isn't very well known in the labor movement."[20] However, Alioto's lack of public visibility was overcome by an extremely well run and well financed campaign, as well as by the candidate's forceful and effective personality. And the "labor problem" was overcome by convincing organized labor that it was in their interest to support Alioto, based on what he could and would do for them, and on the argument that Morrison could not win and to throw labor's support to Morrison would only result in giving the election to the reactionary Dobbs. A recent study of San Francisco politics notes:

Labor was . . . instrumental in the shift to Joseph Alioto. . . There were explicit signs of an implicit set of trade-offs between the mayor's office and the unions, particularly the Building and Construction Trades Council and the longshoremen. In his 1967 and 1971 elections, Alioto received the benefits of labor's campaign workers and fund-raising. . . In return, unions received from his office help in major strikes in the form of mayoralty mediation, sympathetic police in cases of picketing, and zealous efforts to attract construction projects with the attendant jobs.

Too, there were appointments from labor's ranks, giving them access and visibility. . .[21]

The key unions in Alioto's drive were, as indicated above, Local 10 of the International Longshoremen's and Warehousemen's Union (ILWU) and Local 261 of the Laborers International, AFL-CIO, two of the largest unions in the city. Both unions had a large minority membership, Longshore and Warehouse being mostly Black, and the Laborers having a strong position among Spanish-speaking workers in the Mission District. The ILWU gave Alioto additional access to the Black community through the Baptist Ministers Union, one of the earliest Black organizations to support him. The Laborers Union, through its Mission-based district caucus, the Centro Social Obrero, a major neighborhood political force, and through the Centro's influence over the Mexican-American Political Association (MAPA), gave Alioto a

SFRA and the Redevelopment Booster Club

powerful base of support among the city's large Spanish-speaking population. It also gave him a not insubstantial amount of financial backing, secured as political contributions from the union's members, many of whom are recent, and sometimes illegal, immigrants from Central and South America, and who often must submit to high initiation fees, dues and special assessments. Other large, important unions such as the Department Store Employees and the Metal Trades and Industrial Union Council also supported Alioto, and although he was just shy of the two-thirds majority needed for AFL-CIO Central Labor Council endorsement, he clearly managed to win labor to his side.†

The outcome of this joint downtown-labor push was a victory for Alioto, who received 106,000 votes to Dobbs' 90,000 and Morrison's 40,000.

Labor's support was rewarded not only in the long-run provision of construction and other types of jobs for its members, but in immediate appointments to influential city posts. An official of ILWU Local 10 was appointed to Alioto's cabinet, ILWU International president Harry Bridges was appointed to the San Francisco Port Commission, and another ILWU representative, Wilbur Hamilton, went to the Redevelopment Agency board.• Hamilton within a few months applied for—and got—a $24,000 Agency staff job as manager of the Western Addition A-2 project, a move reportedly engineered by Justin Her-

---

† See Dick Meister, "Alioto Gets More Help from Labor," *San Francisco Chronicle*, September 20, 1967, for a description of Alioto's wooing of the ILWU. Among the factors cited by Meister in explaining why union support went to Alioto when he had not been closely identified with labor and when Morrison was clearly more sympathetic to labor were: 1) the timing and rapidity of Alioto's move, which caught Morrison and Burton off guard; 2) the fact that Alioto was making more liberal noises than had been expected; 3) Alioto's friendship with AFL-CIO Secretary-Treasurer George Johns (the two men had served together on the Board of Education and Alioto had been campaign committee chairman for Johns' unsuccessful 1961 race for the Board of Supervisors); 4) Alioto's tactic of using the support of a few key ILWU leaders who had been close to Shelley as a wedge to win over the membership. "Perhaps the most important reason," wrote Meister, "was indicated when Alioto walked into the ILWU [endorsement] meeting on Monday night surrounded by several of Shelley's former campaign aides. It was a graphic demonstration that the men around the man who is San Francisco's first labor mayor in a half century . . . know whom they want to inherit his position."

• At the same time Hamilton was appointed to the Agency Board, Alioto made a second appointment, Michael J. Driscoll, a mortuary owner whose daughter married Alioto's son. (Alioto's appointment of his extended family members to city posts is a standing joke in San Francisco: e.g., his wife to the War Memorial Trustees, his cousin to the Fire Commission, his wife's nephew to a staff job in the mayor's office.) In 1970 Alioto appointed Driscoll to fill a vacancy on the Board of Supervisors and replaced him with James A. Silva, a

man. Alioto thereupon replaced Hamilton on the Agency board with Joe Mosley, another ILWU representative. Dave Jenkins, Alioto's most crucial political link to the ILWU and the local labor movement generally, received a patronage post in 1968 as "labor consultant" to the Redevelopment Agency.† And in late 1969 the Agency awarded the ILWU a choice lot in the Western Addition A-2 redevelopment area, to build its world headquarters (a vote from which Mr. Mosley discreetly abstained.) Local 261 also received its rewards: the head of the Centro Social Obrero was appointed to the mayor's cabinet, the local's president went on the city's Housing Authority board, and one leader of MAPA was appointed by the mayor to fill a vacancy on the Board of Supervisors, another to the Board of Education. Local 261 soon after received an SFRA contract to build "miniparks" on various Redevelopment Agency properties, with the pilot project located next to the local president's house.

Joe Alioto's election appeared to signal the change in the fortunes of the city's redevelopment program that the business-union coalition desired. Alioto immediately named as his Deputy for Development John A. Tolan, Jr., assistant administrator of HUD's Western Region, a long-time friend from college days, a close friend of Justin Herman, and the son of a former East Bay Congressman. At a news conference, held fittingly at Ben Swig's Fairmont Hotel, Alioto pledged his support for the YBC development. "Plans for a grandiose cultural and sports center in the South-of-Market area 'will go forward quickly' in the new City administration, Mayor-elect Joseph L. Alioto said yesterday," reported the January 4, 1968 *Chronicle.* On the same day Cyril Magnin, president of the Chamber of Commerce, vowed to do something to further the downtown sports arena in Yerba Buena Center. Alioto then went to Washington to seek additional federal money for YBC and the Western Addition A-2 project. "It looks like the tide is turning for us," Justin Herman predicted confidently.[22] On March 20, 1968, in a story headed "Alioto Gives His Blessing to Herman," the *Examiner* wrote:

> *Mayor Alioto has reaffirmed his confidence in M. Justin Herman, the controversial executive director of the Redevelopment Agency . . . . The praise*

businessman who previously had been a member of the Parking Authority. (Driscoll ran for the Board of Supervisors on his own in 1971 and lost, whereupon Alioto appointed him to the Port Commission.) Two of the current Redevelopment Agency board members are men first appointed before 1968 whom Alioto has subsequently reappointed: Chairman Walter Kaplan, first appointed by George Christopher, and Stanley E. Jensen of the Machinists Union, who was appointed by John Shelley.

† From August, 1968, through 1973, Jenkins has been paid over $110,000 for his consultant services. (Letter dated January 2, 1974, from Wilbur W. Hamilton, Assistant Executive Director, San Francisco Redev. Agency).

SFRA and the Redevelopment Booster Club

which Alioto heaped on Herman also appeared to be the Mayor's way of telling those leaders of the Negro community who've been demanding the ouster of the redevelopment boss that nothing is further from his mind.

An interesting sidelight to Alioto's strong support for Yerba Buena Center involves a brief, abortive attempt to reintroduce into the plan the South of Market baseball-football stadium Ben Swig originally envisioned but which was dropped when the city built Candlestick Park in an outlying area for the New York Giants. Following Board of Supervisors approval, the city initiated plans in 1967 to expand and remodel Candlestick Park, in part to make it suitable for football use, since the city's professional football team, the 49-ers, was abandoning its old and inadequate home at Kezar Stadium in Golden Gate Park. However, in early 1968 at Mayor Alioto's request, Chamber of Commerce President Cyril Magnin and SPUR Board Chairman Jerd Sullivan set up the Mayor's Joint Committee on Spectator Sports. To no one's surprise, the Committee recommended tearing down eight-year-old Candlestick and putting up a 55,000-seat stadium South of Market (in addition to the indoor sports arena already planned for Yerba Buena Center). Melvin Swig, a member of the Magnin-Sullivan appointed group, was then named chairman of an Alioto task force to develop this plan, and downtown businessmen procured a $150,000 Economic Development Administration grant to study plans for a new stadium.

Examiner columnist Dick Nolan wrote (August 20, 1968): "Politico-financier Ben Swig was money man for the big putsch that putsched Mayor Alioto into office . . . . Now Swig is an 'in' money man again. So it is not surprising that we hear fantastic talk from City Hall about—a colossal downtown sports complex." Seeking a new stadium location was related in part to the racial troubles at Hunters Point, the predominantly Black area adjoining Candlestick Park; in part to the same reasoning that made the Cow Palace inadequate in the eyes of downtown businessmen—that is was too far from downtown to generate restaurant, shopping, and hotel patronage; and in part to the fact that several persons on the mayor's task force owned property in the South of Market area being considered for the stadium. However, the problems of building a new stadium and razing one built only a few years before were insurmountable, and by early 1969 the plan was dropped and the Board of Supervisors gave final approval for the Candlestick Park expansion bond issue. *Examiner* columnist Guy Wright summed up the matter when he wrote on December 30, 1968: "I suspect Mayor Alioto reopened the question of a downtown stadium as a political favor and now wishes he could forget the whole thing."

Labor's Turnaround

Organized labor's strong backing of Joe Alioto in 1967, followed by its strong backing for Yerba Buena Center, was a considerable turn-about from its original stance toward the project. The existing business-es in the South of Market area were highly unionized, and when rede-velopment plans first came to light, the San Francisco Central Labor Council, AFL-CIO, opposed them on the basis that the development would displace thousands of blue-collar jobs and replace them with non-union clerical and service workers.

In the early and mid-1960s, labor leadership generally had express-ed great reservations about the type of economic development being pushed by the Bay Area Council, the Blyth-Zellerbach Committee and SPUR. The April 14, 1963 *Chronicle* reported a statement issued by local AFL-CIO and Teamster leaders, which asserted: "It may suit the purpose of some to make San Francisco a financial and service center, but it destroys the jobs of working people and weakens the City's economic foundations." In the November 3, 1965 Official Bulletin of the San Francisco Labor Council, Secretary-Treasurer George Johns (who was to speak against the YBC plan at the Board of Supervisors 1966 hearings) took a broad look at the YBC project, the Redevelop-ment Agency, and the interests served by urban renewal in San Fran-cisco:

Speculative real estate operators . . . seem to have taken over the planning functions of our City . . . .

Convention halls and sports arenas have their place. But the loss of millions of square feet of industrial space can only extend unemployment, suffering and poverty . . . A redevelopment program is certainly needed there [South of Market]. However . . . a rehabilitation and conservation program makes far better sense than the program of massive clearance . . . .

Certain politically important persons consider the clearance program in Yerba Buena as the beginning of the redevelopment of 1100 industrially zoned acres South of Market. With the support and blessings of the [Redevelopment] agency, they are ready to kick industry out of San Francisco . . . .

In addition to the many workers who will lose their jobs, we wonder if the policy makers of this City have thought of the social and economic effect on over 3,000 single persons, a third of them aged, who will be displaced in the area without realistic provision for relocation. Displacement can mean higher rents and out of the way locations. The hardship such conditions will impose on senior citizens is obvious enough to anyone still sensitive to human needs. . . .

Yet citizens who oppose a policy of rezoning light industry right out of the City are considered "obstructionists." Obstructionism, in fact, has generally become a dirty word for anyone bucking the policies of the redevelopment agency. But isn't it the agency that is really obstructing? Aren't they obstructing efforts to retain industry and therefore jobs in San Francisco by moving away from the preserva-tion and expansion of industrial zoning that is so necessary if we are to maintain the economic balance of this City and the continuance of job opportunities?

SFRA and the Redevelopment Booster Club

> *What they are not obstructing are the special interests of certain groups. The Agency and Mr. Herman must be reminded of their obligations to the rest of the citizens of San Francisco. The Yerba Buena issue is a good place to start.*

The Labor Council's opposition to Yerba Buena Center also led to its hiring a researcher/organizer to help build a coalition strategy against the project (see pages 197-198 below).

But as time passed, and the various pieces began falling into place, pressures began to build up within the ranks of labor and from outside it for a reversal of labor's position on YBC. The politics of the Alioto campaign and election was one major element in the switch. Justin Herman and other SFRA representatives courted labor leaders, trying to convince them that the loss of blue-collar jobs and the transformation of the city into a white-collar administrative center was inevitable, and that labor could reap certain gains from this process. Within a short time the conversion was complete; and by 1970, to prove its fidelity to Justin Herman's and Joseph Alioto's brand of urban renewal, the San Francisco Labor Council even filed an *amicus curiae* brief in the federal court supporting the Redevelopment Agency against charges of inadequate relocation brought by South of Market residents.

Within the Labor Council, it was the Building and Construction Trades · Council (BCTC) that carried the day for YBC. The conversion of downtown San Francisco into the administrative and financial headquarters of the West—particularly through the massive Bay Area Rapid Transit System and the Golden Gateway project—had been good for the various trades and locals in the construction industry. By the mid-1960s the BCTC was a backer not just of Yerba Buena Center, but of any planned construction which would provide employment for members of its affiliated unions. This included such projects as the proposed 550-foot U. S. Steel high-rise on the waterfront and a proposed freeway through Golden Gate Park, both of which earned the hostility of the general populace because of the loss of recreational space and scenic views. As a representative of the BCTC said regarding Yerba Buena Center, "We are in favor of building with no respect to where it is and how it is."[23]

For many San Francisco workers the quest for construction jobs was vitally necessary to survival. The redevelopment master plan for the city was displacing thousands of jobs, and it was not likely that unemployed blue-collar workers would find employment in white-collar jobs. This concern was real and served to push the unions from a position of indifference, and in some instances opposition, to one of key support for redevelopment. According to Dick Meister, former labor reporter for the *San Francisco Chronicle*:

> . . . [U]nion leaders usually agree to whatever projects are proposed by

business–just as long as the projects provide jobs . . . . It . . . has been rare for union leaders to question financial returns promised to business from proposed projects; they merely agree they should be as large as possible to maximize the share granted their members . . . . Unions merely react to the doings of others, occasionally forcing them to alter their plans after they have been unveiled but usually playing only the role of important supporter.

A critic put it this way: ﹐

The unions are an arm of the downtown establishment, playing pretty much of an establishment game. They stand by while business dictates the course of San Francisco and, as long as they get theirs, they don't rock the boat.[24]

Along with the construction trades, those unions associated with the tourism and hotel industries joined the chorus of Yerba Buena Center supporters. These were the Bartender and Culinary Workers and Cooks unions, who had much to gain from more hotel and entertainment facilities. The strong support of the project by the International Longshoremen's and Warehousemen's Union is at least partially explainable by the union's concerns for its future. The ILWU has a historic reputation as one of the most progressive unions in the labor movement, having readily taken stands in support of the civil rights movement and against the war in Vietnam. With the growing mechanization of the West Coast docks, the ILWU was forced to face the prospect of slowly dying or merging with a larger union, such as the International Longshoremen's Association, dominant on East Coast and Gulf docks, or the Teamsters, who were handling increasing quantities of containerized cargo. The ILWU leadership therefore saw it in their best interest to generate more jobs by backing business and political forces determined to advance San Francisco and the Bay Area as a service and trading hub for the Pacific Basin. As union membership declined, the old guard in leadership moved to protect their position by becoming a direct participant in the city's political machine and thus consolidated their power around the union's steadily employed members.

Once labor moved into a pro-YBC position, it became a vocal critic of all activities which hindered progress on the Center, particularly the efforts of TOOR. (See pages 153 and 195 for an account of labor's attacks on TOOR's Legal Services attorneys and the federal judge hearing their suit, and labor's opposition to the proposed hotel tax increase to finance replacement housing for South of Market displacees.) In February, 1972—at a time when the Redevelopment Agency's financing plan for YBC was being submitted to the Board of Supervisors and TOOR's litigation was seriously bogging the project down—the San Francisco Labor Council, Building and Construction Trades Council, and ILWU jointly issued a pamphlet entitled **WHAT EVER HAPPENED TO YERBA BUENA CENTER? AND THOSE 30,000 JOBS!** The widely distri-

SFRA and the Redevelopment Booster Club

buted pamphlet urged progress on YBC, "despite legal harassments by Berkeley lawyers who couldn't care less about the San Francisco wage earner." (According to a labor spokesman, "the pamphlet had been written and distributed to union offices by the Redevelopment Agency."[25])

Labor Council support for clearance in South of Market was not without its irony. Many of the retired residents living in the district's inexpensive hotels and boarding houses had once been active union members, organizers, and even officials, and were supplementing their Social Security with union pensions. Yet the current union leaders were insensitive to the plight of the older men, classifying them as "winos and bums." As one union leader put it when interviewed: "They poor-mouth a lot, but under our system the residents can't remain. A few can't hold up progress."

Propaganda and Property

The downtown interests throughout have found the main outlet for their pro-YBC opinions in San Francisco's major daily newspapers, the *Chronicle* and *Examiner*. The *Chronicle* is an independently owned paper with the largest circulation in Northern California, followed by the Hearst-chain *Examiner*.[26] Both papers are avid supporters of redevelopment schemes, especially YBC, and SPUR, the Swigs, Justin Herman, and others have had no difficulty in finding space for their positions.

San Francisco's dailies, like virtually all major newspapers, have numerous threads binding them to the area's corporate, financial, and political leadership.† However, in the case of Yerba Buena Center, the *Chronicle's* and *Examiner's* stakes are more direct. Headquarters for both papers directly adjoin the project area, and in addition the *Examiner* owns two large and valuable lots adjoining the Central Blocks.

---

† The close relationship among various downtown interests which support and will benefit from YBC, as well as the quality of the city's daily press, is nicely shown in the following item from the September 27, 1972 *Chronicle*, regarding the Emporium, the neighboring major downtown department store, Secretary-Treasurer of which is Walter Kaplan, since 1966 Chairman of the Redevelopment Agency. While newspapers are understandably solicitous toward their large advertisers, this news story, headlined "New Emporium to Open," somewhat exceeds journalistic bounds:

"The Emporium will add its distinguished retailing name to the Tanforan Park Shopping Center in San Bruno with the opening at 9:30 a.m. tomorrow of a new $6.4 million three-story department store. . . .

"The interior of the 197,000 square-foot building features colorful woods, metals, glass and plastics with an emphasis on individual "boutique" departments.

"Major departments include men's, women's and children's apparel, home

Propaganda and Property

As large landowners, both newspapers stand to gain financially from the substantial increase in land values the YBC project will trigger in the South of Market area.

Dozens of editorials supporting Yerba Buena Center have appeared in the two dailies over the past decade. Both papers extol the claims of SPUR and the Convention and Visitors Bureau and heap praise on the Redevelopment Agency. An unfounded and wildly exaggerated CVB statement about loss of revenues from convention activity was duly reproduced in a March 16, 1972 *Examiner* editorial, which proclaimed, "San Francisco has definitely lost $40 million convention business this year. . . . By 1976 the annual loss will reach $80 million." A 1972 SPUR report on the city's redevelopment program received similar treatment. "SPUR is characteristically independent in expertise and outlook," the May 2, 1972 *Chronicle* solemnly stated, in supporting the incredible conclusion that "in all the years of its operations, the Redevelopment Agency has never failed to provide adequately for residents who were forced to seek new quarters." "This extraordinary record," the editorial continued, "has been verified by painstaking study which showed that the Agency has relocated some 2,633 families and more than 400 individuals without once violating federal rules for 'safe, decent, and sanitary housing' for relocated persons." This conclusion relied totally on the Agency's own reports and ignored both the mass of contrary evidence and the numerous persons unaided by the Agency who were left to their own devices in locating new residences.† An earlier *Examiner* editorial, published on November 14, 1969, right after TOOR had filed its relocation suit, asserted: "The Redevelopment

furnishings, sporting goods, appliances and such specialty services as a beauty salon, watch repair center and boutique-registry featuring everything-for-the-bride . . . .

"Convenient shopping hours run from 9:30 a.m. to 9:15 p.m., five nights a week. 9:30 a.m. to 5:30 p.m. Saturdays and noon to 5 p.m. on Sundays...

† In commenting on the relocation claims of local redevelopment agencies, the late Charles Abrams referred to redevelopment administrators as "jugglers of statistics" who have produced "misstatements of fact rare in the annals of official reporting." (*The City is the Frontier*, New York: Harper and Row, 1965, pp. 135, 136.) A National Institute of Mental Health financed study of relocation from Boston's West End urban renewal area showed that 25 percent of the displacees had moved to substandard units, whereas official Boston Redevelopment Authority data showed only two percent in substandard relocation dwellings. (See Chester W. Hartman, "The Housing of Relocated Families," *Journal of the American Institute of Planners*, November, 1964, pp. 266-286.) On the general problem of noncompliance with legal relocation requirements by government agencies, see Edgar Cahn, Timothy Eichenberg, and Roberta Romberg, *The Legal Lawbreakers: A Study of the Nonadministration of Federal Relocation Requirements* (Washington: Citizens Advocate Center, 1970).

SFRA and the Redevelopment Booster Club

Agency is proceeding with meticulous care and compassion in relocating residents of the Yerba Buena area."†

Taking the occasion of Justin Herman's death to plug YBC, the *Examiner's* September 1, 1971 editorial eulogy ended with these words: "The day that Mr. Herman died he was fighting to protect the grand, unified design of the big Yerba Buena Center project south of Market. No memorial to him could be finer than a determination by City Hall to move ahead strongly on that distinguished enterprise." Each of the papers uses any incident involving the project to publish optimistically headlined editorials, such as "The Way Cleared for Yerba Buena" (*Chronicle*, March 29, 1972), "Hopeful News on Yerba Buena" (*Examiner*, June 9, 1972), "Help for Yerba Buena" (*Chronicle*, August 9, 1972), "Yerba Buena Looks Up" (*Chronicle*, February 29, 1972). The overall impact of such editorializing is to create a stampede effect, pushing the project forward with little regard for the consequences. Editorial advocacy even enters the letter columns. When Assemblyman John Burton of San Francisco wrote the *Examiner* (November 16, 1971) regarding responsibility for a hotel fire in the YBC area, the following gratuitous disparaging note was appended to his published letter: "Assemblyman Burton has feuded with the Redevelopment Agency for years.—Editor"

Attacks on the South of Market residents and denigrations of their struggle are commonplace. An editorial in the September 20, 1971 *Examiner* decries "harassing lawsuits." Commenting on a HUD grant of $12 million to cover South of Market relocation costs, a June 29, 1972 *Examiner* editorial notes that the "much belabored Yerba Buena may get off the ground—always assuming the absence of further harassing suits which have added millions of dollars to construction costs. By the way, shouldn't those who file suits like that be held accountable in some degree for the damage their delays inflict?" No note is made of damages inflicted on the residents of South of Market or the fact that the residents' claims had been firmly upheld by a federal court. The January 26, 1970 *Chronicle* editorially put forth the following position

---

† Herbert Gans' reports about press coverage of Boston's notorious West End urban renewal project show marked parallels with the Yerba Buena Center story: " . . .[T]he Boston press not only favored the redevelopment of the West End in repeated and enthusiastic editorials, but also covered the news only from the point of view of the Redevelopment Authority. Press releases or interviews with officials about the West End were never complemented by the West Enders' version of the situation, or, indeed, by their feelings about the matter. Features, moreover, depicted the West End as a vice-ridden set of hovels in which respectable human beings could not be expected to live, thus insulting the West Enders and making them feel like outcasts." (*The Urban Villagers*, New York: The Free Press, 1962, p. 172.)

on statutory rights: "In our assessment of the public interest, redevelopment should be allowed and encouraged to go forward undisrupted by harassing litigation." Again, Herman's death provided an opportunity to comment on Yerba Buena and attack its opponents. On September 1, 1971, the *Chronicle* stated editorially: "The only thing that ever stopped him [Herman] was the poverty lawsuit that ground the Yerba Buena project to a halt. It once drew from him a remark that was a key to his single-minded drive and determination. 'A litigation attorney,' he said, 'can do nothing in the social field. We can.' The truth of this remark will, we think, ultimately prevail and become one of his monuments in San Francisco." In a June 11, 1971 *Examiner* editorial, YBC opponents are put down as "ideologues," and in the same editorial the paper goes on to state about South of Market residents:

> *Neither do we believe that such people should have the right—in the absence of some compelling reason deeply rooted in the public good—to delay and quite possibly kill a major public project of profound importance to the economic well-being of a city that is not really their home community, that they have built no stake in, that they make no attempt to adorn, and to which they are on the whole an unsought burden.*†

News coverage (particularly that of the *Examiner's* urban affairs writer, Donald Canter) and columnists in the dailies tended to be more informative and balanced;• but the papers often used "features" and "human interest" stories, sometimes supplied by the Redevelopment Agency, to distort the plight of area residents. One such story in the December 1, 1971 *Chronicle* transmitted directly, without investigation, the Redevelopment Agency's claims that an "illegal hippie commune" was threatening the project with loss of an $8 million office building and 2,000 new permanent jobs. As it turned out, the three individuals under attack were living and working in an $85 per month storefront

---

† This was the second time the *Examiner* had seen fit to publish the exact same editorial characterization of South of Market residents (see the October 15, 1970 *Examiner*.) In an earlier day—before the residents became troublesome by demanding their rights—the *Examiner* had a different view of who lived in the YBC area and urged more charitable treatment. Its February 24, 1964 editorial stated: "We share Mayor Shelley's concern over one important phase of the project. The area contains 3,165 single residents. These are not drifting derelicts. They are for the most part aged persons living in old hotels on small pensions. They will have to be resettled. Into that task must go as much compassion as energy."

• The principal Yerba Buena reporters for both the *Chronicle* and the *Examiner* are, however, supporters of YBC. A former City Hall reporter for the *Chronicle* who took a more critical stance toward the project quit to take a job with the local education TV station's "Newsroom" program, largely as a result of what he felt was excessive editing and rewriting of his stories on YBC.

SFRA and the Redevelopment Booster Club

completely renovated for residency and a carpentry workshop and were legally protected by a federal court order; they were understandably reluctant to move until the Agency could find comparable quarters. However, it was enough to associate "hippie" and "commune" with the well-developed image of "bums" and "degenerates" housed in South of Market flophouses.

Another story of this character, headlined "The High Cost of Don and His Dog," appeared in the April 1, 1971 *Chronicle* and also was clearly designed to put pressure on "holdouts" to move from the Central Blocks area. The story involved attempts by the Redevelopment Agency to remove the last three residents from the Daton Hotel, since keeping it open was allegedly costing $7,000 monthly. Focus was on Don Caldwell, his dog Tammey, and his "dogged obstinancy" in bringing his case before the Relocation Appeals Board established by the federal court to protect the rights of displacees (see pages 140-42.) Caldwell, who was severely crippled, had refused Agency relocation offers because they all involved climbing hills or stairs or living in places with inadequate fire exits. The story had its intended effect. The *Chronicle's* April 1 story produced "a rash of death threats.... The day before, he (Caldwell) said, he received a special delivery letter saying: 'May God punish you that you may pray to die.' The threat, plus four telephoned warnings taken by hotel clerks, 'scared me to death,' said Caldwell, bursting into tears."[27]

A similar story from the February 9, 1970 *Examiner*, reporting on the only remaining resident of the Colorado Hotel, who was at the time under the protection of a federal court order forbidding his eviction, began: "At the cost of $2,000 a month the government is providing 24-hour doorman service for a Skid Row resident." Another *Chronicle* story (October 23, 1972), headlined "One Man's Battle with Yerba Buena," focused on Peter Mendelsohn, chairman of TOOR, presenting him as a crazed senior citizen's power activist, living in the past, and personally holding up the development of YBC.

Generally speaking, coverage of the Yerba Buena controversy was more searching and more sympathetic to the residents in the non-daily press—in particular, the now defunct underground paper *Good Times*, the muckraking biweekly *Bay Area Guardian*, and the twice-weekly *San Francisco Progress*.

The local television and radio stations are no less supportive editorially of Yerba Buena Center than are the daily newspapers. Frequent editorials are aired with such titles as "Yerba Buena is Key" (KGO-TV, July 5-11, 1971), "Economic Disaster Threatens" (KGO-TV, December 6-12, 1971), and "Time to Expedite Yerba Buena" (KFAX, January 9, 1973). Redevelopment Agency handouts are likewise parroted, and the Agency is routinely praised. ("...[T]he Redevelopment Agency is

Propaganda and Property

aware that unsympathetic displacement of people isn't fair play. And we choose to believe it's been responsive to the rights of affected residents," KPIX-TV, June 12-14, 1970—just a few months before the federal court chose to believe the residents' claims to the contrary.) In a flourish of alliterative indignation, radio station KCBS (January 11-16, 1972) editorialized: "Federally financed lawyers have worked feverishly to frustrate the project which, ironically, is mainly funded by federal tax dollars. Somehow, that seems less than reasonable." The Agency-media route is two-way: supportive editorials, such as that broadcast on KGO-TV December 19-24, 1972, are also mailed out by the Agency to its public.†

The tie-in of the media to the tourism-convention industry was acknowledged (and discounted) in the following editorial (May 6, 1971) by KPIX Area Vice-President Louis S. Simon, which began: "Although I'm President-Elect of the Convention and Visitors Bureau, vitally interested in this subject, I am speaking today solely on behalf of KPIX and our Editorial Board."

These, then—the large corporations and financial institutions, the hotels and other downtown businesses, the Convention and Visitors Bureau and Hotel Employers Association, City Hall, the major labor unions, the newspapers and other media—were the principal members of the redevelopment booster club, who provided the public support for the planning and implementation of Yerba Buena Center.

---

† See form letter dated January 15, 1973, from John B. Dykstra, Project Director, Yerba Buena Center Public Facilities, which notes chummily: "A recent KGO-TV editorial summarized the current problems facing Yerba Buena Center. Thought you might be interested."

3. The Assault on South of Market

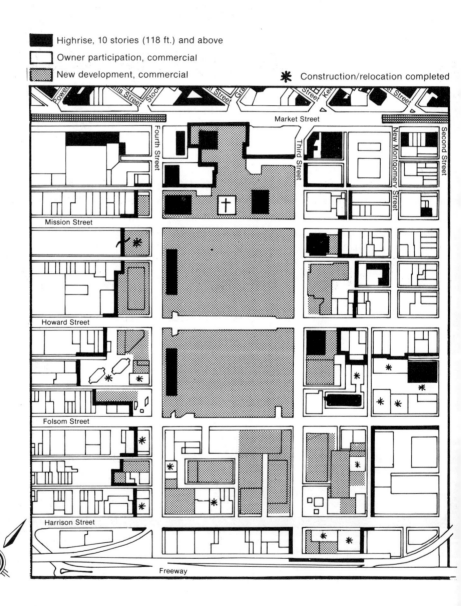

Highrise, 10 stories (118 ft.) and above

Owner participation, commercial

New development, commercial

✳ Construction/relocation completed

Market Street

Fourth Street

Third Street

New Montgomery Street

Second Street

Mission Street

Howard Street

Folsom Street

Harrison Street

Freeway

N

> **Most people in this city don't know**
> **much about Yerba Buena Center . . .**
> **I am disturbed something this big**
> **is not going on the ballot . . . .**
> **If you really want me to tell you,**
> **we have very little control**
> **over the Redevelopment Agency.**
> Member of San Francisco
> Board of Supervisors, 1972

The Redevelopment Agency by the beginning of the sixties had received a clear mandate to redevelop the South of Market area and began to set the urban renewal machinery into motion. Prior to moving in the bulldozers and wrecking balls, the Agency carried out a series of preliminary planning studies. These were necessary in part to provide technical information on which to base rebuilding and relocation plans, but in large part also serve the function of legitimizing such actions, by giving them the aura of objectivity and even necessity. If surveys show overwhelming evidence of "blight," then clearance and removal becomes logical. If economic feasibility studies show that certain uses are "needed," while others are "infeasible," then the nature of the land re-use plan is manifest. The various public bodies at the local and federal level that must approve Redevelopment Agency plans, as well as the public, have little basis to quarrel with the reams of reports by the Agency and outside consultants, on which a final plan is based.

Plans and Approvals

In 1961, with Justin Herman firmly in the saddle, the Redevelopment Agency applied for a federal urban renewal survey and planning grant. Although no specific plan had yet been developed by the Agency, the application outlined the SFRA's proposed treatment of the South of Market area:

- Total removal of residential buildings.
- Removal of business structures blighted beyond conversion or conservation.
- Renovation to renewal and code standards of salvageable commercial and industrial buildings by existing owners.
- Creation of public areas which contribute to a wholesome working environment, with provision for needed public facilities.
- Realignment of streets to permit efficient circulation of traffic.

The Assault on South of Market

• Replotting of parcels to allow better use of the land and encourage new investment.

• Development of all vacant or open land by existing owners.

In addition, while outlining a redevelopment study area slightly larger than that in Ben Swig's 1955 plan, the application moved the site closer to Market Street and also omitted the segment the City Planning Department had identified as the most blighted blocks. Changing project area boundaries was neither capricious nor scientific: the Redevelopment Agency determined and even gerrymandered these boundaries in response to real estate values and the demands of the politically influential. As the *Wall Street Journal* later noted (May 27, 1970):

. . . *[I]t's clear that the redevelopment agency considerably broadened the meaning of the designation "blight" in order to achieve the current boundaries. Ironically, the project now bears a remarkable resemblance to a plan first suggested in 1954 by Benjamin Swig, prominent Democrat and owner of the prestigious Fairmont Hotel on Nob Hill. However, Mr. Swig's "San Francisco Prosperity Plan" was rejected by the redevelopment and planning agency in 1956 on the grounds that it "perverted" the basic reason for redeveloping the area.*

The revised boundaries were well suited to benefit adjacent owners, whose land values could be expected to skyrocket as a result of the renewal project.   the beneficiaries included some of the more powerful and influential individuals and concerns in the city: the Hearst Corporation (publisher of the *Examiner*), the *San Francisco Chronicle*, Pacific Telephone and Telegraph, Ben Swig, Standard Oil, Litton Systems, United California Bank, the Emporium, and others —all of whom owned property in or near the revised area. Particularly interesting is the case of the Emporium, one of the city's major department stores, located on Market Street between Fourth and Fifth and adjacent to the new redevelopment area. Secretary-Treasurer of the Emporium Walter Kaplan also, in his civic role, sat as chairman of the Redevelopment Agency board. He was also president of the city-sponsored Fifth and Mission Garage Corporation. Under the redevelopment plan, Mr. Kaplan's garage was to expand over to Fourth and Mission, all the better to serve Mr. Kaplan's Emporium customers, via land made available through Mr. Kaplan's Redevelopment agency.†

The application sailed through the Board of Supervisors and on to

---

† Kaplan was not the only Redevelopment Agency board member with interests in property adjacent to the YBC project area. Stephen Walter, a Redevelopment Agency commissioner from 1964-1968, is executive vice-president of D. N. and E. Walter & Co., a firm that owns and partially occupies a six-story office building on Mission Street, just east of Second Street.

the Housing and Home Finance Agency, which in October, 1962, approved a planning grant for over $600,000. With federal monies in hand and Swig's conception of a sports-office-convention complex in mind, all survey and planning efforts were directed toward total clearance. The Swig family itself re-entered the YBC picture when in 1962 Ben's son Melvin became part-owner, with Albert Schlesinger, of the city's professional basketball and hockey teams. Swig hired the architectural firm of Skidmore, Owings and Merrill to draw up schematics of a revised Yerba Buena Center plan, focused around an indoor sports arena and convention center. According to Swig, "I was after Justin to get something going arenawise and conventionwise .... I went to see Justin with a plan for a sports arena in Yerba Buena. And he liked the idea very much."[1]

The Agency had hired its own planning consultants, the firm of Livingston & Blayney, to supplement its staff; and they maintained close contacts with the business community. As the February 21, 1964 *Chronicle* reported: "The consultants planned closely with civic leaders and businessmen, many of whom have already expressed interest in the proposals and will serve on a committee created by [Mayor John] Shelley to evaluate it." And the same story added, "Melvin Swig, who proposed the sports arena, will be on the committee."

Although there were important inputs from outside, Justin Herman's general strategy was to keep all planning within his own agency and wherever possible circumvent the City Planning Commission, whose staff, as shown in the past, could not be relied upon to come up with the proper supportive studies. Although California law directs the City Planning Commission to decide project boundaries and devise a Preliminary Plan, James McCarthy, then staff director of the Commission, in a later interview described his agency's role in YBC planning as only "the tail of the kite." The Commission first saw the YBC redevelopment plan upon its completion when the SFRA asked for the planners' approval. The Planning Commission expressed strong resentment at the Redevelopment Agency for having bypassed the city's official planning staff and taking its approval for granted.[2] And SFRA assistant director Robert Rumsey later told the Planning Commission, "I respectfully suggest that you leave the decision to the Board of Supervisors. I doubt that Mr. McCarthy (director of Planning) could find a staff capable of evaluating our planning."[3]

Another tactic in the Agency's *modus operandi* throughout the protracted planning and approval period was to use the presumed (and actual) tentativeness of its plans as a way of manipulating, maneuvering, and remaining in control. Thus initially, when application was being made for a federal planning grant, the Agency asked for approval of its preliminary plan on the basis that it was not binding;

The Assault on South of Market

criticism was deflected and dismissed through the Agency's assurances that all redevelopment plans were tentative, serving only to point directions, and that there would be ample opportunity to change them before they bcame final. When the Agency and its planning consultants completed their final redevelopment scheme in 1964, it asked for approval on the basis that the plan was really nothing more than a detailed elaboration of the preliminary version.

But there was still a good deal of public confusion about Herman's plans for YBC. At first the Agency gave assurance that it was not intending a massive clearance project: according to the February 28, 1961 *Chronicle*, "As Herman foresaw the project, it would require razing only a quarter of the existing structures . . . . Herman cautioned against regarding the projected demolition in terms of 'vast, cleared blocks.' " "We will keep what's rehabilitable, and raze the rest," said Herman.[4] The *Examiner* later (February 1, 1966) noted that: "[T]he Redevelopment Agency itself is definitely not blameless for some of the confusion and discontent among property owners. When the agency asked the supervisors in 1961 to designate the South of Market redevelopment area, it listed as its major aims 'spot clearance' and 'extensive conservation techniques.' " However, the project as developed by the Agency during the years 1962-1965 retained only 15 percent of the buildings originally on the site, and the Central Blocks portion was totally cleared, except for St. Patrick's Church. (The pastor of St. Patrick's, Msgr. Vincent McCarthy, approved the project mightily: "I think Yerba Buena is the greatest thing to come along. When it's built I won't have to stand in the center of Mission Street on Sundays and apologize for the heart of San Francisco."[5])

The Agency unveiled its plans for the South of Market area in February, 1964, and following some revisions applied to the Housing and Home Finance Agency for an urban renewal grant reservation. In June, 1965, the federal agency announced it was setting aside a $19.6 million grant for the project, and the official hearings process began. The Redevelopment Agency board approved the plan unanimously (with Walter Kaplan tactfully abstaining). In January, 1966, the Planning Commission likewise approved the plan unanimously.† And in April the Board of Supervisors by a 9-2 vote (Supervisors Jack Morrison and George Moscone in opposition) gave its approval.

---

†The appointed Planning Commission (to whom the Planning Department staff is responsible) then, as now, included many influential members of the downtown San Francisco business establishment, and Justin Herman was able to lobby the Planning Commissioners sufficiently to gain their general support for his plans, despite interagency rivalry on the staff level.

The Planning Commission's current appointees are: Walter Newman

Non-Supervising Supervisors & DHUD

These rapid-fire approvals were the result of extensive lobbying on the part of the Swigs, Herman, Schlesinger and others, as public and "civic" representatives fell in line behind the plan. Albert Schlesinger of the Convention and Visitors Bureau, along with Herman and one of the Swigs, had talked with each of the Supervisors individually. According to Schlesinger, the plan went through the Board "like shooting fish."

Some opposition voices made themselves heard during the hearings. Labor representatives at that time were upset over the lack of industrial re-use in the area and the loss of blue-collar jobs. Official data were later to show that between 1960 and 1970 manufacturing employment in San Francisco decreased by 19 percent, while employment in finance-insurance-real estate rose 37 percent, and service employment rose 41 percent.[6] Herman promised at least 25 percent of the land in the YBC area would be devoted to industry.[7] The controversial issue of how to relocate 4,000 low-income persons was conveniently side-stepped. Social workers, ministers, and representatives of the city's Human Rights Commission appeared, carrying petitions with several hundred names, to register protest over the lack of relocation housing. Herman promised that he would be able to get federal relocation money when it was needed and emphasized that the plan was flexible within its basic outlines. The *Chronicle* (February 22, 1966) reported that "Herman, responding to a question from Supervisor Terry Francois, said some of the old hotels in the 87-acre area might possibly by rehabilitated instead of demolished." The opposition was weak and unorganized, and Justin Herman knew how to respond to their concerns, at least verbally. But the project in its final form contained few industrial uses, and Herman's negative reaction to a proposal to rehabilitate some of the area's hotels is described on pages 119-21.

The Non-Supervising Supervisors and DHUD

Justin Herman's handling of the Board of Supervisors during the Yerba Buena hearings was typical of Redevelopment Agency relations

---

(chairman), vice-president of I. Magnin and Co., a major department store chain and son-in-law of Cyril Magnin, head of the Port Commission; Mortimer Fleishhacker, a director of Crocker Citizens Bank and a partner in the Golden Gateway urban renewal development; John Ritchie, one of the city's major realtors and former president of the Real Estate Board; Hector Rueda, a representative of the Elevator Constructors Union; and Julia Porter, the member with the longest service and the only commissioner not originally appointed by Mayor Alioto. The two ex-officio members are the general manager of the city's Public Utilities Commission and the city's Chief Administrative Officer (see pages 185-86). Needless to say, such persons have in the past been sympathetic to downtown development projects like YBC.

The Assault on South of Market

with city agencies. As the city's elected legislative body, the Board holds crucial powers in the renewal process because it must approve or disapprove plans before the federal government will release funds reserved for a project. Since Supervisors' positions are only part-time and lack the necessary staff to investigate or evaluate proposed urban renewal plans, the SFRA can overwhelm the Board with a mass of data and federal administrative regulations.

One of the important tools used by Herman to "snow" the Supervisors, and the public in general, were feasibility studies by outside private consultants, employed not only to supplement the Agency's staff capabilities, but to give the image of disinterested objectivity. These various reports were commissioned to show that the federal urban renewal program was absolutely necessary for redevelopment of the area, that redevelopment would have to be total, rather than mere spot clearance, that projected demand for office space and shopping facilities would support large-scale new construction, and that the development as a whole would show a profit.[8]

Consultants' reports inevitably seem to reflect the thinking of the Redevelopment Agency. Rarely are such reports commissioned out of a real desire to amass facts and outside advice for the purpose of making policy decisions. Rather, consultants selected are those who can be relied upon to share the Agency's views, and under these conditions it is the rare outside consultant who will risk future contracts by producing a report sharply different from what is known to be the desired outcome.[9]

Confusion and ignorance as to the technical details are only part of the problem. More basic is that the Supervisors do not really concern themselves with the results of such massive redevelopment projects unless there is extensive public opposition. From their point of view, if the project is held out as costless to the city, fully paid for by federal funds or project-generated revenues, as Herman constantly assured, then there is no reason to dig too deeply into the proposal.

The 11-member Board of Supervisors is elected at-large, and the history of such campaigns has been that candidates with the greatest financial backing get elected. Successful supervisorial campaigns have in the past cost in the vicinity of $100,000—for a part-time job that pays $9,000 a year; a campaign spending limit of 12 cents per registered voter, enacted in time for the 1973 municipal elections, put a $51,000 maximum on campaign spending, but as the December 8, 1973 *Chronicle* noted, the law "did not . . . change the type of contributors that regularly finance elections." Board members for the most part have close ties to downtown business interests, and most reside in the city's wealthy neighborhoods, such as St. Francis Wood, Pacific Heights-Marina, and Nob Hill.[10]

Non-Supervising Supervisors & DHUD

At least two Supervisors in the 1968-73 period had direct interest in seeing the Yerba Buena project completed. Supervisor Robert Mendelsohn was an employee of Lawrence Halprin and Associates, landscape architect for YBC. He also had been a Redevelopment Agency official from 1961-64. Supervisor Peter Tamaras owns the Tamaras Supply Company, which provides janitorial services and supplies to most major hotels in the downtown area. Other Supervisors have an interest in some aspect of city-wide face-lifting, through their real estate and business activities, employment by downtown interests, or union ties. With few exceptions, the Board has been a willing supporter of plans for downtown renewal and other redevelopment projects, displaying caution only when there was a likelihood of incurring strong public disapproval.

Board of Supervisors approval of the Yerba Buena Center plan in April, 1966, gave the SFRA and downtown corporate and financial interests the go-ahead they had been seeking since the late 1950s. While actual land clearance and forced relocation of South of Market residents was still a year or two off, the Redevelopment Agency could now take action and turn the proposals into a plan that could be nicely packaged and sold to the public—a prelude to the actions that would come along with the wrecking balls and bulldozers.

The Board of Supervisors was not the only government entity which processed the YBC plans without exercising control over the evolution of the project. Their posture of ceding effective responsibility to private interests and the Redevelopment Agency, and their unwillingness and inability to marshall independent evaluation and re-direct the project, were matched or exceeded by the U.S. Department of Housing and Urban Development—the federal agency charged with overall supervision of redevelopment projects.[11]

Created in 1965 to give cabinet status to the Housing and Home Finance Agency, HUD evolved as essentially a conduit of funds to local agencies. As its legislative mandate to *control* projects has developed, its philosophy and staff capacity have not kept pace. HUD staff tend to favor large-scale downtown development. There has been a movement of personnel between HUD and local government agencies and private companies undertaking this type of development. Moreover, HUD staff have traditionally subordinated themselves to local initiative. It is signficant that Justin Herman moved *up* to the directorship of the San Francisco Redevelopment Agency from his position as regional director of the HHFA with jurisdiction over all HHFA activity (including urban renewal) for the entire Western United States. HUD's deference was related to the composition of the Agency. The SFRA staff by the late 1960s was approximately five times greater than that of the entire regional office of HUD which was nominally supervising it and all other HUD activity in 11 states.

High staff turnover, combined with a cadre of "deadwood" protected by federal civil service requirements, have left HUD (or, as it is sometimes acronymized by its critics, DHUD) with a staff that does not have the capacity to control the more stable and technically competent staffs of large redevelopment agencies such as the SFRA. Within HUD the enormous paper flow involved in project approval was distributed among a range of highly specialized technicians' offices over a very long period of time; overall assessment of the project was almost nonexistent. Prior to neighborhood protest and litigation the YBC relocation plan had been processed and approved in isolation from the rest of the project activities and the legal counsel's office had routinely signed approvals as to the legality of the project. Only after the deficiencies in HUD's supervisory role became so blatant as to embarrass the Department publicly did it intervene in the project.

Urban Design: Form Follows Finance

In December, 1966, the Redevelopment Agency and HUD signed the urban renewal loan and grant contract making available the federal funds reserved for YBC, and by July of 1967 site preparation commenced. Properties and buildings were purchased and condemned, design plans prepared, and the search for a developer launched. All efforts focused on the Central Blocks, the 25 acres of YBC bounded by Third, Fourth, Market and Folsom Streets, which were to contain the principal convention and sport facilities (see page 83). The surrounding 62 acres would primarily contain office buildings on some two dozen parcels, and their design, although subject to Redevelopment Agency approval, would be handled by individual developers and their architects, once the central lodestone of public facilities had been fixed.

It was Justin Herman's decision to produce a detailed urban design plan as soon as possible, before selecting a developer—rather than follow the more usual urban renewal practice of having developers bid on a plan and then hire their own architects. He felt this would give him more control over the project, for in theory it meant that the Redevelopment Agency, not the developer, would be in charge of locating the facilities and determining their configuration. Herman was determined to retain as much control over the project as long as possible, knowing that once the developer entered the scene practical considerations of profitability and capability would begin to fix its details. He also wanted a visually striking project, stemming from both his general interest in design quality and his desire to attract adequate financing and prestigious developers from outside the Bay Area.

To head the Central Blocks urban design team, Herman chose the internationally known Japanese architect Kenzo Tange; and to insure a

Urban Design: Form Follows Finance

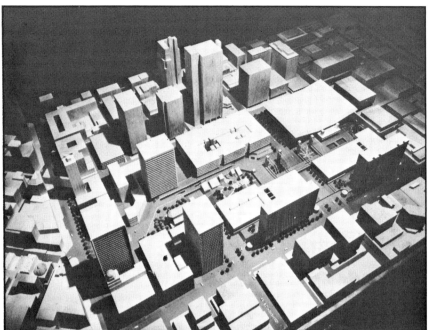

Yerba Buena Center, facing southeast from Market Street

functionalist approach, local inputs, City Hall contacts and high quality landscape design for the extensive malls and plazas, teamed Tange with local architects John Bolles and Gerald McCue and landscape architect Lawrence Halprin. However, as planning for YBC moved ahead, it became clear that rather than the design dictating the behavior of the developer, the financial needs of both the city and the private developer would dictate the design.

This design team was named in January, 1968, and unveiled its product in June, 1969, with great fanfare. (Fittingly, the unveiling took place at the annual luncheon of the Convention and Visitors Bureau, hosted by Richard L. Swig, the Bureau's president.) It was a beautiful package designed to impress the public and attract a major developer. Since the basic decisions and guidelines for the YBC Central Blocks design had already been set in the earlier work of the Redevelopment Agency's planning consultant, Livingston & Blayney, the design team's task was really how to fit all the facilities into 25 acres and how to accommodate such bulky structures as the exhibition hall, sports arena and parking garages.

The urban design team's plan provided for a 350,000 square foot exhibition hall, a 14,000 seat sports arena, an 800 room hotel, a 2,200

The Assault on South of Market

seat theater, an Italian Cultural and Trade Center,† parking for 4,000 cars, an airlines terminal, four office buildings, shops, restaurants, pedestrian malls, and landscaped plazas. Most prominent visually were two massive multi-story parking structures, while the convention center was placed underground. These "unique visual elements" (a representation of which was used by the SFRA as its logo for the YBC project) well symbolized the financial importance of the garages to the project: the construction cost of these parking structures was to be the principal element in the city's local contribution required under the federal urban renewal financing formula, and the largest revenue source from YBC facilities for repaying the bond issue that would be required for their construction (see pages 162-67). The fact that the garages were the only sure revenue-producers *and* the best means to get urban renewal credits exerted some pressure on the design team to make them as expensive as possible, in order to garner more credits. (Under the urban renewal financing formula, a locality can substitute construction of public facilities for a cash contribution in providing the local share of the renewal subsidy—see pages 160-61).

These financial demands also led to disregard of the overall transportation picture in the area. YBC will be served by two BART stations, is bordered by two regional bus terminals and the Southern Pacific commuter station, and is surrounded and criss-crossed by several municipal bus and trolley lines. Automobile traffic in the vicinity is already dense, and the main auto feeders to the area will be the freeway exits serving downtown, which for many years have been inadequate during rush hours. (The auto-centeredness of the project and the values it represents are well illustrated by the fact that the YBC urban design plan allotted each car 500 square feet of space, whereas the typical resident of the area was living in a room of about 100 square feet. The two parking structures contained enough room to house nearly 4,000 people in two-bedroom high-rise apartments under FHA minimum standards, or as many people as were to be displaced by the YBC project!)

The truth of that important but rarely acknowledged architectural canon that "form follows finance" was revealed *a fortiori* after selection of the developer for the Tange et al. Central Blocks design (as de-

---

† The Italian Cultural and Trade Center was later dropped from the plan in favor of a location nearer North Beach, the city's Italian population center. Other major elements (such as a new home for the San Francisco Museum of Art and a San Francisco campus for the University of California) have been in and out of the YBC plan over the years. Some Agency critics have charged that facilities such as the Italian Cultural and Trade Center were publicized as part of the plan in order to garner public support, even though the Agency knew these elements would eventually be dropped or shifted to another location.

Urban Design: Form Follows Finance

scribed below), when one of the parking structures was magically trans-
formed to another use. The developer had already lined up tenants for
a one million square foot apparel mart which was not part of the urban
design plan, and since it was central to his profit-making plans, room
simply had to be made. In an embarrassment of the notion that form
follows function, the architects simply fit the apparel mart inside a
wing of one of the parking structures, and the now useless spiral automobile ramps in this newly designated section were retained as a
formal part of the mart. Later, at the developer's insistence, the parking was to be placed underground, and the number of spaces was
reduced to 2,450 (600 under the apparel mart, 1,850 under the exhibition hall).

In addition to changes in the parking structures, the luxury hotel
planned for the area was moved from its original site on Third
Street—across from the Del Monte Corporation's planned headquarters building directly adjacent to the Central Blocks—and over to
Fourth Street, closer to the BART station and the downtown hotel
district. At the time Del Monte was originally scheduled to own and
manage the luxury hotel, the "best" site to be found was across from its
planned world headquarters; when the hotel came under the charge of
the developer the notion of "best" location changed and the hotel and
other supporting conference facilities were accordingly transferred.†
The more recent changes in the Central Blocks plan were carried out
by the firm of McCue Boone Tomsick, of the original design team.
McCue's locally based office was retained by the Agency to work with
the developer on any needed plan revisions and now bears the title of
Executive Architects for the project. Funds for design and engineering
work amounting to several million dollars had already been provided
for in the hotel tax increase passed in 1967 to create a special fund for
this purpose.

More questionable from an urban design standpoint is the wisdom of
creating a massive convention complex in the middle of downtown, set
off from the city that surrounds it. It is likely that the area will suffer
from monumental deadness at various times of the day and during
periods when it is not in use; set-up and take-down times before and
after large conventions, lasting several days, guarantee that there will
be considerable "dead time" in the complex. As one critic put it:

*Yerba Buena is designed for people who do not live in San Francisco. It won't
belong to the city; it will remain aloof, luxurious but dead, attractive but sterile,
recreating the hollowness and helplessness of an airport terminal . . . . The
Redevelopment Agency is missing an opportunity to develop an integrated community to meet the diverse needs of San Francisco . . .*[12]

†See also note to page 55.

The Assault on South of Market

Selecting a Developer

Once the basic YBC urban design plan was produced, the Redevelopment Agency's task was to designate a developer for the Central Blocks. The 1949 Housing Act, which initiated the urban renewal program, does not authorize local redevelopment agencies to engage in building activities directly; rather, their role is to assemble land for resale, at a marked-down price, to developers who agree to build according to agency plans. In the case of Yerba Buena Center the private developer was to have special importance, for it was Justin Herman's decision that the development of the entire 25-acre Central Blocks area, public as well as private facilities, would go to a single private group. Public facilities would then be leased back to the city.

Herman's reasons for this rather unusual step were several. Private development of the sports arena, convention center and other public facilities would obviate the need for public construction financing and hence bypass the need for a public vote on a general obligation bond issue. Failure to approve the bonds would jeopardize the entire project, a possibility neither Herman nor others pushing the project wanted to risk. Herman and his agency wanted direct and exclusive control over the development and could exercise their control most effectively by having to deal with only a single partner. The development process would be speedier, Herman felt, and the "package" more attractive to the private developer if fees for construction of the public facilities were included. Herman made his decision despite the fact that his consultants' studies had shown a general obligation bond issue would be cheaper; that Supervisor Roger Boas' South of Market Advisory Committee (see note to page 33) had recommended this type of financing; and that, based upon the information given out by the Redevelopment Agency, the Board of Supervisors presumed this would be the method of financing when it approved the project in 1966. The August 25, 1965 *Chronicle*, for example, describes the YBC plan developed by the Redevelopment Agency as follows: "It would include the convention center and sports arena and parking for 3300 cars, financed by a $42 million general obligation bond issue, supplemented by a one percent increase in the city's three percent hotel tax."[13] Herman felt that the delays and risks involved in a general obligation bond issue and public vote were to be avoided at all costs.

Herman's decision to rely on a single developer compounded the risks inherent in urban renewal projects. What is finally constructed on renewal sites tends to be more the product of subsequent negotiations between developers and agency officials, rather than procedure strictly according to the formally approved plan. A study of redevelopment in Newark in the late 1950s found that: "It is self-evident to NHA [Newark Housing Authority] officials that decisions on sites and their uses must be adapted to the demands of the investor if projects are to be successful."† And as one experienced corporate developer put it:

A private redeveloper has got to have a lot of confidence in his local rede-velopment authority to buy one of these programs. . . . He needs confidence that if he commits for a redevelopment which obligates him to build to a specific program over a substantial number of years, the redevelopment agency will be reasonably flexible in its insistence upon time schedules and in revisions of the program, where experience indicates the original concept to be uneconomic. [14]

Indeed, a redevelopment plan often represents little more than an open invitation to developers to engage in speculative promotions. Once a redevelopment plan is approved, the developer, not the public, becomes the single most influential client of the redevelopment agency.

Finding a single super-competent developer (with diversified talents in bonding, leasing, planning, and construction) willing to take on the entire Central Blocks area proved difficult. SFRA advertised for bids on the Central Blocks in June, 1969, making use of an elaborate brochure based on the work of the urban design team. The search went slowly, and the initial deadline had to be extended. Efforts were directed at finding a major national developer, since Justin Herman felt that only a development corporation of substantial size and reputation could guarantee completion of the project. *Fortune* ads notwithstanding, only 14 would-be developers expressed any interest in the YBC Central Blocks, and of these only five actually entered the competition, one of whom immediately withdrew.

Of the four bidders only two proved to be final contenders. Clement Chen, a San Francisco architect, was unable to secure financing. A second, the Dillingham Corporation, withdrew in October, 1970, because of internal problems. Dillingham, a family corporation which began as the Oahu Railway and Land Company in 1889 and expanded and prospered as a heavy construction and engineering firm throughout the Pacific Basin in the wake of World War II and U.S. military adventures in Southeast Asia, came closest to meeting the Agency's

---

† Harold Kaplan, *Urban Renewal Politics: Slum Clearance in Newark* (New York: Columbia University Press, 1963), p. 29. This fact was dramatized in the 1950s when redevelopment agencies all over the country cleared thousands of acres of urban land only to discover that they could not convince developers to purchase the land and build in accordance with the agencies' original plans. One way to avoid this type of failure was the approach taken by Robert Moses in his mammoth New York City clearance programs in the 1950s: private negotiations between speculative developers and the redevelopment agency over sites, plans, and land prices prior to public announcement of urban renewal projects or solicitation of bids. These practices, and the scandals they gave rise to, are described in Jeanne Lowe, *Cities in a Race with Time* (New York: Random House, 1967), pp. 70-72.

The Assault on South of Market

aesire tor a major corporate developer. The firm had constructed
hotel, condominium and office building projects in Hawaii and also
had wide experience in design, planning, financing, leasing and management. Its mainland experience included the Bunker Hill downtown
renewal project in Los Angeles and San Francisco's new Union Square
Hyatt House high-rise hotel.

Dillingham joined with Albert Schlesinger of Convention and Visitors Bureau fame to form a YBC partnership. Schlesinger, who was
the former Chairman of the City's Parking Authority and had an
entrepreneur's penchant and talent for packaging and financing major
projects, was central to this team. The Dillingham group was clearly the
strongest of the four contenders, and its sudden withdrawal due to
internal corporate disagreements about the wisdom of the venture was
a blow to the Redevelopment Agency's hopes for a major corporate
developer. The third bidder was Terra California, a local consortium
headed by San Francisco developer Harold Moose, whose previous
ventures included the so-called "Chinese Cultural Center," otherwise
known as the Chinatown Holiday Inn.†

Finally, there was Arcon/Pacific, a partnership consisting of talented
but relatively unknown figures led by Lyman Jee, an architect-
developer with several small commercial buildings to his credit, and
Elijah McCartt, who had formerly worked as a city planning intern with
the Redevelopment Agency on YBC surveys. Jee and McCartt, having
previously collaborated, formed a YBC partnership with the support of
Bay Securities, a subsidiary of the Texas-based ISI Mutual Fund. When

---

† The Chinese Cultural Center is a recently completed floor of the $15
million 27-story Downtown Holiday Inn built in 1970 on the site of the old Hall
of Justice (police department headquarters) under the auspices of the Redevelopment Agency. The hotel and the $600,000 foot-bridge connecting the Inn
with Portsmouth Square and Chinatown sparked considerable controversy. The
Redevelopment Agency wanted commercial development on lands adjacent to
its Golden Gateway project, while residents of notoriously overcrowded
Chinatown wanted housing. As a "compromise," the Agency and developers
agreed to dedicate one floor of the new hotel for use as a Chinese Cultural
Center, providing the community would come up with the money needed
($4-600,000) to construct the center. As a recent (January 28, 1973) *Examiner*
story noted, "To date, the most culturally redeeming aspect of the building is the
fact that its predominantly Caucasian clientele is served by a largely Chinese
staff." After numerous delays and difficulties, the Center opened in October,
1973. The economic and political details of this project, in many ways a mini-
YBC, may be found in Mike Miller, "The Inscrutable Chinese Cultural
Center—It's a Holiday Inn," *San Francisco Bay Guardian*, March 28, 1972,
and in the two-part series by John Burks, "Chinatown's Dream Delayed" and
"Chinatown's Bridge of 1,000 Controversies," *San Francisco Examiner*, July 26,
and 27, 1971.

"Protecting" the Central Blocks

ISI decided to drop all speculative projects, McCartt formed Pacific National Equity. The partnership selected R. W. Pressprich, a New York bond house, to advise them on bonding and Damon Raike, a large local realtor, to arrange pre-leasing agreements. Jee and Damon Raike were able to obtain leasing commitments from the Del Monte Corporation for managing the YBC hotel and convention center. Meyer Brothers Parking Systems, an RCA subsidiary, was committed to the parking facilities. Schlesinger, left adrift with the collapse of the Dillingham venture, joined up with the Jee group, in a marriage reportedly arranged by Justin Herman.

In this greatly reduced competition, Schlesinger-Arcon/Pacific won handily. The group was a far cry from Justin Herman's original boast—"The development is of such proportions that I don't think there are more than three or four combines in all the world big enough to handle it"[15]—but under the circumstances it was the best that could be found. The group's proposal was conditionally adopted by the Redevelopment Agency's commissioners at their October 22, 1970 meeting, and in March, 1971, the decision was made final. Events, however, were to dictate that the city would jettison Justin Herman's plan to have a single private developer for the Central Blocks and would itself take over development of the public facilities.

"Protecting" the Central Blocks

One of the key planning concepts applied under Justin Herman was the "protected environment."† In essence, the idea is to create a *cordon sanitaire*: surround the central development of a renewal project with peripheral construction that will provide an effective physical barrier to deter former residents from moving back into or adjacent to the area.• In San Francisco the notion originally took shape with the Western Addition and Golden Gateway projects. As applied to Yerba Buena Center, "creating a protected environment" obviously meant large-scale demolition and people removal; it served as a code word for

---

† The phrase "protected environment" appears frequently in Agency publicity about Yerba Buena Center. See, for example, the Agency's brochure inviting developers to bid on the Central Blocks, "A Major Opportunity to Invest in Downtown San Francisco" (n.d. [1969]), which speaks of YBC being large enough to "guarantee a protected, quality environment. . ."

• Most relocation studies, particularly of downtown area displacement projects, indicate that persons tend to relocate in a highly centripetal pattern. In a Minneapolis study, for example, 70-80 percent of the displacees moved within a one-mile radius, and in a New Jersey study 74 percent of the displacees moved within six blocks. See Chester W. Hartman, "The Housing of Relocated Families," *Journal of the American Institute of Planners*, November, 1964, pp. 266-286.

The Assault on South of Market

ridding the area totally and permanently of its poor and skid row populations. As the September 5, 1971 *Examiner* put it, "the late M. Justin Herman had planned to dot [the surrounding blocks] with office buildings,. . .to create a powerful urban fortress." In the more graphic words of a Del Monte executive interviewed for this study, "You certainly can't expect us to erect a 50 million dollar building in an area where dirty old men will be going around exposing themselves to our secretaries." While the gentleman expressed concern for the sensibilities of secretaries, in reality his concern had far more to do with the calculations of investors.

The Redevelopment Agency's plan was to surround the Central Blocks with high-rise office buildings totaling nearly five million square feet, classy shops and restaurants, and similar uses. This served the dual function of protecting the public facilities and providing a large number of office building sites to house the Bay Area's corporate activities. Several private high-rise buildings were constructed in this periphery during the 1960s in anticipation of YBC, and a number of office buildings and other structures have been erected or rehabilitated in the blocks adjacent to the YBC project area. Eighteen redevelopment parcels are slated for sale to private developers, and "owner-participation agreements" are slated for some three dozen existing owners of buildings in the surrounding redevelopment area who have agreed to renovate their structures according to Agency plans and standards.

Activity in this surrounding area has been slow, pending resolution of the controversy over the Central Blocks development. As of February, 1973, the Agency had designated private developers on only three of the 18 sites outside the Central Blocks area, and a firm commitment had been signed with only one.[16] In addition, the San Francisco Community College District will be constructing a seven-story vocational education center on a site adjoining the Central Blocks. One major developer, Crocker-Citizens Bank, dropped plans for constructing a computer center in YBC. Another, the Del Monte Corporation, abandoned its plan to construct a headquarters building in YBC and will instead lease space in a new building outside the project area.[17] The continued delays and uncertainties of the project, stemming from litigation and controversy, have so far made it difficult to flesh out the protected environment concept.

Ridding the area of its existing population was thus a key part of the Redevelopment Agency's goals in the South of Market area and was regarded as a necessity if the downtown office area was to be successfully propelled across the Market Street divide. While no forced displacement of the 4,000 residents could take place until the Agency's plans were given final approval, not so subtle campaigns to purge the

"Protecting" the Central Blocks

area were begun before the official starting date for the project. In early 1966 the Agency flooded the South of Market area with a pamphlet, illustrated by photos of napping and wine-sipping skid-row residents amidst heaps of rubbish, which stated: "They say this is good enough for you. . . . We say you deserve better." Several thousand of these pamphlets were mailed out, to all known residents of the renewal project area, although "the envelope in which the pamphlets were stuffed bore no return address."[18] Such propaganda efforts also nourished the image of South of Market as an area harboring people who were of little value to society and who might without qualm be transferred elsewhere.

The concern expressed at the public hearings about proper relocation was handled with similar pamphleteering. Several weeks before the January, 1966 Planning Commission hearings on the YBC plan, the Agency distributed to area residents a brochure headed, "Of course Urban Renewal wants you out, but into safe, decent, comfortable housing you can afford." A photo was also included of Justin Herman presenting someone with a check for $457, headed, "Money for the Holidays." (In a small block of tiny type the recipient was identified as a former resident of the Golden Gateway project site. The leaflet was condemned as misleading and unethical by a group of concerned ministers working in the South of Market area.[19])

The machinery was cranking up to begin implementation of the plan to cast out the old and bring in the new.

4. South of Market Fights Back

Howard Street, South of Market, 1953

Nor do we believe that such people
should have the right—in the absence
of some compelling reason deeply rooted
in the public good—to delay and
quite possibly kill a major public project
of profound importance to the economic
well-being of a city that is not really
their home community, that they have
built no stake in, that they make no attempt
to adorn, and to which they are on the whole
an unsought burden.

Editorial, *San Francisco Examiner,*
October 15, 1970, and again on June 11, 1971

One of the greatest injustices in South of Market redevelopment has been the callous obliteration of its past. The name chosen by the Redevelopment Agency to dignify its project, "Yerba Buena" (Spanish for "good grass" or "good herb"), was the name of the original Spanish settlement which in 1847 became San Francisco. While rhetorical continuation of the old pioneering tradition serves public relations, in reality the project represents destruction and eviction of a human past regarded as not worth acknowledging, much less honoring. The irony here is compounded by the fact that the original settlement was wrested from Mexican Californians by American pioneers in the Mexican-American War: the redevelopment process is but a more sophisticated wrinkle in the long American tradition of land-grabbing.

Workingmen's Quarter[1]

For nearly a century the South of Market area, where Yerba Buena Center is to be located, has been a home to men and women whose lives and labors form the rich tradition of San Francisco and the West. Once also a haven for the wealthy, who moved out as the human and industrial wellsprings of their wealth closed in around them, South of Market gradually became a neighborhood populated mainly by single men: the workingmen, immigrants, transients and hoboes who gathered to live, work, or just spend time there.

Jack London, himself born South of Market, described the division of the city's downtown area that persisted until the YBC project was devised to obliterate it. In his story "South of the Slot" (after the cable slot of the Market Street cars), he wrote: "Old San Francisco . . . was divided by the Slot. . . . North of the Slot were the theatres, hotels, and shopping district, the banks and the staid, respectable business houses. South of the Slot were the factories, slums, laundries, machine shops, boiler works, and the abodes of the working class."

There are South of Market areas in most American cities. Their

South of Market Fights Back

primary economic function has been the sheltering and maintenance of a reserve army of skilled and unskilled workers. Here grew up the workingmen's institutions: the hotels and lodging houses whose proprietors acted as bankers so that men spending their regular off-seasons in San Francisco had safekeeping for their money and could not splurge it on a single spree; saloons which furnished the men smorgasbord "free lunches" for ten or fifteen cents and sometimes doubled as informal employment agencies; pawnshops where a person might put up a tool or some clothing to pay for food, drink or shelter; and, at one time, a dense network of second-hand stores (51), employment agencies hiring mainly for out-of-town jobs (seven on a single block), pool rooms, movie theaters, barber colleges where apprentice barbers could practice and men get free haircuts, and the missions, varying in number with the season and the state of the economy. Until the mid-1920s, there was the local headquarters of the Industrial Workers of the World. Often on opposite street corners bands, choirs and preachers from the various missions, along with the IWW, could be heard singing different words to the same tunes, and making altogether different arguments. This network sheltered and supported the homeless: seamen, miners, woodcutters, men who built the railroads, agricultural and other seasonal workers, hoboes, bums and the "home guard" of casual laborers who worked regularly or irregularly at unskilled jobs in the city.

The last quarter of the nineteenth century saw the beginning of a large-scale influx of both skilled and unskilled workers, resulting from greatly increased exploitation of western resources and the opening up of commercial activities in the Pacific region, stretching all the way to Asia. Between 1870 and 1880 the South of Market district became more congested as the city absorbed the many German, Irish, and English immigrants, families as well as single men. These same years marked a great expansion in the hotel, lodging, and boarding house population, continuing a tradition from the 1850s Gold Rush, when winter rains and snow drove thousands of miners to the Bay towns. Miners still returned to pass the winter pursuing the amusements of the city, joining sailors on leave and agricultural laborers from the valleys. Cyclical unemployment and the seasonal nature of many of the jobs held by South of Market residents led to great mobility; in none of the periods 1871-1876, 1880-1885, and 1890-1895 did more than 21 percent of the residents stay at the same address.

The 1906 Earthquake and Fire did heavy damage to the "made ground" over the large swamp originally covering South of Market and razed many of the area's wooden structures. Yet within three years the city was largely rebuilt, including South of Market. Apartment and boarding houses and smaller dwellings reappeared along narrow alley-streets, and hotels resumed their places along the major thoroughfares. By 1907, 58 new hotels and 80 new lodging houses had been built. Small manufacturing, wholesaling, and warehousing concerns gradually rose again among these residences. The Irish and Germans who returned to their old neighborhood were joined by a large Greek community. This settlement, which occurred between 1910 and 1920, was at first largely composed of men who had worked their way across the country on railroad crews. They often opened tea or coffee houses and inexpensive restaurants, serving the Greek and other single men's community. Other immigrants opened pawnshops and new and second-hand clothing stores. The formerly genteel South Park neighborhood just to the south became a mixed area of warehouses, machine shops, and flats housing a Japanese community. South of Market thus became a neighborhood of every nationality.

Two "main stems" grew up after 1906 and remained for over 50 years. Along Third Street men came to gamble in the many saloons with their special back rooms that doubled as "bookie joints," legal until 1938. On Howard Street, the men spent most of their time on the street, looking at the blackboards advertising work, drinking, or pitching pennies on the sidewalk. The Howard Street area became known as the "slave market" due to the extraordinary exploitation and suffering that migratory and unskilled workers were subject to. As most available employment was temporary, and located away from the cities, the men forced into casual labor were left to the mercy of employment agencies and employers. The employers contracted with agencies to provide workers, and in turn the agencies sold the jobs for a fee, either paid in advance or out of a man's earnings. It was to the advantage of the employers and the agencies to have a large pool of unskilled and unemployed workers who formed an industrial reserve army. Because they moved from job to job and from employer to employer it was difficult for migratory workers and transients to organize for better pay and conditions. When they did take action, usually inspired by the IWW, it was by walking out on a temporary job, doing as little work as possible or briefly striking. With the Depression even the "slave market" disappeared, as there were no jobs to either sell or buy, and those able to work were directed to public works projects.

In addition to fostering, sustaining, and relying on this industrial reserve army of job-hungry men, capitalist development as it occurred in California and other western states used men up in another sense. Exposure to the elements in rural jobs, the hazards of mining, logging, and construction work, lack of medical attention, insufficient diet and arduous work made men either unable or unwilling to continue. Men wore out early, with little provision by society for premature old age and premature retirement. Thus were created groups of retirees and causal workers who settled in the quarter they knew to pursue easier part-time or irregular work.

During World War II, heavy unemployment no longer characterized South of Market as huge work demands provided ready jobs. In the war years San Francisco became a dormitory metropolis housing war industry workers and military personnel. As newly arrived workers, seamen, soldiers and sailors joined the traditional residents in the hotels, boarding houses, bars and restaurants, South of Market temporarily revived. After the war the cheap hotel district remained, and by 1950 unattached men represented 72 percent of the area's population.

Wartime brought to the South of Market one obvious change that occurred in most other northern cities as well as in other parts of San Francisco: a substantial immigration of non-whites. This migration of mainly Black workers was followed by an influx of Asians. South of Market was to become during the 1950s a reception area for a Filipino population of seasonal workers and, later, of family groupings.

South of Market remained as a workingmen's quarter after the Second World War. Joining the transients and migratory workers were men who worked on jobs at the docks, warehouses and factories surrounding the residential neighborhood; and, increasingly, those too old to work who found the network of cheap hotels and restaurants the only way of surviving on fixed pensions or welfare.

This was the character of South of Market when the redevelopment forces entered the picture in the 1950s, beginning the project which was to wipe the area clean of all this past.

"Skid Row" or Community?

About 4,000 persons were living in the South of Market area slated for destruction to make way for Yerba Buena Center. Apart from about 300 families, residents of South of Market were for the most part single, elderly, male and poor, surviving on the meager proceeds of Social Security and small pensions.† Some were alcoholics. Most, however, were retired or disabled working men who had come to the South of Market to spend the remaining days of their lives. The area and its 48 residential hotels provided them with inexpensive housing• and

---

† According to surveys undertaken for the Redevelopment Agency, 75 percent of the individual householders were over 45 years old, 94 percent were men, and 57 percent had incomes of less than $200 per month. Nearly 90 percent of all individual householders were white, although families living in the YBC project area were predominantly non-white. See E. M. Schaffran and Company, "Relocation Survey Report, South of Market Redevelopment Project" (December, 1963 and July, 1965).

• The condition of these inexpensive residential hotels varied, but a large

"Skid Row" or Community?

eating places. It was sunny and flat, in a city where hills and fog abound. It was downtown, near Market Street, the city's transportation hub, and other facilities they needed. Most of all, it provided them with a community of other single men with common backgrounds, experience and problems. People looked out for each other and took care of one another. Men gathered to talk, watch television, and just be with other people in the hotel lobbies, streets, restaurants and bars. South of Market was their family and their home. An *Examiner* feature story from late 1965 gave some flavor of the positive aspects of life South of Market:

William Colvin, a retired painting contractor, is typical. For years, he has lived in Room 409 of the Albany Hotel at 187 Third Street, where operator James W. Walker spent $15,000 last year for a new fire prevention sprinkler system. The rooms are clean, with a homey warmth.

"Most people don't understand" Colvin said, "But let me tell you something. A man can enjoy freedom here. All of us have many friends. To us, this has been home for years. We enjoy life.

"If you're ill, or hungry, your neighbors help. I don't think you'll find any finer people in the world. We're good citizens . . . ."

"But most of all there is something spiritual about all this. It's something money couldn't buy. We have something that couldn't be replaced with all the money our federal government could put in here. We like it the way it is. We want to stay. We don't want to be regimented by some agency."[2]

All through the hearing and planning stages for YBC, the fate of these people was considered a minor matter. The area was referred to by the planners, newspapers and city officials as "skid row," and the people who lived there were "bums," "drifters," and "transients."[3] Official agencies and the business community played on class prejudices, particularly of suburban commuters who daily pass through South of Market on their way between the Southern Pacific station and nearby office buildings and stores in the financial district and downtown shopping area. This carefully cultivated image of the residents of South of Market enabled the planners of Yerba Buena Center to present their project as a two-fold public service: they were providing economic revival through construction jobs and increased tourist and convention business, and were also assisting the city in clearing out an

portion was decent and sound housing, and still more was rehabilitable. That it by no means was the worst segment of the city's housing stock was indicated when the city's Public Welfare Commission in mid-1964 sent notices to 118 residential hotels warning that housing allowances to Old Age Security recipients (mainly single men and women) would be shut off in three months unless the buildings were fixed up; according to the May 22, 1964 *Examiner*: "Of the 118 buildings on the list, only five were in the South of Market district which formerly was regarded as the center of substandard housing here."

South of Market Fights Back

"undesirable element."

But such labels were patently false. The most comprehensive social study of the area's population, prepared by a Redevelopment Agency consultant, noted that "Alcoholism, either alone or in concert with other disorders, accounted for only 15 percent [of the individuals living in the YBC area], although it stands out as the chief disorder among those enumerated."†[4] However, labeling of this sort permitted the power structure and the public at large to disregard or dismiss injustices being done to those who lived in the area. Property and profits were far more important than people.

But the South of Market residents did not see it this way. When the Redevelopment Agency moved in and began to intimidate the residents and take away their homes, there were many who decided to resist. First acting individually, later collectively, the residents moved to oppose the destruction of their neighborhood. The heart of their struggle was an involved court battle in which they tried to secure their legal rights to decent relocation housing, and to be free of the harassing tactics of the Redevelopment Agency.

Housing: The Key

Given the formidable backing for the YBC project and its lengthy period of preparation, the prospects of stopping the juggernaut altogether seemed remote. What these South of Market residents were thus compelled to focus on—and what according to law was their right—was decent, safe, and sanitary housing at rents they could afford.• Their principal issue was that the Redevelopment Agency was either unwilling or unable to relocate properly the 3,000 single residents and 280 families in the area.

Since these people were single, mostly poor, and for the most part

---

† The Agency's attempt to dismiss the YBC area as a skid row also, of course, denied the important function the area served as a support system for persons afflicted with alcoholism. As sociologist Ronald Vander Kooi notes: "The social character of skid row, with its easy acceptance, friendship, and money for lodging, makes it a desirable place for those who have no home affiliations. . . .Since skid row is so very social, with only the most pathological of men drinking alone in their rooms or seeking isolation, demolition of skid row means that gathering places are razed and cronies separated. . . .[S]kid row residents. . .suffer from loneliness as old friends disperse to other parts of the city or even to other towns. . . .[W]ell over 100,000 skid rowers today face an immediate crisis in their new homelessness caused by the destruction of skid rows and their dislocation by urban renewal." "The Main Stem: Skid Row Revisited," *Society*, September/October, 1973, pp. 67, 71.

• Federal law requires the local renewal agency to guarantee "that there are or are being provided, in the urban renewal area or in other areas not generally less desirable in regard to public utilities and public and commercial

elderly or physically disabled, their housing was a special type: furnished residential and transient hotels at very low rents, which were not available in many other parts of the city. The Agency's survey of the project population found that 37 percent of the individuals paid a monthly gross rent of less than $30, while 79 percent paid less than $40.[5] In addition, it was likely that another 3,000 people in the surrounding area would be displaced from their hotel and boarding house residences as these were sold to take advantage of rising property values in the vicinity of YBC.[6]

The full dimensions of the problem could be seen only in the context of other concurrent public projects involving large-scale displacement. The Golden Gateway project, also in the downtown area, had destroyed the homes of 200 single men and two dozen families living near the San Francisco waterfront. The Western Addition A-2 project, in the mostly Black Fillmore district, was displacing about 13,500 people.[†] Even though neighborhood opposition to Western Addition A-2 had resulted in the construction of several publicly assisted housing projects, there was a gap of up to five or six years before completed projects could provide housing for residents displaced years before, the number of replacement units did not equal the number torn down, and new rents were far higher than old rents. Displacement was occurring in the predominantly Black Bayview-Hunters Point area, as well as from minor public projects (such as the extension of a state highway and a city street that destroyed two residential hotels totaling 150 units in the vicinity of YBC), code enforcement in nearby

---

facilities and at rents or prices within the financial means of the families and individuals displaced from the urban renewal area, decent, safe, and sanitary dwellings equal in number to the number of, and available to, such displaced families and individuals and reasonably accessible to their places of employment." Housing Act of 1949, ch. 388, s. 105. The Housing Act of 1964, s. 305(a)(1) gave to individuals displaced from renewal sites the same protection given to families under the 1949 Act.

† ". . . [T]he Fillmore began to lose its identity a few years ago, when it was swallowed up in that huge area known as the Western Addition, target for the United States' most costly, longest-lasting redevelopment project.

"The idea of tearing down the Fillmore's substandard, shabby buildings and replacing them with garden apartments and green space sounded great on paper, but 18 years have passed since the project was started; and now Helen Erickson [president of the Fillmore Street Merchants and Improvement Association] and others in the Fillmore believe that Redevelopment is the villain, the scourge that swept through their neighborhood, slashing it down the middle with the Geary Street Expressway, razing houses, driving away the residents and leaving gaping lots and empty buildings instead of the promised low-cost housing." Joan Chatfield-Taylor, "The Grand Old Lady of Fillmore Street", *San Francisco Chronicle*, February 22, 1974.

South of Market Fights Back

Chinatown, and private clearance. According to a 1969 City Planning Department report, some 6,000 housing units had been destroyed in redevelopment areas, while only 662 units of publicly aided (i.e., low- or moderate-income) housing had been built in these areas.[7]

Further cause for alarm was the Redevelopment Agency's record on relocation, particularly in the late 1950s and early 1960s in the Western Addition A-1 project. There, over 4,000 households, mostly low-income Black and Asian families, were dispersed throughout the Bay Area. Many displaced families and persons had to move to other cities and communities either in the East Bay or on the Peninsula; others settled in the area adjacent to Western Addition A-1—thus finding themselves in the path of Western Addition A-2 bulldozers just a few years later. The poor housing, higher rents, and generally unsatisfactory relocation experience of the Western Addition A-1 residents had been well analyzed, after-the-fact, by scholars and government agencies, and the accompanying condemnation of the Redevelopment Agency served to alert others to the dangers of relocation.† It was from Western Addition A-1 and projects like it around the country that redevelopment and urban renewal became known as "Negro removal."

SFRA's relocation plans for South of Market had been approved by the U.S. Department of Housing and Urban Development in 1966, along with federal approval of the entire YBC plan. Under the plan, only 276 units of new housing were to be built for displaced residents. These were to be in Clementina Towers, a San Francisco Housing Authority project for senior citizens located in a corner of the project site, well away from the Central Blocks. This small number of replacement units for 4,000 persons was supposedly justified by surveys which used a "turnover factor" to calculate the number of rooms available to displaced persons on a city-wide basis.

"Turnover" is an incredible piece of statistical legerdemain. The game involves estimating the frequency with which an occupied unit is vacated and reoccupied. If it is assumed that on the average all residen-

---

† See Nathaniel Lichfield, "Relocation: The Impact on Housing Welfare," *Journal of the American Institute of Planners*, August, 1961, pp. 199-203, and "Review of Slum Clearance and Urban Renewal Activities of the San Francisco Regional Office, Housing and Home Finance Agency, 1959," Report to the Congress of the United States by the Comptroller General of the United States, July, 1960, pp. 32-43. The Comptroller General's study of San Francisco Redevelopment Agency files on Western Addition A-1 relocatees listed as satisfactorily closed found that nearly half of those examined had moved to unsatisfactory housing or were forced to accept massive rent increases. About one-fourth of the dislocated A-1 residents were moved into deteriorated housing in the A-2 area and subsequently forced to undergo relocation a second time.

tial hotel rooms are vacated and reoccupied once every three months, a "turnover factor" of 4 then is applied to get the annual number of vacancies, and to project available vacancies over a five-year period a turnover factor of 20 is applied. Based on this reasoning, the Agency estimated that over a five-year period no less than 30,000 vacant low-rent hotel rooms would be available for occupancy by YBC displacees.[8]

The turnover concept is obviously invalid and misleading, since it confuses normal mobility from one unit to another with true vacancies—those which are excess housing supply, above the amount needed to house local residents and provide for normal mobility. Only units in the excess housing supply can legitimately be counted on for relocation purposes, else relocation becomes a game of "musical chairs"—an apt metaphor, given the constant destruction of low-rent units for urban renewal and other programs and the removal of still other units from the low-rent stock through rent increases caused in turn by increased competition for the decreasing number of available units. (HUD regulations now require one-for-one replacement of units destroyed by HUD-assisted actions when the vacancy rate drops below three percent; the federal government and most real estate experts consider a vacancy rate of four to six percent as necessary to a healthy housing market, to allow for population growth, mobility, adequate housing choice, and systematic removal of substandard units.) Downtown San Francisco hotel rooms renting for $45 and $50 per month in 1967 when YBC displacement began were renting for between $65 and $80 per month by the summer of 1971. And a 1969 citizens' group report, based on City Planning Department studies, found that "for units, other than studios, renting under $100 per month, the vacancy rate is zero percent."[9]

A good illustration of the callousness of the "turnover" formula is the case of the residents of the International Hotel, home for over 100 elderly and poor Filipino men. In 1969, the owner of the International Hotel, Walter Shorenstein, a local real estate tycoon, political financier, and president of the City's Recreation and Parks Commission, sought City sanction to convert the hotel into a parking facility and received prompt official endorsement, with a commitment from the Mayor's Office and the Redevelopment Agency to help him relocate the residents. Over a three-year period city officials worked in vain to locate anything remotely acceptable to the Filipino pensioners. At one point, the Mayor's Office made an apparently serious offer to assist International Hotel residents to relocate *en masse* to the Imperial Hotel, at that time a fully occupied hotel within the boundaries of the Yerba Buena redevelopment area. Because of the obvious fallacies in this technique of "relocation planning," HUD in 1968, two years after it had approved the YBC relocation plan, barred the use of the turnover methodology by local renewal agencies.

South of Market Fights Back

Official Lawlessness

While coordinated population displacement and hotel demolition had in fact been going on in the area for many years, official displacement of YBC residents began in 1967 and accelerated in 1968-1969, as the Redevelopment Agency came in, bought hotels and other buildings and cleared land wherever it could. The attempt by private investors in the 1958-1961 period (after the Board of Supervisors had removed the area's "blight" designation—see page 42) to undertake non-assisted redevelopment of the area had led to the demolition of ten hotels and displacement of some 500 persons. And city housing code enforcement had the effect, if not the intent, of further reducing the population. Parking lots, the profitable "interim" use (sometimes lasting over a decade) to which urban renewal sites are often put,† were studding the area as hotel after hotel came down.

By mid-1969, the Agency had acquired 44 percent of the land in the project area. On taking over hotels, the Agency adopted a "no vacancy" policy, designed to keep up pressure on residents to move out of the area; a further consequence was to turn hotels into lonely, partially occupied, intimidating and dangerous places, hastening the departure of remaining residents. Often displacement was carried out by private owners in anticipation of Agency takeover of their properties, which meant giving almost no notice to residents.[10]

For many pensioners, accustomed to $40 and $50 per month rents, relocation was a terrifying experience. Those who could afford it moved across Market Street, into the "Tenderloin District," where rents were steep, hills steeper, and the crime rate steeper still. Others found another hotel South of Market, keeping one step ahead of the Redevelopment Agency's bulldozers. Eviction and demolition were swift, sometimes not even allowing residents the full notice required by law.

One early instance of what the *Chronicle* labeled the "swift, sharp slum ax" involved the Irwin Hotel, on the site needed for expanding the Fifth and Mission Garage—the development incorporating Walter Kaplan's three roles as chairman of the Redevelopment Agency, president of the Downtown Parking Corporation and secretary-treasurer of the Emporium department store directly across the street from the garage expansion site. In its rush to tear down the Irwin, the Agency neglected to give residents the full 90-day notice they were

---

† In Boston's West End urban renewal project, a parking lot was operated for nearly ten years on a "temporary," month-to-month basis, grossing for the private owners some $1.4 million over this period, while rental payments to the redevelopment agency amounted to only $132,000. See the "Spotlight" report in the *Boston Sunday Globe*, September 27, 1970.

entitled to by law, which evoked a protest—but nothing more—from HUD officials.[11]

As housing was torn down, area residents desperately began to search for a way to stop this forced removal. Many began coming to the South of Market office of the San Francisco Neighborhood Legal Assistance Foundation (SFNLAF), the OEO-funded Legal Services agency for low-income clients. They complained vehemently of the tactics employed by SFRA's relocation workers in emptying the hotels, the quality of relocation offerings made to hotel residents, and the housing to which many had already been forced to move.

The first real step toward resistance came in 1968, when the Legal Services attorneys, acting on behalf of a group of tenants principally living in the Milner Hotel, filed a petition with HUD asking for an administrative hearing on the Redevelopment Agency's relocation plan. HUD denied the residents' petition on the remarkable reasoning that little actual displacement had yet occurred. But residents were being displaced, and the HUD response, together with City Hall indifference, made them even angrier and more determined to fight it out.

In the spring of 1969, South of Market residents and their SFNLAF attorneys tried once again to get HUD to re-examine the feasibility of the Yerba Buena relocation plan. Several letters were sent to HUD over a four-month period; the responses were uniformly evasive and unreasonable, contending that since HUD had no mechanism for hearing residents' complaints about relocation it was impossible to entertain these objections. In a letter to the Secretary of HUD, the residents' attorney warned that unless a full administrative hearing was granted within 30 days, suit would be brought in federal court to enjoin the project until it was modified to provide for adequate relocation housing. But the warnings went unheeded.

Added to the residents' inability to get a hearing before official agencies was the intimidating and sometimes violent activity initiated against them both by Agency officials and by hoodlums seemingly unattached to official San Francisco, yet well versed in the identities and whereabouts of protesting area residents. Such actions, sometimes reminiscent of a Chicago gang war, intensified once an actual lawsuit was brought.

● Eddie Heider, one of the named plaintiffs, was viciously attacked on the day the suit was filed. The incident took place as he was returning to his Tenderloin hotel following a conversation with an attorney in the SFNLAF office. Witnesses to the attack, including several federal employees, stated under oath that Mr. Heider, who weighs scarcely 120 pounds and is nearly 65, was jumped by a large man who made no attempt to rob him and warned a young VISTA employee who tried to intercede, "I'll get you next."[12]

South of Market Fights Back

● Frank Hagan, an elderly resident, was beaten in his own hotel by a drunken security guard hired by the Redevelopment Agency. He later sought damages.

● Another named lawsuit plaintiff, Joseph Padron, came to the SFNLAF office with a paper a relocation worker had asked him to sign. Padron recounted a bizarre tale of several night visits to his hotel room by an Agency relocation worker, who wanted Padron's signature on a slip of paper saying:

I, Joseph Padron, under penalty of perjury, hereby state that I have secured a place of my own that is convenient to my plan of employment and where I have friends.

I have no objection to the Agency Personnel and Service in helping me to move from the Colorado Hotel.

Since I have been able to move to a better place, I have no further wish to be assisted with the lawsuit by the San Francisco Neighborhood Legal Assistance Foundation on behalf of the Engineered Group known as Tenants and Owners in Opposition to Redevelopment (TOOR).[13]

There were numerous other examples of Agency pressure on South of Market residents.[14] One case in November, 1969, involved a young couple who complained to California gubernatorial hopeful Jesse Unruh, during a walking tour of the neighborhood, that rent on their room had been substantially raised by the Redevelopment Agency, and that they had been threatened with eviction for no apparent reason. Right after Unruh's visit the head of relocation in the Agency's Yerba Buena site office, who had overhead this complaint, reported to the Shore Patrol that the young man, who was home on leave, was AWOL from the Navy.

According to the April 29, 1970 *Daily Commercial News*, Justin Herman denounced reports of such incidents against YBC displacees as a "complete hoax" (following an investigation by three high-ranking Agency employees) and even charged SFNLAF attorneys with "deliberately and scandalously" staging a series of phony incidents designed to discredit the Agency. But the federal court in December, 1969, was to issue the first of several restraining orders against interference with First Amendment and statutory rights of the residents (see page 126). And in early 1972 Frank Hagan was awarded $1,200 in damages against the Agency as a result of injuries received at the hands of their employee. (Another Agency response to the residents' charges was to publish a pamphlet extolling its New Start alcoholic treatment program—see below—with a cover drawing of one man beating another, and titled, "Here's How the San Francisco Redevelopment Agency has Beaten, Robbed, and Threatened the People in Yerba Buena Center." The pamphlet was distributed by the thousands and mailed to the business community.[15])

Added to the residents' list of grievances were the management practices of the Redevelopment Agency, which, combined with the absence
of repair and code enforcement services by other city agencies, markedly hastened the deterioration of the South of Market area. Partly in
order to insulate itself from public criticism, the Agency contracted for
outside management of hotels until the time came for relocation and
demolition. Old-time hotel staff, who performed important and
friendly functions in the lives of the old people, were replaced by often
insensitive and incompetent clerks and maintenance personnel. In
large part as a result of Agency policy to hasten the departure of
remaining guests, conditions and services at the hotels deteriorated
rapidly. Heat and hot water were shut off because of "boiler problems"; lobby doors were kept locked and residents admitted only upon
showing identification; linens were unavailable and maid service ter-
minated; hall toilets were locked; comfortable lobby chairs were replaced by benches and camp chairs; mail and messages got lost; rubbish
stood uncollected; desk clerks and security guards drank, slept on the
job, and were insolent to and on occasions physically abused
residents.[16]

In hotel after hotel, residents signed petitions demanding better security and improved maintenance, and clergymen or staff from various
social service agencies would accompany the protesters as advocates in
attempting to negotiate with the Redevelopment Agency for better
living conditions. Conditions in the hotels taken over by the Agency
turned dangerous as well. Many of the older men became afraid to
leave their rooms because of increasing robberies and threats. The
most violent of these attacks was the robbery and murder of James
Gregory in December, 1970, in the Agency-owned Westchester Hotel.
Ironically, the month before Gregory had been one of the signers of a
residents' petition to the Redevelopment Agency asking for improved
security at the Westchester, a move which the Agency rejected.[17]

A somewhat more ingratiating approach was taken by the Agency in
its New Start Center, an alcoholic treatment program located in a YBC
hotel and run in conjunction with the City's Departments of Public
Health and Social Services. The Center was established in 1966, largely
as a response to social workers' protests against the project voiced at the
time of the public hearings. The Agency has held up the New Start
Center as an example of its humane treatment of YBC residents and its
people-oriented approach (see the pamphlet put out by the Agency
and the two city departments in August, 1972, entitled "Breaking the
Frisco Circle: The True Story of an Innovative Approach to the Problem of Alcoholism in San Francisco's Skid Row"). But residents and
other critics of the Agency have charged that the Center is merely a

South of Market Fights Back

"soft cop" approach to population displacement, facilitating the task of moving people out of the hotels. The Agency's publication suggests that the Center has at least some propaganda functions: Posing the question, "Who are the people in the Yerba Buena Center area who need New Start's medical, psychological, social and economic help?" the brochure, after responding that not all are skid row alcoholics and that there are no "typical" residents of the area, answers: ". . .those seen most frequently on television protesting rehousing are not truly representative either." One of the more obvious questions to ask about New Start and similar attempts by renewal and relocation officials to stress the "human services" aspects of their work, is why these services, if they are so valuable, could not be and were not made available independent of the displacement and relocation process.

TOOR

In all the planning and creation of support for Yerba Buena Center in the 1950s and 1960s, the one group conspicuously absent were the residents of the area. Federal urban renewal statutes contain a somewhat vague "citizen participation" requirement, calling for involvement of individuals, organizations, and interest groups in the planning process. During the 1960s, when Yerba Buena planning was carried out, the group designated to fulfill the citizen participation requirement for *all* the city's renewal projects was SPUR (see pages 37-38). As the city's official Citizens Action Committee, required under urban renewal statutes, SPUR in 1966 issued a publication entitled *Prologue for Action*, from which are taken the following statements, made at the time the Yerba Buena project was receiving its approvals from the Board of Supervisors and other city agencies:

If San Francisco decides to compete effectively with other cities for new "clean" industries and new corporate power, its population will move closer to standard White Anglo-Saxon Protestant characteristics. As automation increases, the need of unskilled labor will decrease. Economically and socially, the population will tend to range from lower middle-class through lower upper-class. . . .

Selection of a population's composition might be undemocratic. Influence on it, however, is legal and desirable for the health of the city. A workable though changing balance of economic levels, social types, age levels, and other factors must be maintained. Influence on these factors should be exerted in many ways —for example, changing the quality of housing, schools, and job opportunities.

Thus, the welfare of the elderly, single, poor workingmen of South of Market was placed in the hands of the city's corporate and financial interests. The people in the area were kept in the dark about their fate. An *Examiner* series on YBC residents quoted people as saying, "We

TOOR

don't know what they're going to do. . . ." "Nobody has spelled out the details. . . ." "We're all confused. . . ." "When the plans are ready—they're ready."[18] It was only when the Redevelopment Agency began to acquire buildings, evict occupants, demolish structures, and urban renewal became a living, frightening reality, that real participation of the area's residents began as they organized to defend themselves.

In summer of 1969 residents began meeting together in the lobby of the Milner Hotel, one of the better maintained and more prestigious hotels in the area; Milner residents were to become the backbone of the struggle against the Agency and for the rights and welfare of area residents. As one Milner resident put it at the first meeting, "Nobody invited me down here, and nobody is going to invite me out." Out of these meetings came the decision to establish a formal organization, Tenants and Owners in Opposition to Redevelopment.

(The opposition mounted by TOOR was not without antecedents. In early 1965 a small group of organizers came into the area and attempted to put together a coalition to oppose the Yerba Buena project and substitute an alternative development plan. The effort was initiated by Harry Brill, who had been hired by the San Francisco Central Labor Council; joining him were Michael Miller, Carol Brill and Jerry Mandel, all of whom had previously been involved in organizing efforts against the Western Addition A-2 project and were interested in developing a city-wide coalition against Justin Herman's brand of people removal. Their strategy was to fashion a coalition around the issue of blue-collar jobs and low- and moderate-income housing. The core of this coalition was to be union locals whose members would be losing their jobs as a result of YBC—garment workers, longshoremen, building service employees, printers, hotel-motel workers, culinary workers, painters, and machinists. The locals would then try to ally with the building trades unions to create a massive program of construction work, stressing light industrial plants, the rehabilitation and conservation of existing housing and construction of new units and supportive community facilities—schools, medical and recreation facilities, etc. The union coalition could then develop linkages with organizations representing the aged and with Black, Mexican-American and other minority organizations in need of jobs and housing. The idea was to produce an alternative plan for the YBC site which could be put forth during the 1967 city election campaigns.

While the organizers had some initial success with the labor unions, it proved impossible to carry out this grand scheme of opposition. At the April, 1966 Board of Supervisors hearings and in the months prior to these hearings, the Central Labor Council issued some strong statements against YBC, particularly regarding the blue-collar jobs being destroyed by the project. The South of Market Improvement Associa-

South of Market Fights Back

tion, formed by Lou Silver, owner of the Milner Hotel at Fourth and Mission and spokesman for many other hotel-owners and small businessmen in the area, was also brought into the alliance, as were several neighborhood, civil rights and church organizations. But by mid-1966, after the Supervisors had approved the Redevelopment Agency's plan, the organizers drifted away from the area to undertake other activities—principally helping to organize the fight against redevelopment in the Mission district—and by 1967 and the Alioto takeover the dominant union position had changed to wholehearted support for Yerba Buena Center. TOOR arose independently nearly three years later, with a different set of characters and a narrower focus: securing decent treatment for displacees, rather than challenging the project as a whole and offering alternative development strategies.)

TOOR's organizing efforts took the usual forms, distributing leaflets and literature in the area's hotels to inform people of their rights and urge them to come to meetings. Some of the more active residents, along with a few young VISTA volunteers working and living in the area, went around the neighborhood to talk with people in hotels and with families living in flats located on the side streets. But the best organizing tool throughout was the extreme pressure tactics of the Redevelopment Agency. It was in direct response to being harassed and hurt that people came to meetings.

For the many retired trade unionists living in the area, organizing their fellow residents against the bulldozer harked back to organizing efforts in building the labor movement three and four decades back. TOOR's elected chairman was 80-year old George Woolf, an organizer and first president of the San Francisco-based Alaska Cannery Workers' Union, and earlier president of the Ship Scalers Union (now an affiliate of the ILWU). Woolf was intimately involved in the progressive labor movement in the late 1920s and early 1930s in San Francisco, and had his front teeth knocked out during the city's 1934 General Strike. After his retirement in 1954, he organized his fellow ILWU retirees into the Pensioners' Club, a "union within the union."[19] He described himself by saying, "I've lived my life so that I can look any man in the eye and tell him to go to hell." His attitude toward the Redevelopment Agency was uncompromising. A newspaper interview with George Woolf noted that "it was a casual remark by Redevelopment Director M. Justin Herman which started him in battle." Herman had reportedly called the residents of the South of Market area "nothing but a bunch of skid row bums." Woolf was indignant—"I'm not a bum and I resent being discredited and discounted."[20] He responded by helping to establish TOOR.

Co-chairman of TOOR was Peter Mendelsohn, for 40 years a merchant seaman who lived on the same South of Market block when he

TOOR

Ira Nowinski

"I've lived my life so that I can look any man in the eye and tell him to go to hell."
— George Woolf, chairman of TOOR

Ira Nowinski

TOOR meeting, Milner Hotel lobby, 1973. TOOR chairman
Peter Mendelsohn (with microphone) flanked by attorneys
J. Anthony Kline and Amanda Hawes; with TOOR
organizers Stephen Dutton (far corner) and Sandra Marks
(at table, back to camera). *from S. F. State*

South of Market Fights Back

returned from sea. Although 65 years old, Mendelsohn had more
energy than most people 30 years younger. Like George Woolf, Mendelsohn was a union organizer and also organized for the Communist
Party in the 1930s. When Mendelsohn returned from his final voyage
in the summer of 1970, he discovered that the Redevelopment Agency
had taken over his hotel. He briefly visited relatives and on his return
found that his room had been broken into and robbed of all his valu-
ables, which were quite substantial, as he had been a coin collector for
years. Referring to the Agency's plans to move him to another neighborhood, Mendelsohn said: "I've lived on this block for 40 years. I
know everyone here and they know me. To move me even five blocks
away would be the same as moving me to another city. It'll take years
for me to build up new relationships, and years off my life in the
process." George Woolf died in June, 1972, following a brief illness,
and upon his death Pete Mendelsohn assumed the chairmanship of
TOOR.

From the beginning, TOOR was able to draw on outside assistance.
In October, 1969, Canon Kip Community House, a small settlement
house located in the South of Market, hired Sandra Marks as a community organizer to pull together an umbrella group of community
organizations. This move was designed to assist area residents in affecting decisions related to the South of Market community. Prior to this
time, Canon Kip had confined its role to more traditional recreational
programs, social clubs, tutoring, and a part-time medical clinic for
indigents. Events dictated that Marks' work in the community would
focus on TOOR, as most of the other organizations in the area were
inactive. Although static soon arose from some members of the Canon
Kip board of directors regarding her work,† the settlement house continued to pay Marks' salary and also provided funds for mimeograph-
ing and telephone service (TOOR's one room office in the Milner
Hotel was virtually rent free, and between 1969-1973 it received less
that $500 in contributions, mostly used to cover postage and incidental
costs for the office).

Joining Marks on the TOOR staff, such as it was, was Stephen Dut-

---

† Like most charitable organizations, Canon Kip's board of directors was
largely a collection of "blue ribbon" business and civic personalities. One board
member who owned a construction firm felt delays in building YBC would be
"bad for business"; others who had friendships with city influentials did not
like being put in the position of having to explain the agency's involvement
with Yerba Buena renewal foes. The controversy between Marks and some
members of the Canon Kip board came to light when the Redevelopment
Agency's YBC area director made a self-publicized refusal to donate his usual
contribution to the United Bay Area Crusade, which funds the settlement
house, because one of its staff members was "fomenting dissent" and "using
techniques of the radical left." (*San Francisco Chronicle*, October 14, 1970.)

ton. A graduate student in urban studies at San Francisco State University, he was working as an intern for State Assemblyman Willie Brown and first learned of TOOR when he came across a request for assistance from the organization. In the summer of 1970 Dutton became a full-time TOOR staff member, supported by small grants from Lou Silver, from SFNLAF, the Housing Law Center, and a local foundation. Dutton worked with TOOR until August, 1972, when he took a staff position with the city's anti-poverty agency, concentrating on the development of a federally aided housing rehabilitation program, a project which would help the South of Market displacees. He subsequently returned to work directly for TOOR on developing replacement housing, which the community group will sponsor (see page 198). At various times social work graduate students from San Francisco State University have also assisted TOOR as part of field work assignments.

It was Woolf, Mendelsohn, Marks and Dutton who provided the backbone for the TOOR organization. The poor health and advanced age of many of the area's residents left them incapable of engaging in militant activity and precluded TOOR's becoming a true membership organization. Solidarity was achieved through bulletins and leaflets sent regularly to residents and through mobilizing actions around Redevelopment Agency and Supervisors hearings and carefully planned protests and demonstrations. Monthly informational meetings were held, attended on the average by 60-80 persons, and the group also sponsored free Friday night films and provided members referrals for health and welfare problems. The office became a dropping-in spot for area residents who wanted to discuss their problems. TOOR was not an angry mass of people disrupting meetings and sitting-in; it was a relatively small organization whose leaders represented the residents' interests, and its organizing strategies were adapted to the particular conditions and limitations of its constituency.

Early protest activity principally made use of petitions calling for improved conditions in hotels taken over by the Redevelopment Agency. On occasion, a great many residents were mobilized for public protests, some quite creative, which captured publicity usually denied TOOR by the media (except in its litigation activities). One example was the construction of a "people's minipark" on an Agency-owned cleared site in October, 1971, and named "The James L. Gregory Memorial Park." (Gregory's violent death in an Agency-owned hotel is noted on page 105). This action, designed to symbolize the Agency's unwillingness to use its land to benefit area residents in any way, was planned to coincide with the national convention of the American Institute of Planners being held at the San Francisco Hilton, at which a group from the Housing Law Center was to present a report critical of

South of Market Fights Back

the entire YBC plan. TOOR staff enlisted outside design, financing and construction assistance in prefabricating a pergola, which would be placed on the site together with some instant landscaping. Neighborhood residents were asked to turn out, and on the designated day a large crowd of residents appeared to assist in constructing the park, a colorful event well covered by the media. True to the symbolism of the event, Redevelopment Agency maintenance men tore the mini-park down the next day, and then later that day the Agency apologized for its action, claiming it was "a mistake"—as one TOOR member wryly remarked, "Yeah, they thought it was a hotel."†

Another example was a demonstration held at a tasteless event sponsored by the Convention and Visitors Bureau in the spring of 1971. CVB decided to celebrate the destruction of a building on the Central Blocks site, one of the last buildings standing in the way of the convention center. On demolition day, the CVB hosted a gala luncheon for 500 people, pitching a huge tent on the site for the event. Mayor Alioto was the CVB's keynote speaker. Attending the luncheon were many of the city's notables, who stepped through the surrounding rubble, cocktails in hand, to witness the steel-ball crane deliver the blow which residents saw as symbolically marking the destruction and passing of their community. TOOR's response was to pitch two small tents of their own across from the CVB's tent, with residents passing out literature to those attending the luncheon, making the point that the city had not so much as "pitched a tent to accommodate Yerba Buena residents in this convention-happy city." It was the TOOR protest, and not the CVB luncheon, which received the majority of the day's publicity.

Another avenue of activity was building alliances with other groups in the city. TOOR attempted to link up with community housing organizations from Chinatown, Western Addition, the Haight-Ashbury, Bayview-Hunters Point and other areas. But TOOR's uncompromising stand against the YBC project, while appropriate for a group being totally uprooted for a plan that would not benefit them at all, conflicted with other areas and groups which had a more ambivalent stance toward redevelopment, as in the Western Addition, the Mission and Bayview-Hunters Point, where there existed federally funded community organizations designated as official representatives of the community in overseeing Redevelopment Agency housing activity. These groups, such as the Western Addition Project Area Committee (WAPAC), the Mission Coalition Organization, and the Hunters Point Model Cities Council have moderately cooperative relations with the

---

† The Redevelopment Agency spokesman stated, "We had intended to leave it up, but inadvertently it got taken down." "How a park 'died' South of Market," *San Francisco Progress*, October 29, 1971.

Redevelopment Agency. In the Western Addition, most of the project moneys to date have been used for demolition and relocation; future allocations will go for production of housing, which the community desperately needs and wants. In these areas too, the most vocal community leaders tend to be co-opted by the Agency, which places them on its staff in well-paying jobs connected with the Project Area Committees. Given the interlocking nature of local financing arrangements for urban renewal projects (see pages 160-61), organizations in other neighborhoods were reluctant to oppose Yerba Buena Center, which was vital to the continuation of other projects in the city. A not atypical threat was that publicized in the February 4, 1970 *Examiner*:

The people of the Western Addition can forget about new low cost housing projects in their area unless the planned $200 million Yerba Buena convention complex South of Market gets built fast.

That warning was sounded yesterday by M. Justin Herman, executive director of the Redevelopment Agency.

Despite difficulties, however, TOOR continued to foster city-wide links wherever possible. It was common to find Pete Mendelsohn testifying at public hearings on the side of other neighborhood groups. And on occasions, such as the Redevelopment Agency's proposal to move South of Market residents to a Western Addition hotel already promised to Western Addition relocatees, TOOR and WAPAC joined forces to oppose official actions; at a joint press conference held to protest this plan, a WAPAC spokesman stated, "We will not be tricked into fighting other poor people, be they black, brown, yellow, or white."[21]

"We Won't Move"

Throughout its life, TOOR has centered its organizing and activities around one goal: decent rehousing for South of Market residents. The residents, and TOOR, were under no illusions that housing conditions in the area were adequate, and they conceded that some of the neighborhood's hotels needed to be torn down—although they pointed out that the advanced state of deterioration of many hotels was due to the Agency's intentional neglect, its failure to maintain the buildings. While the problem was seen in part as an overall city-wide shortage of decent low-rent housing, TOOR put forth explicit demands to be rehoused in the same neighborhood. The desirability of the area in terms of older residents' needs; their familiarity with the surroundings; the obvious defects of alternative nearby areas which contained residential hotels (high rents, crime, and hilly topography in the Tenderloin, the skid row atmosphere of the Sixth and Howard neighborhood just west of the project area); and their adamance not to be bulldozed out of San Francisco altogether, all meant that the residents took their stand in

South of Market Fights Back

and for the South of Market neighborhood they knew and inhabited.
These demands obviously clashed with Justin Herman's concept of a
"protected environment" for Yerba Buena Center (see pages 89-91).
They also were completely contrary to Justin Herman's sentiments
about YBC, expressed at a lawyers' conference in the mayor's office:
"This land is too valuable to permit poor people to park on it."

TOOR's slogan was "We Won't Move," but it had a less than literal
interpretation. Clearly many persons would have to move, since some
of the existing hotels were unsalvageable and remaining on the Central
Blocks slated for the convention and sports facilities did not appear
feasible. "We Won't Move" therefore meant: we won't move from the
blocks needed for the public facilities unless we are given decent relocation housing, and housing that is in the same general neighborhood.
The organization was convinced that the Redevelopment Agency and
the City would meet its demands only if they had no other choice.
TOOR's central tactic therefore became holding onto its turf as long as
possible. The lawsuit filed by TOOR, and the subsequent injunction
and other judicial and administrative intervention (discussed in Chapter V), enabled TOOR to hold the Central Blocks hostage for several
years. Its goal was to force the city to build or rehabilitate in or immediately adjacent to the project area relocation housing that would be
permanently reserved for South of Market displacees and other low-
income persons. For TOOR was determined to foreclose the possibility
that in the years to come concessions made in the heat of battle would
be wiped out by additional public and private development plans South
of Market.

The corporate community's plans to make South of Market part of
the city's central office district were obvious to anyone with even a
minimal understanding of the economic and political forces at work in
the Bay Area. As an SFRA brochure trumpeted: "Yerba Buena Center
is only the beginning. Much of the remaining area South of Market is
seriously blighted. Hopefully, Yerba Buena Center will stimulate private rebuilding on this land to provide the best in urban living."

TOOR's fears of a complete transformation of South of Market and
new difficulties to come were not based on speculation; there was good
evidence of other development projects in the works, or shortly forthcoming:

• A considerable amount of private office construction already taking place directly east of YBC. According to the December 9, 1973
Sunday Examiner & Chronicle, the "location of high rise office towers has
largely shifted from the old financial district core to what was once
considered peripheral territory. South-of-Market . . . is being trans-
formed into a speculative high-rise office center."

• Planned reconstruction of the Transbay Transit Terminal at First and Mission calling for several million square feet of office space on air rights above the terminal.[22]

• Probable demolition of low-rent residences to the west and south for more profitable parking lots, thereby threatening one of the last areas of single room occupancy housing in the city, along with a growing Filipino community located between Sixth and Ninth Streets. A recent Environmental Impact Report on YBC commissioned by the City noted that one impact of the project on its surroundings would be: "Probable future displacement of some South of Market residents as a result of private development stimulated by the project and as a result chiefly of parking lot construction where older housing now exists outside the project area."[23]

• Housing development studies for two nearby sites, commissioned by the Chamber of Commerce. The Chamber report, according to the April 30, 1972 *Sunday Examiner & Chronicle*, concluded "it appears that this study area which is adjacent to the city commercial and convention core must find a higher use intensity if an economical investment return and tax base is to be realized."

• A Chamber of Commerce plan for a new industrially oriented project south of YBC, which was heard before the Supervisors' Planning and Development Committee in June, 1973.[24]

• A plan unveiled in early 1972 by Ron Pelosi, President of the Board of Supervisors, worked out with the Redevelopment Agency, for a massive commercial and residential development covering 37 acres, situated two blocks west of YBC, and crossing over Market Street into the Tenderloin. (The project was in many ways similar to YBC, even to the point of requiring relocation of some 4,000 low-income tenants.† While the Board of Supervisors, wary of beginning a massive new project while YBC was in limbo, refused to approve application for a federal planning grant, the vote was only six to five, and it is more than likely that expanded South of Market renewal proposals will be revived in the near future.)

• A plan, announced in early 1972, by some owners to evict tenants and renovate low-rent hotels and housing for a middle-income housing and shopping complex in the small Black South Park enclave just south of YBC. (A realty company was also buying up buildings in the area for purposes of speculation. The director of the Central City Anti-Poverty Program told the Board of Supervisors that at least 100 people had already been evicted from the South Park area in 1971, under pressure from the Yerba Buena project. The speculative owner of these proper-

†One of the principal arguments given for moving ahead quickly on the project was the availability of surplus local urban renewal credit (see page 160) from YBC, which would shortly expire. See *San Francisco Chronicle*, February 26, and April 18, 1972, and *San Francisco Progress*, April 21, 1972.

ties justified his plans by noting that the people of the area are "alcoholics and welfare people. . .pretty low on the totem pole, society-wise."[25] TOOR saw these evictions as its struggle, too, and largely through its efforts further displacement of South Park residents was stopped, at least temporarily.)

Out of Site, Out of Mind

TOOR's insistence that South of Market residents not be moved out of the area was based on evidence and impressions that forced relocation was causing and would continue to cause economic, emotional and health problems. These conclusions were borne out by the results of several surveys (undertaken in conjunction with the legal battles around Yerba Buena Center).

A HUD report "found that one-third of these [remaining] South of Market single residents were incapable of paying more than $40 per month rent. Another 47 percent can pay no more than $60" at a time when units renting for under $60 were "acutely tight" in San Francisco.[26] A similar study was undertaken by the Housing Law Center showing parallel results.† Among the 71 relocatees found and interviewed, almost all had relocated into other downtown hotels, mainly in the Tenderloin and around Sixth and Howard Streets, just west of the project area. It was clear that South of Market residents were moving a very short distance from their old neighborhood, because the only alternative quarters were located in these areas and because they wanted to remain in a central location.

As for housing costs, the survey showed that the median monthly rent in the YBC area prior to relocation was $45; after relocation it was $64, an increase of over 40 percent. Almost everyone had experienced a rent increase—some as high as $30, $40, $50 and more per month. A study by Arthur D. Little, Inc. and URS Research Company of Redevelopment Agency records on persons displaced from the YBC area between December, 1969, and December, 1972, showed that of the 250 displacees for whom such information was available 87 percent had experienced a rent increase, eight percent a rent decrease. The median rent increase was $36 a month.• And with the city's general shortage of

---

† This survey was undertaken during the summer of 1971 and was based on interviews with a one-third sample of all persons officially relocated by SFRA since December, 1969, whose current addresses could be found. The interviewers were university students working on a summer project through the San Francisco Neighborhood Legal Assistance Foundation, under the supervision of Melvin Mitnick and Chester Hartman. The interviewers were: Andrea Ach, Travers Baer, Wendy Chaikin, Susan Chu, Jo Ann Majid, Gerry Palast, Christopher Peck, Alan Ramo, Stephen Wiman, Kathy Zelinsky.

• See draft copy of environmental impact study of the Yerba Buena

Out of Site, Out of Mind

low-rent residential hotels, which YBC was exacerbating, ever spiral-ling rents in the coming years were an inevitability. One-fourth of the persons interviewed in the Housing Law Center survey had within a few months after moving to their new quarters already received a rent increase. For persons living on low fixed incomes of around $200 and often less per month, an added rent burden of even a few dollars can be catastrophic, forcing corresponding cuts in their budgets for food, medical care, transportation, and other necessities of life.

Even those former residents receiving "relocation adjustment pay-ments"—less than a third of those for whom adequate Agency records are available, and doubtless a considerably lower proportion of the total displaced population—faced serious difficulties.† Under the 1970 Uniform Relocation Act, tenants relocated by urban renewal projects are entitled to up to $1,000 per year for four years ($83 per month) to make up the difference between what the resident can afford (based on 25 percent of income) and the cost of decent replacement housing. One-fifth of those interviewed reported that the payment did not cover the actual amount of the rent increase. And all recipients must face the problem that after a few years the subsidy ends and they will be forced

Center project, cited in footnote 23, this chapter, Part E, "Social and Displace-ment Relocation Impacts," Table E-9. Of the 654 displacees in the Agency caseload during this three-year period no rent information was available for 404, or 62 percent of the total. At least as many persons as were on the official Agency caseload were displaced from the area without entering official Agency relocation statistics. Detailed information on rent increases was deleted from the report as released to the public (although TOOR had obtained a copy of the original draft and its attorneys had submitted this draft as part of some legal papers filed with the federal court challenging HUD's approval of the Redevelopment Agency's relocation plan). According to the May 2, 1973 *San Francisco Progress*: "The Arthur D. Little report endured numerous rewrites before the company felt it was suitable for submittal. A segment of the rough draft on relocation submitted to Judge Stanley Weigel several months ago is barely recognizable. Most of the strong words and critical comments have been deleted.

"For example, the report no longer states that: elderly residents (most of the present population in YBC) do not adapt readily to change; adequate housing for those who will be relocated is lacking; community residents cannot expect jobs from the project; relocation may cause an instant skid-row downtown, in the Mission district or elsewhere South of Market."

†The draft of the Arthur D. Little-URS study cited in the footnote above reports that only 31.5 percent of the displacees for whom Agency records are available received rental assistance payments. Since it can safely be assumed that no one not on the official caseload is receiving these government pay-ments, which are administered by the Redevelopment Agency, the percentage of total displacees aided by these subsidies is substantially lower, probably half the known figure.

South of Market Fights Back

either to accept the full cost of renting or to move to less expensive locations, likely also to be less adequate. (For those relocated prior to 1971, the maximum annual amount was $500, and the grants lasted only two years.) Problems like these do not seem to bother the Redevelopment Agency. Addressing a class at San Francisco State University, a key Agency official, in response to a question of what happens to people in the YBC area after relocation payments run out, answered: "Life is short."

But life would not be too short to avoid other financial difficulties revealed in the survey interviews. Many persons reported that landlords were requiring security deposits to move into relocation housing, sums which displacees either could not afford at all, or which proved very burdensome to persons with few savings. And most relocatees indicated that their expenses for food had increased since moving from South of Market, which was known for its cheap restaurants.

One of the most disturbing survey findings was the high proportion of relocatees who were not traceable within a short time after having supposedly been satisfactorily relocated by the Redevelopment Agency. Over one-fourth of the names on the Agency's official list of persons relocated since December, 1969, were not living at the address indicated by the Agency and were no longer traceable at the time of the Housing Law Center survey in the summer of 1971. And 18 percent of the persons on the official 1969-1972 Agency caseload whose records were examined for the Arthur D. Little-URS study were listed as being in an "unknown location." Once officially "relocated," the Agency's legal responsibility for and interest in the fate of South of Market residents was at an end—as one of TOOR's attorneys later put it, the Agency's "out of site, out of mind" policy.

The interviews also revealed the disruption of social networks. For older people in particular, personal friendships are perhaps the most important aspect of day-to-day life. Loss of familiar faces in the streets and in the hotel lobbies, of people to talk to, eat, drink, and play cards with is a severe shock. Similarly, the loss of stores, restaurants and other commercial institutions can rob people of an important basis of stability, a place to obtain credit, and a place to meet friends. According to an account in the November 19, 1969 *San Francisco Progress:*

These [1900 remaining] people are finding it tougher to get along South of Market. The grocery stores and saloons they went to are being closed and ripped down. The cleaning establishment they took their clothes to is closed up—the place boarded up—the little hotel next door is a sandy depression behind the high Redevelopment Agency fence.

This isn't the same place it was, two years ago before demolition began in earnest.

The balance is being tipped in favor of Yerba Buena Center. It is frightening, bewildering and angering to the people who remain. They don't want to leave.[27]

The popular image of South of Market put forth by the Redevelopment Agency and its booster club, i.e., extremely transient and therefore easily dismissible (see, for example, the *Examiner* editorial quoted on page 71), was flatly contradicted by data from the Housing Law Center survey: more than half of the persons interviewed had lived in the same hotel for at least six years, and one-third had lived in the same hotel for ten years or more. Roots in the South of Market neighborhood as a whole were doubtless even deeper, given the frequent movement from one hotel to another within the area. Moving from South of Market was not merely a matter of details such as locating a new room or apartment or packing; for many residents it represented a complete disruption of their lives.

TOOR's Rehab Proposal

TOOR realized that the Redevelopment Agency was not about to accept the residents' demands to remain in the area, much less acknowledge their feasibility, and in the fall of 1971 they decided to take the initiative. Following issuance of a HUD report to the federal court critical of the Agency's relocation plan (see page 144), George Woolf, TOOR's chairman, sent a copy to each member of the Board of Supervisors and asked support for a TOOR proposal to retain and rehabilitate several specified hotels in the project area. The letter also suggested use of the city's hotel tax to provide the subsidies needed to undertake the project. The proposal was intended largely to demonstrate to the city and the public that what TOOR was demanding could be incorporated into the YBC plan; it was not anticipated that the specific plan would be found acceptable. Yet by one of those chance comic events that occasionally occur in the game of politics, TOOR's proposal was greeted positively by the city, a response dictated solely by narrow political considerations.

Peter Mendelsohn, TOOR's co-chairman, had decided to run for the Board of Supervisors in the November, 1971 election, basing his campaign on the issue of urban renewal and more generally on a "senior power" platform. It happened, however, that incumbent Supervisor Robert Mendelsohn was up for reelection. Robert Mendelsohn, an up-and-coming young politician and close ally of Mayor Alioto, had just finished plastering the city with his election posters, which simply said, "Mendelsohn for Supervisor." Understandably, Robert panicked at the thought of Peter running for the same office, especially since he (Robert) had a good chance of receiving the most votes and thereby becoming the president of the Board of Supervisors. This prospect was attractive not just to him, but to Mayor Alioto, who wanted his ally in this post. With Peter Mendelsohn having filed, and the deadline for

South of Market Fights Back

withdrawal fast approaching, a series of meetings involving both Mendelsohns, the mayor, other city officials, TOOR and its attorneys was hastily convened. The subject of the meetings was simple: what concessions could the city make to TOOR that would persuade its co-chairman to drop out of the Supervisors race? The agreement, finally signed by the mayor and accepted by Peter Mendelsohn†, committed the city administration to the "rehabilitation and retention" of four YBC hotels containing a total of 420 units "unless and until an equal number of permanent new replacement housing units are produced in or adjacent to the project area." Three of the four hotels were on the west side of Fourth Street, and thus fit in with TOOR's desire to preserve low-rent housing on the western edge of the project area outside the Central Blocks.

Having secured an agreement, TOOR moved quickly to force the mayor to meet his commitment. Given the widely advertised shortage of federal funds for new construction, TOOR proposed in mid-October, 1971, that it sponsor the renovation of these hotels through a non-profit housing development corporation formed for the purpose. In December TOOR carried its proposal one step further by requesting that San Francisco apply to HUD for designation as a "Project Rehab" city in order to obtain funds to rehabilitate the hotels. Under this federally funded program, cities receive subsidies and government assisted loans to undertake large-scale, rapid rehabilitation projects. With the assistance of the Housing Law Center and the University of California's Community Design Center, TOOR prepared all the background work necessary for an application, and through some intensive lobbying had a resolution introduced to the Board of Supervisors calling for the city to make such application. TOOR managed to get this resolution through the Supervisors' Planning and Development Committee in mid-February, 1972, complete with specific mention of the four South of Market hotels named in the mayor's agreement. But at a later full Supervisors meeting the Redevelopment Agency carried the day, with the resolution being amended to exclude mention of any hotel rehabilitation South of Market.

Defeat of the Project Rehab proposal by the Board of Supervisors revealed the flimsiness of the agreement Mayor Alioto had signed with TOOR in the heat of "l'affaire Mendelsohns." Supervisor Robert Mendelsohn, originally a co-sponsor of TOOR's Project Rehab resolution, pulled a classic political double-cross: he withdrew his support and would only vote for the resolution after deletion of specific reference

---

† Mendelsohn fulfilled his desire to run for the Board of Supervisors in the 1973 election, where he made a very respectable showing, garnering 22,000 votes and finishing ninth in a field of 28 running for five available slots.

to the four hotels. The Redevelopment Agency was totally committed to creation of a "protected environment" and removal of all poor people from the YBC area (with the exception of the Clementina Towers project neatly stuck off in a corner). Agency spokesmen repeatedly asserted that the four hotels TOOR wished to rehabilitate were unsalvageable, despite the fact that engineers and architects retained by the Community Design Center had produced rehabilitation plans and cost estimates demonstrating the feasibility of TOOR's proposal.

TOOR's proposal to allow some of the older hotels and their residents to remain as part of the shiny, new Yerba Buena Center evoked the full anguish of the redevelopment booster club, and its propaganda apparatus moved into full gear. Supervisor Peter Tamaras, leading the opposition to Project Rehab, declared that retention of the hotels could "kill the project and destroy our dreams."[28] The Redevelopment Agency's executive director told the Supervisors that TOOR was "chipping away at the integrity and viability" of the project.[29] In its February 18, 1972 editorial entitled "A Mistake," the *Examiner* castigated the two members of the Supervisors' Planning and Development Committee who had approved inclusion of the YBC hotels in the Project Rehab resolution. The *Examiner's* February 25, 1972 editorial said of the proposed rehabilitation: "That would be like building a lovely garden without removing a pile of rusty tin cans stacked in one corner of it." And in an editorial condemning the Project Rehab proposal, entitled "Good Money After Bad," the February 24, 1972 *Chronicle* asserted "it would certainly blight the whole Yerba Buena project"—in reference to hotels which would have been rehabilitated to Federal Housing Administration standards.

(A different view from that of the Redevelopment Agency and the daily newspapers appeared in the February 18, 1972 *San Francisco Progress*, which noted: "In fact, the old hotels are quite charming, according to various architects. . . . Progress art critic Prudence Juris examined the buildings and remarked on 'their essential elegance, their humanity in the midst of a dehumanized downtown.' With the street clutter removed and the old brickwork sandblasted free of its accumulated grime, 'these buildings could be the most happy feature of the Yerba Buena area.' ")

What YBC supporters and planners meant by "blight" was not the physical characteristics or condition of the hotels. It was a social and political description—the poor are a blight on everyone else.

Although TOOR's rehab proposal was shot down in 1972, the essence of that idea—providing area residents with several hundred units of permanent low-rent housing within the project area, providing the needed subsidies through the hotel tax, and giving TOOR responsibility for developing these units—became the core of a settlement agreement to which the city was to accede two years later.

5. The Yerba Buena Legal Battle

Ira Nowinski

> After all this is a world of
> the survival of the fittest.
> And what bothers me is
> that some of the people opposed
> to this project are trying
> to protect the weaker members
> of society from the stronger.
> This is in conflict with
> the law of the land.
>
> Lyman Jee, developer for
> the Yerba Buena Center Central Blocks, 1972

*Now has other projects going
in Chinatown & with a church.*

While the struggle of South of Market residents against the Redevelopment Agency's oppressive people-removal tactics had some minor successes, it had not really become a public issue. Once the conflict moved into the courts, however, it became a matter the Agency, the city, and the general public could not avoid.

TOOR's goal for those displaced was firmly decided and, at least in principle, guaranteed by federal statute: decent, safe, sanitary relocation housing, conveniently located and at rents they could afford.[1] The next step was to use the courts to make the Agency obey the law. Attempts by the residents and their Legal Services attorneys to secure these rights, actions by the federal court, and the city's evasive response to the litigation were to consume three and a half years.

The Western Addition Precedent

The decision to bring suit against the Yerba Buena project was inspired by a partly successful action the year before which the San Francisco Neighborhood Legal Assistance Foundation (SFNLAF) took against the Western Addition A-2 project. There, the Western Addition Community Organization (WACO) had begun a drive in the mid-1960s to exact from the Redevelopment Agency guarantees of decent housing for all displacees. Failing to get these guarantees, and having experienced the havoc wrought by the Western Addition A-1 project (see page 100), WACO enlisted the aid of SFNLAF and filed suit for a federal injunction against relocation, demolition and federal funding in Western Addition A-2 until a valid relocation plan was developed. Both SFRA and HUD responded by claiming that residents of renewal areas lacked standing (i.e., had no legal right) to challenge inadequacies in relocation plans, and that HUD's decision on the adequacy of such plans was at the sole and unreviewable discretion

The Legal Battle

of the HUD Secretary. (The Agency later used the same two claims in its response to TOOR's Yerba Buena relocation suit, despite the court's unwillingness in the WACO case to accept these claims or the lack of any cogent Agency explanation as to why residents of HUD-assisted renewal areas were not allowed to defend their own interests and why HUD's Secretary should be protected from judicial review.)

WACO's case had been aided by strong evidence of inequities. HUD's own records revealed that its approval of relocation in Western Addition A-2 hinged upon satisfying several stipulations. Finding that these conditions had not been satisfied, Federal Judge William T. Sweigert held in December, 1968, that HUD's approval was arbitrary, capricious and therefore invalid. Under these circumstances, the judge found it necessary, in order to avoid irreparable injury to residents, to halt further relocation, demolition and financing of the A-2 project until a plan could be lawfully and unconditionally approved by HUD.[2] Judge Sweigert dissolved his preliminary injunction against the project less than four months after imposing it, when the Redevelopment Agency filed and HUD unconditionally approved a slightly revised relocation plan.†

The court's Western Addition decision, while a useful precedent for the Yerba Buena litigation, was by no means a far-reaching protection of people's rights. The court did not rule on the substance of the SFRA's relocation plan, nor did it feel that the courts should pre-empt the HUD Secretary's judgement on these matters. The court merely ruled that HUD must comply with its own regulations and the provisions of the federal statute.

Nonetheless, for the first time in the 20-year history of urban renewal a court had actually enjoined an urban renewal project[3]—and that was more than enough to inspire TOOR and its attorneys.

Into Court: The Quest for Compromise

HUD's unwillingness to provide administrative relief to Yerba Buena relocatees (see page 103) gave the residents no choice but to follow the

---

† The legal troubles of the Western Addition A-2 project were not to end with this action, however. In February, 1971, the federal district court issued a temporary order barring SFRA from dislocating anyone from the area unless HUD certified, on a case-by-case basis, that the relocation housing met federal standards with respect to housing quality and the tenants' rent-paying abilities. In April, 1971, HUD ordered the Redevelopment Agency not to relocate any more residents of the Western Addition project until new housing was available for them within the project area. Such rulings, while welcome to the residents, came late, as most of those living in the project area had already been removed. See *Dept. HUD Review*, "Findings and Determination of HUD Pursuant to Sec. 105 (c) (3), Western Addition A-2" (Cal, R54, April 1, 1971); also *San Francisco Chronicle*, April 2, 1971.

The Quest for Compromise

litigation route laid out in the WACO suit. On November 5, 1969, represented by half a dozen named individuals and the unincorporated association Tenants and Owners in Opposition to Redevelopment, they filed a complaint in federal district court against both HUD and SFRA, contending that the Redevelopment Agency had not located decent, safe and sanitary housing for displacees according to rights contained in the 1949 Housing Act. The action was accompanied by an immediate motion for injunctive relief. As counsel, South of Market residents obtained two lawyers from the SFNLAF central office—Sidney Wolinsky (who had previously brought the WACO suit) and Amanda Hawes—and as co-counsel, J. Anthony Kline of the Housing Law Center at the University of California, Berkeley.

At the core of the residents' plea were the flaws in the turnover formula underlying the YBC relocation plan.† Over three years had passed since HUD's original approval of the YBC relocation plan. Since 1966 the city's low-rent housing supply had actually decreased, contrary to the turnover formula's projections. TOOR filed with the court compelling exhibits supporting its motion for injunctive relief. Inspection sheets of the building inspectors employed by SFRA showed that many "approved" relocation resources were in poor physical condition, had illegal wiring, an absence of dual means of egress and fire exit signs, access to fire escapes through locked doors, and other serious infractions. Most of this evidence was available to HUD in 1966; it evidently chose to look the other way.

TOOR shored up its evidence by commissioning the nationally known Bureau of Social Science Research to conduct a vacancy survey of those hotels the Redevelopment Agency was using for relocation purposes. After eliminating vacant units renting for over $100 per

---

† The plaintiffs' brief also raised the point that the Agency had failed to consult with minority groups regarding its relocation plan, as required by federal urban renewal law (about three-fifths of the families living in the site area, and a small percentage of the individual householders, were nonwhite.) To support their point, the following Agency statement, made in its official application to the Housing and Home Finance Agency for the YBC loan and grant, was produced:

"Representative leadership of the minority community has not been consulted on this project because of the events which have taken place in relation to the Western Addition Area 2 Project. . . The leaders of local civil rights groups have been alerted to take a strong position in opposition to urban renewal . . . particularly with reference to the Relocation Program." (Report on Minority Group Considerations, submitted by San Francisco Redevelopment Agency to HHFA, December 1, 1964, Part I, Application for Loan and Grant [Sec. R215, pp. 1-2], for Yerba Buena Project, South of Market Area D)

In other words, minority groups were not consulted because they might not support the project!

The Legal Battle

month and those for which Agency inspection sheets showed gross physical deficiencies, the survey team counted slightly over 200 vacancies city-wide. This survey exposed the extraordinarily small number of standard low-rent units in San Francisco at a time when "turnover theory" predicted just the opposite.[4] TOOR also submitted official crime statistics from the San Francisco Police Department to show the high incidence of crimes against persons in the areas into which most YBC displacees were being relocated—Sixth Street and the Tenderloin. These data were particularly important, since older persons and alcoholics are especially vulnerable to muggings and street crime. Impersonal statistics were accompanied by some 60 affidavits from present and former residents of the YBC area describing personal experiences as displacees and their fears of being displaced. This factual demonstration of the housing crisis faced by YBC displacees contrasted dramatically with the official relocation plan HUD had earlier approved.

Action on the suit got underway in December, 1969, when Federal Judge Stanley A. Weigel conducted the first of three hearings on TOOR's contentions. Influential in these court hearings were SFRA data showing that among the first group moved out of the area 44 percent were forced to pay at least one-third of their income for rent; and two-thirds of these persons had moved via Agency referrals. At the conclusion of the first day, the court, expressing its concern that YBC residents were not receiving fair treatment, issued a temporary restraining order halting involuntary relocation and demolition inside YBC pending an opportunity to rule on the motion for an injunction. In hotels where relocation efforts had not started, the court order was greeted with great relief, but in those hotels where relocation workers were already making their rounds the order afforded little protection.

The Agency still posted notices in hotel lobbies, informing residents they had to move by March 4, and Agency workers were visiting site residents in some cases four, five and six times in a single day, trying to persuade them to move voluntarily. The Redevelopment Agency viewed the order as merely stopping state court eviction proceedings against tenants failing to move within the 90-day period set by the relocation plan.[5]

The week before the third and last full court hearing in March, 1970, TOOR's counsel appealed to Judge Weigel for a protective order preserving the residents' status quo pending a decision on the basic relocation and housing issues. At this hearing the court dictated an order prohibiting all relocation activities except in instances where residents signed a statement before a notary attesting to the voluntariness of the action.

Still, SFRA relocation workers zealously pursued their quarry. One

The Quest for Compromise

of the last residents of the Daton Hotel was visited in the hospital by two relocation workers and a notary. The relocation workers had already placed the woman's possessions in storage "for safekeeping" when she was hospitalized, making her forcible relocation an accomplished fact.

While the Redevelopment Agency demonstrated outright resistance to preliminary court orders, Judge Weigel continued to urge the parties to reach a relocation settlement to avert judicial decision. Shortly after the March hearing the court convened a settlement discussion at which the SFRA, to avoid the possibility of a favorable court ruling on TOOR's request for an injunction, agreed to produce 1,500 units of low-cost housing. Under this agreement, the court required the Redevelopment Agency to submit regular reports on the promised units, reserving the right to release the parties from the agreement at any time and rule on the original motion.

Almost immediately it became clear that the Agency had no intention of fulfilling the spirit of the agreement. TOOR learned the Agency was planning to discharge its promise of 1,500 units by counting city public housing already scheduled for construction, and not through housing it would provide especially for YBC displacees. This meant TOOR would be taking low-rent housing away from others equally in need. Because of this, and because intimidation of YBC residents was intensifying, the residents on April 16, 1970, returned to court and renewed their request for an injunction. Supporting their motion was evidence that: (1) an elderly YBC resident had been beaten by a drunken security guard employed by the SFRA; (2) the Agency had deliberately halted operation of a hotel elevator, even though an epileptic was still living on the fifth floor; (3) hotel management had been grossly negligent in failing to protect a tenant's room in the Daton Hotel when she went away for two days. She returned to find her door kicked in and possesssions gone. (Because she had told the desk clerk about the trip she suspected an "inside job," and so advised her relocation worker, who told her, "If you don't like it at the Daton, why don't you move?") Further evidence included a lengthy affidavit from a West Hotel resident describing the lack of even routine maintenance; this was reputed to be the area's cleanest and most popular hotel before it was acquired by the Redevelopment Agency. Receiving this evidence, the court made a final request for the parties to settle their differences and report back in a week. The effort at compromise was futile. Judge Weigel accepted the parties' representation that no settlement could be reached and took the motion for an injunction under submission.

Two weeks later, on April 30, 1970, he ordered the most sweeping injunction against an urban renewal project ever issued, immediately halting all demolition and relocation and setting July 1, 1970, as the

The Legal Battle

date for cutting off federal funds if the YBC relocation plan had not been satisfactorily revised.

The Injunction: Maneuvers and Politics

In his opinion accompanying the YBC injunction, Judge Weigel concluded that the Secretary of HUD "had not been provided with any credible evidence at all" in regard to the Agency's YBC relocation plan and that "the record shows that at this very moment there is not adequate relocation housing in San Francisco which meets the requirements of the [1949 Housing] Act and is available for persons yet to be displaced from the Project Area." The statute make[s] it abundantly clear," wrote Judge Weigel, "that Congress intended residents of blighted areas to be beneficiaries, not victims, of . . . urban renewal."[6]

The next move was up to the Redevelopment Agency. On May 3 the Agency filed an appeal of Judge Weigel's decision to the Ninth Circuit Court. To reinforce its legal maneuvers, the Agency even brought in special counsel—none other than Mayor Joseph Alioto. This was an extraordinary and blatantly political move, particularly since the City of San Francisco was not a named defendant, and the Agency already had hired special counsel to handle the TOOR litigation. During the same week the mayor convened a bargaining session with TOOR's legal counsel, Justin Herman and other city officials. Alioto was furious at TOOR's unwillingness to bargain away gains won in court and berated the TOOR attorneys with such statements as: "You can't have everything, you know. You're not dealing with children." "There's no feeling of weakness on our side, you know. No federal judge in the country is going to stop the Yerba Buena project. I won't permit it. I've known Stan Weigel for 20 years and he is not about to do that."[7]

But sensing Judge Weigel might just do that, the city's next move was to attempt to maneuver around him. On May 8, attorney Alioto moved in district court to have the injunction "modified," in order to permit relocation and demolition to proceed on all sites in which commercial developers had expressed an interest. The city claimed it was fearful that developers who had agreed to build on parcels outside the Central Blocks, such as Del Monte, Crocker-Citizens Bank, and Taylor-

Woodrow, would back out if the sites were not delivered on schedule. Immediately after issuing his decision on YBC Judge Weigel had left for a six-week vacation. The Redevelopment Agency asked for an immediate hearing on its motion to modify the injunction. Presiding Judge George Harris, well known in Democratic circles and a close friend of Ben Swig, got the case. Judge Harris ordered a hearing for the following Monday on the motion to modify the injunction.

TOOR felt its back was against the wall, that it was about to see the victory it had just won go down the drain. Its attorneys were understandably fearful that Judge Harris would grant the Agency's request to modify the injunction, an action sure to unleash a furious rash of eviction and demolition activity within a matter of days, thereby ending the relocation issue for all practical purposes. As a legal matter, they argued that Judge Harris' district court had no jurisdiction over the injunction, since the Agency had already filed its appeal to the Circuit Court; attorney Anthony Kline even served a writ of prohibition on Judge Harris in his chambers to dissuade him from going ahead with the hearing. TOOR's attorneys also protested the proceedings and asked for a continuance on the grounds that papers filed by the SFRA did not show any different circumstances from the time Judge Weigel made his decision. However, Judge Harris was convinced by Attorney Alioto that the new hearings should be held, and TOOR's request for a delay was denied.

During the noon recess of the hearing on the SFRA's motion, TOOR's attorneys decided to try a long shot and raise the issue of Judge Harris' personal friendship with Ben Swig and others with a financial stake in the YBC project, and ask that he remove himself from the case. Among other things, a photograph in the judge's chamber showing him arm-in-arm with the senior Swig, combined with his membership in the Bohemian Club, the preeminent men's social club in the state of California,[8] gave South of Market residents concern over Judge Harris' ability to be impartial when the interests of Del Monte, Crocker-Citizens Bank, and Pacific Telephone and Telegraph were pitted against people whom Justin Herman had called "skid row bums." The heightened public concern with probity in the judiciary branch that had arisen about this time around the confirmation hearings for Supreme Court nominees G. Harrold Carswell and Clement F. Haynsworth, Jr. increased everyone's sensitivity to this issue.

Judge Harris granted TOOR's request to meet in chambers and reacted positively to the suggestion that the issues in the litigation might be resolved by means other than the federal judiciary. TOOR's counsel Anthony Kline then suggested the appointment of a Special Master (an officer appointed to take testimony and make a report to the court) to devise a way for the Yerba Buena project to move ahead while insuring adequate housing for displacees. Kline proposed the

The Legal Battle

Democratic ex-governor of California, Edmund "Pat" Brown, a choice which was immediately acceptable to both Judge Harris and Special Counsel Joseph Alioto, a large contributor to the recent successful campaign of Brown's son for Secretary of State.† Kline, a former speechwriter for Brown, had confidence that the ex-governor, whom Kline regarded as something of a populist, would be able to work out a compromise acceptable to both sides.

During May and June, 1970, Brown conducted several conferences, took a walking tour of the area, and called in many officials to obtain a complete view of the problem. TOOR took advantage of the opportunity presented by appointment of a Special Master and with the help of a team of architects and planners assembled by the University of California's Community Design Center prepared a rehousing plan which they submitted to Brown. The TOOR-CDC plan called for 2,000 units of new and rehabilitated low-rent housing, in the YBC project area but outside the Central Blocks. A working model of the proposal, together with lengthy documentation of financial feasibility and a schedule for phased on-site relocation, were included in the plan. By leaving the Central Blocks development intact and concentrating on the fringe area, it avoided engendering staunch opposition on the part of those interests pushing the convention and sports facilities. The plan was at once something Brown could support, technically sound, and consonant with TOOR's basic objectives.

TOOR's initiative caught SFRA off guard. The Agency assumed an alliance with Brown and was not prepared for a serious presentation of an alternative plan, or a contest for Brown's mind. On June 24th, with Judge Weigel back from his vacation, Brown issued his report, essentially supporting the residents' proposal to require SFRA to produce 2,000 units of low-rent housing. This report limited YBC relocation to new or permanently rehabilitated units, and thus recognized the inability of the existing San Francisco housing market to absorb more YBC displacees. The Special Master gave the Agency the option of selecting sites inside or outside the project area; but it could only take the latter option if units could be produced as quickly and cheaply. Further, no one would be forced to move away from the area unless it were into a newly completed unit.

---

† Brown was also very close to Ben Swig, as Brown indicated in the following anecdote regarding his loss in the gubernatorial race of November, 1966: "Ben was with us that night, having dinner. It was a real low point, but I remember he said, 'Pat, you'll be a much happier man now.' Then and there, he made me his legal counsel and put me on retainer. I was down that night, all right. But Ben's gesture was the difference between being down and completely out." Walter Blum, *Benjamin H. Swig: The Measure of a Man* (San Francisco, 1968), p. 77.

Maneuvers and Politics

The TOOR plan was an important turning point in the battle. Brown's partial endorsement of it served to shift attention from simple relocation to the provision of replacement housing. The plan was reasonable and feasible; it was clear that the real obstacles were the Agency's lack of will and Justin Herman's personal intransigence.

To no one's surprise, the Redevelopment Agency promptly and emphatically rejected Brown's report, claiming that its own vacancy survey† (which Brown had seen before issuing his report) indicated sufficient relocation housing; and the report was simply filed by the court. The Agency also believed that Judge Weigel would dissolve the April 30th injunction when it submitted the revised relocation plan Weigel had called for. The key element of the "revised" plan was a detailing of how the existing public housing supply was to be captured for Yerba Buena displacees. This feature was the result of pressures both from Mayor Alioto and Justin Herman on the commissioners of the San Francisco Housing Authority (all of whom are mayoral appointees) to admit Yerba Buena displacees into public housing on a "superpriority" basis, in exchange for granting the Authority some additional urban renewal land on which to build more public housing.•

Federal statutes require that families and individuals displaced by public action receive priority status for admission to public housing; practically, this means that displacees get housing over others on the waiting lists no matter how long they have been waiting. The effect of this superpriority plan was to turn the victims of redevelopment projects against each other and against other poor people in their desperate search for replacement housing. The Housing Authority waiting list at the time numbered 3,900 households, 600-800 of whom were Redevelopment Agency displacees from the Western Addition A-2

---

† According to a newspaper account, the survey was sloppily undertaken, with information on vacancies derived primarily by querying hotel managers and owners. "Individual rooms were rarely inspected. One Redevelopment Agency official told The Progress he looked at 'one room in every other hotel.'" Many vacancies were in poor locations and too expensive for YBC displacees. See Patrick Corman, "A Hasty Hotel Survey", *San Francisco Progress*, June 5, 1970.

• Although the San Francisco Housing Authority has eminent domain powers, there is a tacit understanding in the city that it will not obtain public housing sites through exercise of this power. The Housing Authority relies principally on the Redevelopment Agency to grant it sites at marked-down prices in urban renewal areas. Little public housing, particularly family-sized units, was built during the 1960s. "One of the reasons no housing has been built is that the Redevelopment Agency has not made suitable land available for public housing, [housing] authority officials say. It has been a point of bitterness and dispute between the two agencies for a long time." (*San Francisco Chronicle*, April 1, 1970.)

The Legal Battle

project. Elderly South of Market residents would be able to "bump" black families displaced from both Western Addition and Hunters Point. The relocation plan also ignored the fact that most South of Market residents, like urban renewal displacees all over the country, did not want to relocate into public housing. Three-fourths of the residents interviewed in the Housing Law Center survey during the summer of 1971 stated they did not wish to move to the new Clementina Towers public housing project in the South of Market area.† Yet this superpriority plan was accepted by the Housing Authority in June, 1970, and used by the Redevelopment Agency to challenge the April 30th court order. The sentiment underlying "superpriority" was well articulated by Housing Authority Chairman William Jack Chow, who stated in the June 30, 1970 *Chronicle*: "The economic importance to the city (of Yerba Buena) is more important than some inconveniences (to people on the [waiting] lists)."

Throughout this period, the Agency continued to evade the spirit of Judge Weigel's protective orders, which led TOOR's attorneys in late July to file a civil contempt action against the Agency. "Advice" and "informational" notices to hotel residents had the effect, if not the intention, of intimidating persons protected by the court. According to an *Examiner* report: "He [Weigel] noted that the agency, composed of 'sophisticated people' was dealing with 'unsophisticated people who would be sensitive and frightened by such a notice.' Weigel said residents would interpret the notice as one of probable eviction. . . . Weigel said he 'believed. . .the agency. . .had pursued a policy of moving people out willy nilly, regardless of the injunction, and as close to the line

---

† Nationally, only 19 percent of all families displaced by redevelopment relocate into public housing (see Hartman, *op. cit.*, footnote 3, this chapter). The reasons given by the YBC residents interviewed for rejecting Clementina Towers had to do mainly with its isolated location and the need to spend several hundred dollars to buy furniture and linens in order to live in public housing, items supplied in the residential hotels. In addition, many persons on welfare who previously received special food allowances stated they would lose these extra allowances by moving into units with kitchen facilities, even though they would not cook since their life-style involved eating in low-priced restaurants. Residents of Clementina Towers have voiced considerable protest against safety conditions in the project. See letters in the July 14, 1971 *Examiner* and news account in the December 1, 1972 *Chronicle*. At a press conference called by the Clementina Towers Tenants' Association in early August, 1972, tenants "charged again. . .that they are living in fear and terror because of inadequate protection from South of Market marauders." "There is no security in Clementina Towers. We have had a murder here and there have been countless robberies and beatings," the Association president asserted. Tenants also complained of insanitary conditions and poor maintenance. See *San Francisco Chronicle*, August 9, 1972.

as possible without violating the injunction.' Weigel said he was 'not at all sure but what the notice constituted a deliberate, outright violation of the injunction.' "[9]

In September the Redevelopment Agency in fact moved to have the injunction lifted, on the grounds that HUD had approved its new relocation plan. As the September 7, 1970 *San Francisco Chronicle* noted: "...Agency officials are obviously hoping that other factors, more political than legal in implication, will count for something in the court's consideration of the bid to have the injunction dissolved."

TOOR immediately challenged the validity of HUD's approval for this revised relocation plan, but the matter was never adjudicated. A hearing was set for late October with Judge Weigel presiding; but it was never held, for by this time attorneys for both sides were meeting to work out a settlement and avoid prolonged litigation. By the date set for the hearing a settlement had been worked out by the attorneys, with final acceptance contingent on TOOR's approval.

The Consent Decree

SFRA and SFNLAF attorneys presented Judge Weigel with their proposal in lieu of arguments on the revised relocation plan; and the court, after receiving a promise from TOOR's attorneys that they would recommend acceptance of the settlement package, lifted its injunction—reserving the right to reimpose it if a majority of TOOR's following rejected the settlement. Three days later, TOOR held a meeting at the Milner Hotel to vote on the proposal: the tally was nine votes for, 135 against. In George Woolf's words, "It was a lousy deal."

Hopeful that the parties could still work out their differences, Judge Weigel ordered another settlement discussion. When it failed, he drafted a consent decree, based on the proposed settlement package but with more safeguards for the residents. Its basic features were:

● The Redevelopment Agency will produce within three years (i.e., by November, 1973) 1,500 to 1,800 new or rehabilitated units of low-rent housing anywhere in the city, in addition to those units the city already had programmed when the YBC injunction was imposed. The figure 1,500 will apply if YBC residents have priority to 300 of those units, 1,800 if they do not.†

† The incentive provided by this range apparently was designed not to insure that YBC residents received benefit from the agreement, but (proceeding on some rather insulting but probably accurate assumptions about the city government) to attain a larger number of units of replacement housing. According to the November 10, 1970 *Examiner*: "If, at the end of the three year period, the City has built 1,800 instead of 1,500 new units, no priority at all will have to be given to Yerba Buena residents. Judge Weigel said he made his stipulation to 'encourage' the City to build more low-rent housing."

The Legal Battle

• Pending construction or rehabilitation of these units, the Agency will house relocatees in decent, safe, and sanitary housing within their means. (This was a restatement of existing federal law.)

• With the above guarantee, the Agency may proceed with relocation and demolition. A grievance mechanism is to be established through appointment of a three-person arbitration board to hear and decide any claims brought by relocatees that the housing offered them fails to meet statutory standards.

• Four project area hotels, outside the Central Blocks, are to be retained as "hostages" until the 1,500 to 1,800 replacement units are completed, with $150,000 to be spent by the Agency in the interim to refurbish the hotels.

• The Agency is required to fulfill all promises made in its revised relocation plan.

• The Agency will maintain a rent-free office for TOOR and permit the organization to hold meetings in one of the hotels.

Judge Weigel urged the Redevelopment Agency to agree to the decree, thereby avoiding the necessity of ruling on the adequacy of the revised relocation plan. On November 9, 1970, Justin Herman signed the document. In return, Judge Weigel dissolved his injunction but retained jurisdiction over the case to insure the production of the 1,500 to 1,800 units by November, 1973. By contrast, the proposed settlement package the residents had rejected called for TOOR to drop its lawsuit entirely, included no deadline for Agency performance, and contained no arbitration procedure; all TOOR was getting was the Agency's promise of 1,500 additional units. As George Woolf put it, according to the October 24, 1970 *Chronicle*, the original agreement would have "allow[ed] clearance of the central blocks 'and [would have] shove[d] half of us into some of the worst hotels in the project and [left] the rest of us to be forced into Sixth Street and the Tenderloin.' "

In the context of the history of urban renewal litigation, Judge Weigel's disposition of the TOOR suit was a landmark case. For the first time a court had thoroughly scrutinized the record underlying HUD's approval of a relocation plan. Examining the claim that federal relocation standards were not being met, Weigel found that the Agency's plan definitely failed to provide housing within the financial means of the relocatees and contained no indication that the relocation housing would be decent, safe, and sanitary. In requiring that replacement housing be built concurrent with demolition and displacement, the court explicitly recognized the effects of residential displacement on the city's housing market as a whole. Weigel not only was intervening in the renewal process further than had been done to date, but was also to an extent assuming a planning function in specify-

The Consent Decree

"They want to drive all the working-class and all the lower middle-class out of the city." — Peter Mendelsohn, chairman of TOOR

The Legal Battle

ing the type of housing to be built.† The TOOR-CDC plan had clearly done much to shape the thinking of the court.

But progressive as it was in the context of previous urban renewal litigation, the court's action still gave higher priority to completion of Yerba Buena Center than to firm guarantees that the residents' rights would be protected. Therefore, it was not a settlement TOOR fully approved. The final consent decree, while an improvement over the original proposed settlement package, was not regarded by TOOR as guaranteeing protection of their rights—an evaluation which time has proven correct.

Given the fact that some 4,000 units were being removed by the project, TOOR felt that the 2,000 units recommended by ex-governor Brown was a minimum replacement figure; the 1,500-1,800 units which the Agency had consented to produce was a disappointment. (The 1969 Housing Act, it should be noted, requires replacement of occupied low- or moderate-income residential units removed by a renewal project with an equivalent number of units constructed or rehabilitated for low- or moderate-income families. This stipulation only applies to projects approved after passage of the 1969 Act and to family, not individual, units; hence, it is inapplicable to Yerba Buena. But it does indicate Congressional thinking about the direction and responsibilities of the renewal program and, as with other Congressional reforms of urban renewal abuses, it is likely that within a few years, after the magnitude of the problem has been irrefutably demonstrated, Congress will move to expand this statutory protection of the housing stock to include units for individual householders as well.) TOOR also felt that only by constructing replacement units in or adjacent to the YBC site would this housing be satisfactory with respect to maintaining social ties. And to minimize dislocation and insure the Agency would keep its construction promise, they also wanted guarantees that no one would be forced to move until new or rehabilitated housing was available.

Under the consent decree, the Agency was allowed to proceed with its project essentially as before, although the price exacted for this

† Similar developments have occurred in public housing. See Note, "Public Housing and Urban Policy: Gautreaux v. Chicago Housing Authority," 79 *Yale Law Journal* (1969), 712. In a more recent case, a federal court found that the urban renewal plans and program of Hamtramck, Michigan (a suburban enclave totally surrounded by the city of Detroit) were designed to remove Negroes from the town permanently and has ordered the city to implement a detailed housing construction and integration plan. (See *Garrett v. Hamtramck* 335 F. Supp. 16 [ED Mich 1971] and 357 F. Supp. 925 [ED Mich 1973]; *Journal of Housing*, May 1973, p. 244; and note to page 208 and the references cited therein.

permission was its commitment to provide replacement units, which obligation the court stood ready to review. True relief for the residents would have required their satisfactory relocation *prior* to continuing work on YBC. This would have delayed the project, but it would have been the only real way to guarantee the rights of displacees to decent low-rent housing. The lifting of the injunction took pressure off the Redevelopment Agency and raised the possibility that its promises would never be fulfilled. Judge Weigel had proven unwilling to go much beyond the settlement negotiated by the lawyers to protect the rights of the community. In the settlement discussions urged by the court, the attorneys had spoken for the community, and even when the South of Market residents rejected the settlement, the judge was responsive to what the attorneys had thought reasonable, implying that the residents' demands were unreasonable and extreme.

TOOR's rejection of the settlement highlighted the substantial differences not only between it and the Redevelopment Agency, but between those who are victims of urban redevelopment and those who are their outside professional advocates.

People vs. Professionals

Underlying the schism between TOOR and its attorneys, brought to light by the group's overwhelming rejection of the settlement proposal its lawyers had negotiated and tentatively agreed to, are some important questions regarding community organization and struggle, particularly in lower-income neighborhoods, and the role played by outside, usually middle-class advocates.[10] TOOR was not a mass-based, Alinsky-type organization; while it was able to communicate well and regularly with its constituency, bring them out for selected hearings and events, and convince large numbers of them to take the politically most important step of all—staying put—its real muscle was the court injunction. But the organization's reliance on the courts and attorneys had its drawbacks as well. Its tangible victories and publicity were won by and associated with the lawyers. And it was the lawyers who, during 1969 and 1970, provided the spark for the organization. The inherent difficulties in building a strong, mass-based organization among elderly, oftimes alienated and disabled persons were exacerbated by the powerful role which the attorneys assumed and TOOR allowed them to assume.

By playing out its struggle in the courtroom, TOOR found itself caught up willy-nilly in the style of the game as it is played there, and involved with the kinds of persons who are the key actors in that arena. Thus Judge Weigel was assiduously pushing both sides to reach a compromise solution, and sought to avoid making a definitive ruling on the Agency's relocation plan or enjoining the project longer than was

The Legal Battle

necessary to extract a substantial concession from the Agency. The attorneys for their part also sought middle-ground solutions that would advance their clients' interests to the maximum extent they thought possible, given their view of the political and legal realities of the situation, while at the same time permitting the project to go ahead. TOOR was in the position of having allowed its attorneys to take over the negotiations, a role they did not at all mind playing, but then rebelling against the attorneys when the settlement they had tentatively agreed to was revealed. In TOOR's view, by agreeing to drop the lawsuit in exchange for the Redevelopment Agency's promise to build 1,500 - 1,800 housing units, the attorneys had left the community defenseless. Based on past experience with the Agency, the community group felt that SFRA promises were useless and that without the lawsuit TOOR no longer would have its only real weapon—the ability to hold YBC land hostage—which the injunction and continued court supervision offered. Thus TOOR decisively rejected the proposed settlement—which the October 28, 1970 *San Francisco Progress* characterized as "obviously a bad deal for the . . . elderly South of Market residents"—regarded it as a "sell-out," and at one point even discussed dismissing its attorneys.

Blame for this situation is attributable to both sides, and may be regarded as an inevitable product of community struggle in which by mutual assent the tail is allowed to wag the dog. TOOR by and large adopted the principle that "lawyer knows best" and placed its fate in the hands of its professional advocates, regarding their judgment and skills as superior to those of the community. The lawyers by and large seemed to share this assessment. For their part, the attorneys were not given adequate guidance by the community and were put in the position of making the political decisions that under a strong community organization they would not have been permitted to make. In this situation, the style, predilections and values of the attorneys came to influence the outcome.

The attorneys were in uncharted waters in carrying out their suit. They did not know how far the court would go in protecting TOOR's interests; generally speaking, courts in the past had not been notably solicitous of the rights of displacees, and the attorneys to a large extent were seeking to make new law. There was a possibility that Judge Weigel might accept HUD's approval of the Agency's revised relocation plan, although since the court had rejected the previous plan and the revised one was not much different, this was somewhat unlikely. In terms of a settlement as opposed to a court order, the proposed agreement was probably the most that could have been gotten voluntarily from Justin Herman. He staked his reputation on the YBC project; he was incensed at the roadblocks being thrown up by the residents; and

People vs. Professionals

he had a particular dislike for advocate planners and Legal Service attorneys. Sidney Wolinsky, SFNLAF's director of litigation and chief attorney for the TOOR suit, was a special target of Herman's wrath. When Wolinsky et al. filed the TOOR suit, Herman, referring to the Neighborhood Legal Assistance Foundation's previous suit on the Western Addition project, retorted: "This is the last straw. This time we are going to beat this bunch and we are going to beat them good."[11] Herman was quoted as calling Wolinsky " . . . a clever, well-financed, able, ambulance-chasing lawyer who has no respect for poor people, is wrong and is intellectually dishonest. There is a benefit of being in redevelopment. You can go to bed each night knowing you have helped the people in the slums. Wolinsky can't do that. That man has contributed nothing. Nothing."†

The attorneys' acceptance of the settlement agreement may also have stemmed from an understandable desire on the part of some of them to consolidate a victory and go on to other things. The litigation had lasted for over a year and was very time-consuming; given Judge Weigel's obvious preference for a settlement rather than a clear judicial finding, a settlement that represented an advanced instance of judicial protection of displacees' rights would have been a significant legal victory, one for which the attorneys could take a great deal of justifiable credit. There was probably also some real concern about the strength and durability of the community organization they were representing. A further consideration might have had to do with the broader consequences of pursuing the Yerba Buena suit. If delay continued, developers might possibly drop out and the whole project fall through. If this happened, TOOR and its attorneys would be blamed, and perhaps neither wanted to push matters this far.

In retrospect, it seems clear that there was inadequate participation by the community in the various settlement discussions that took place between attorneys for both sides. These discussions were lengthy and exhausting, with the settlement proposal finally reached after a 15-hour session in Mayor Alioto's office ending at 7 a.m. The Redevelopment Agency had hired special counsel, a highly skilled negotiator named Frederick Furth. (Furth was a former law partner of Mayor Alioto and was hired on the mayor's personal recommendation; he was paid a total of $120,000 for his $65 an hour services to the Agency in helping fight the TOOR suit.) The discussions were taken over by the lawyers, without adequate consultation with TOOR or adequate sensitivity to the residents' needs and desires—even given the physical limitations on participation by the organization's leaders and

---

† *San Francisco Chronicle*, January 20, 1970. The *Chronicle* reporter, Scott Blakey, notes in the same article: "The mere mention of Wolinsky's name enrages. . .Herman."

The Legal Battle

constituency.

As a routine matter, the attorneys had planned to hold a brief meeting the morning of the settlement with those TOOR members coming to court for a scheduled hearing on the Agency's relocation plan. TOOR's officers and staff argued that before any settlement could be made they had to call a general TOOR meeting so that the attorneys could make the terms of the proposed agreement known to the full body. The attorneys agreed this was a sensible step, and by the time that meeting was held they too had developed doubts about the wisdom of the proposed agreement and the lack of direct community involvement in the negotiations.

The conflict between TOOR and its attorneys highlighted the organization's difficulties in militantly defending the South of Market neighborhood as the basis for negotiating a good deal with City Hall, particularly given the limitations of its membership. Militancy, in the course of the residents' struggle, was defined in terms of litigation, a strategy and style congenial to the talents and predilections of the outside advocates to whom the community turned for assistance. But that same choice of strategy and allies tended to reduce even further the slim possibility of developing an alternate or complementary mass-based political organization and set of tactics. Dependence on the attorneys meant deference to outsiders who likely would be acting out of a different set of priorities from those of the residents. And as it turned out, legal protections offered no firm guarantees, for as the next three years were to show the Redevelopment Agency and the City were determined to avoid and undermine the November 9th decree.

Arbitration and Back Into Court

The limitations of the November 9th decree for protecting TOOR's interests showed themselves almost immediately in the operations of the Relocation Appeals Board established as part of the protective apparatus. The Board's activities did not begin until March, 1971, mainly due to difficulties in defining procedural groundrules. Each side was to appoint one person sympathetic with its interests, with the third member jointly selected. The Agency chose Arnold Baker, director of the city's Centralized Relocation Services; TOOR chose Chester Hartman, Senior Planning Associate with the Housing Law Center; and the mutually acceptable third party and chairman was Morris Watson, a retired ILWU official.

From the beginning the arbitration procedures proved unwieldy, unpopular and unworkable. The Agency's appointment of the city's relocation chief showed its low esteem of the appeals mechanism, since the man responsible for relocation in the Yerba Buena site area was not likely to overrule his own actions. The Redevelopment Agency held that the Board was unnecessary since its relocation referrals always met statutory requirements. From TOOR's view, it was unjust to make a dissatisfied relocatee go through arbitration, since the legality of the entire relocation plan had never been adjudicated.

Only three cases were brought before the board, although during the several sessions required for each an enormous amount of material on Agency relocation practices was revealed in both lengthy arguments and supporting documents. The Convention and Visitors Bureau, it turned out, had paid the owners of 24 hotels $50 per room to reserve a total of 203 rooms for YBC relocatees, with a guarantee that rents would not be increased or services decreased for twelve months. The Bureau, which as noted earlier is supported principally by city tax moneys, was trying to rig a short-term private solution to a public problem, apparently with no concern for the residents' fate after this twelve-month period.

The real issue was providing permanent relocation housing for YBC site residents; the Bureau's interest was only in clearing them off the Central Blocks as expeditiously as possible. Moreover, several of the hotels with which the CVB has made these arrangements were clearly substandard. One, the Jefferson, in the Tenderloin, was categorized as "unacceptable relocation housing" by the Redevelopment Agency itself, a judgment proved accurate by a fatal fire which occurred in mid-1972. The aggrieved displacees who came before the board reported in detail the deterioration of their hotels once acquired by the Redevelopment Agency; offers of hotel jobs to residents as an inducement to move; relocation offers to substandard or unsuitable hotels (or to hotels such as the Embarcadero, just one block from the Golden Gateway project, which would clearly be appreciating in value and rezoned for higher use in the near future); and practices such as refusing rent from Central Block hotel residents (urging them instead to save the money for moving expenses), and then presenting them with huge bills for back rent and demands for immediate removal.†

The weakness inherent in the arbitration procedure was that it approached the Yerba Buena relocation problem one case at a time, rather than taking the overall comprehensive review required in the statutes. It allowed the Agency to throw its full weight against individual tenants and escape the requirement to produce a satisfactory relocation plan for *all* residents. Further, throughout the short life of

---

† Among the several affidavits attesting to this and other Agency practices filed before the arbitration panel and in state court (to counter attempted eviction actions by the Redevelopment Agency) was one from a former Agency relocation worker, who was assigned to a Central Blocks hotel from July, 1969, to September, 1970.

The Legal Battle

the appeals body, the Agency held that no displacee had the right to come before it until he or she received an actual eviction notice; TOOR argued that this approach would allow SFRA to harass and wear down individual residents by making endless referrals to inferior housing. While the Relocation Appeals Board examined the three cases microscopically, the Agency continued to drive out anyone it could convince or coerce to leave. After two months of meetings, however, the bottom fell out of the Redevelopment Agency's revised relocation plan. The Board stopped meeting, and the action shifted to another front.†

The surprise development came in May, 1971, when the San Francisco Housing Authority suddenly dropped its superpriority policy for YBC displacees. For the year this policy had been in effect the Authority had been under constant criticism from neighborhood groups all over the city because it threatened to rob them of sorely needed housing. TOOR itself did not want to see its housing problem solved by harming other poor people, and had even attempted to enjoin the Housing Authority from implementing the superpriority policy in a motion denied by Judge Weigel in May, 1971. The Housing Authority staff also resented this policy, because it put them in the position of denying housing to those already on its waiting lists, thus becoming the target for anger and frustration which properly belonged in the lap of the Redevelopment Agency. As one Housing Authority commissioner put it, "We're not the tail on anybody else's kite."[12] There had been longstanding ill will between the housing and redevelopment agencies, and the last straw was the SFRA's failure to produce the public housing sites promised at the time the superpriority deal had been arranged.•
(The Housing Authority had twice requested a site for 250 units of

---

†The Relocation Appeals Board has not met since May, 1971. The TOOR-Redevelopment Agency agreement ending TOOR's lawsuit (see pages 192-201) retains this protective mechanism, although with altered ground-rules. The new appeals board formed in February, 1974, consists of Henry Davis, Counsel to the San Francisco Redevelopment Agency; Chester Hartman; and Howard Durham, a professional arbitrator. As of this writing, it has not yet begun to hear cases.

• A recent manifestation of the feud involves the Housing Authority's unanimous opposition to demands from HUD, Mayor Alioto and the Redevelopment Agency that a 191-unit low-rent housing project in the Hunters Point area be torn down as a condition for releasing federal funds to continue a redevelopment program in the area. The rundown public housing project is regarded by the Agency and HUD as a "blighting influence" on the new moderate-income apartments to be built nearby. The Housing Authority, while acknowledging the poor condition of the project, is insisting that the 191 low-rent units be replaced or funds be made available for renovation of the project. The dispute once again reflects the differences in the economic and social characteristics of each agency's constituency. See Larry Liebert, "The Politics of Public Housing", *San Francisco Chronicle*, January 10, 1974.

family-sized public housing in the YBC area, but the Redevelopment Agency each time turned down its request.) This failure was due to Justin Herman's intransigence regarding TOOR and its demands and to Mayor Alioto's unwillingness to expend any political muscle pressuring Herman and the Redevelopment Agency into assisting the Housing Authority. With the Redevelopment Agency already facing serious trouble over YBC, the Housing Authority took the opportunity to get even.

The withdrawal of "superpriority" completely undercut SFRA's revised relocation plan. Immediately, TOOR and its attorneys went back to Judge Weigel, claiming that the November 9th decree had been violated. In addition they submitted evidence that the Agency had shown no significant progress in producing the 1,500-1,800 housing units. Rather than risk waiting until 1973, only to learn that the Agency had failed to produce housing, TOOR moved at once for renewed protective relief against further destruction of housing and dispersal of the South of Market community. On June 2, 1971, TOOR's lawyers† filed for a second preliminary injunction. Capitalizing on the Housing Authority's feud with the Redevelopment Agency, TOOR included an affidavit from Housing Authority Executive Director Eneas Kane refuting the Agency's contention that it could meet the November, 1973 deadline for production of the 1,500-1,800 units; Kane asserted that the majority of public housing units claimed by the Agency as eligible to meet the quota had been programmed prior to April 30, 1970—contrary to the clear wording of the consent decree that units under commitment prior to that date could not be counted.•

The collapse of the Redevelopment Agency's revised relocation plan

---

† Two of TOOR's attorneys, Sidney Wolinsky and J. Anthony Kline, had by this time left SFNLAF and the Housing Law Center, respectively, to form (together with several other attorneys) a non-profit public interest law firm, Public Advocates, Inc., located in San Francisco. Amanda Hawes left SFNLAF in 1972 to work with a Legal Services group in nearby Alameda County. All three remained active in the case, despite the change in their base of operations.

• Affidavit in Support of Plaintiffs' Motion for Preliminary Injunction, June 14, 1971. Kane's affidavit also made clear his resentment about the Agency's attempted use of the Housing Authority: ". . .[W]e are not in a position to make our units available strictly and solely as a relocation resource for the Redevelopment Agency. In addition to the several hundred persons facing displacement from Yerba Buena, . . .the Housing Authority has a constituency—persons on the waiting list. This constituency includes large numbers of persons already displaced by government action, including those from the Redevelopment Agency's own Western Addition A-2 and Yerba Buena Center redevelopment areas. Other persons on our waiting list have been waiting as long as 1961."

The Legal Battle

served to bring the Area Office of the Department of Housing and
Urban Development into the fray as well. Up to this point, HUD had
been a virtual rubber stamp for the Redevelopment Agency, particularly with respect to relocation matters (see pages 81-82). Its principal
interest was in the re-use of the land, not in the people being displaced.
According to an assistant to the director of HUD's San Francisco Area
Office, "Our main concern is for the city to get a developer and redevelop so that we can unload the land . . . ." [13] The YBC litigation was,
however, causing HUD some embarrassment. In mid-June, during the
hearings on TOOR's motion for a new injunction, HUD's San Francisco Office advised the court that it wanted to review once again the
relocation plans and practices for YBC. Area Director James Price
submitted an affidavit stating that his staff did not have sufficient information to say whether the Redevelopment Agency was obeying the
relocation statutes. "We question whether agency relocation plans are
adequate or whether any plan is being carried out adequately," said
Price,[14] although these doubts did not lead HUD to withdraw its cer-
tification of the YBC relocation plan. Angered by this admission, Judge
Weigel ordered HUD to report back to the court in 60 days the results
of its relocation study, and in the interim reimposed the original April
30, 1970 restraints against all relocation and demolition. As the June
23, 1971 *Chronicle* noted, "The allegations [Price's acknowledgment of
possible law violations requiring further investigation] upset Judge
Weigel, who viewed them as an effort to shift full responsibility for
enforcement of housing law from the Department of Housing and
Urban Development to himself."

HUD's sudden involvement was probably attributable to political factors as well. Mayor Alioto, a Democrat, had some national visibility and
gubernatorial aspirations, and the Republican Administration in
Washington was probably not adverse to making him look bad.
Another factor was the Nixon Administration's move to cut back on
urban renewal expenditures nationally, as part of general budget-
pruning; any delays on the expensive YBC project would save money,
at least for a time. The city charged Price with even more specific
political motives: retaliation for a lawsuit Mayor Alioto, the Redevelopment Agency and the Housing Authority had filed two weeks
earlier against President Nixon and HUD to compel release of funds
already authorized for HUD programs. (The suit, generally considered
a grandstand play, was dismissed in federal district court.)

HUD's intervention proved not to be a one-shot affair. After exten-
sively interviewing displacees and surveying relocation resources,
HUD in late August filed with the court a startling report, which concluded: "There are not now nor will there be, sufficient rehousing
resources to allow the relocation of Yerba Buena Center residents to

continue unabated."[15] The Department thereupon ordered the SFRA to file within 120 days a refined relocation plan, updated to include developments since filing its previously approved plan. During this four-month period no relocation or demolition activity was to be permitted unless specifically approved by HUD. An Agency request filed soon thereafter for permission to demolish two hotels was turned down by HUD pending submission of an acceptable relocation plan.

The Redevelopment Agency was typically unmoved by HUD's findings, adhering adamantly to its stance that there was no relocation problem and people ought to leave the Agency alone so that it could continue its work of building Yerba Buena Center. The Agency's deputy executive director said that the previous 60 days had been wasted and that the next 120 days would also be wasted as the Agency prepared a new relocation plan: "The report sets up more paperwork, more hurdles, more obstacles to the project. . .which will continue to slow down the project to a point in time where it simply cannot move."[16]

Thus, prompted by Judge Weigel, HUD substituted for the court injunction what in effect was a continuing administrative injunction. When the Agency in December, 1971, submitted its revised relocation plan, HUD rejected it outright. In a letter to Mayor Alioto dated February 23, 1972, HUD Area Director James Price stated that the Agency's new relocation plan "does not meet the test of Federal law, nor in our opinion will it pass the scrutiny of Judge Weigel's Court since it does not include any commitment on the part of the City to provide *permanent* replacement housing for YBC displacees." And in February, 1972, HUD advised the Agency that the four-year relocation payments provided for under the new Uniform Relocation Act (see page 117) did not qualify as permanent housing subsidies. Once again, in July, 1972, the Agency attempted to get a relocation plan through HUD, only to have it returned as "lacking clarity" specifically regarding plans for temporarily relocating project residents and using the city's locally funded rent assistance program.[17] Finally, in September, 1972, the Redevelopment Agency submitted a relocation plan that met with HUD's approval (and TOOR's disapproval: the plan was immediately challenged in court by TOOR and subsequently remanded to HUD for further documentation supporting its approval).

Housing Progress (?)

Although Justin Herman in November, 1970, voluntarily signed a consent decree committing his Agency to produce 1,500-1,800 low-rent units within three years, it is unlikely that he regarded this as a serious commitment, as is illustrated by the Agency's lethargic response to this promise in the two years following its issuance. In the words of a

The Legal Battle

high city official who knew Herman well, "He was damned if he was going to build those units. He never believed the feds would make him."[18] As of August, 1972, by the Agency's own records, only 11 units were actually completed.

Providing low-rent housing had always been the job of the Housing Authority, and it was not until YBC that the Redevelopment Agency had to deal directly with the effects of its people-removal activities. Since by law local redevelopment agencies cannot themselves be developers, the SFRA's task was to "cause" the 1,500-1,800 units to be constructed, either through the Housing Authority or private developers. The Housing Authority's unwillingness to redirect its entire effort to bail out the Redevelopment Agency and its Yerba Buena Center project, combined with HUD's sudden announcement in November, 1971, that it was cutting off funds previously committed to San Francisco public housing construction,† meant the Redevelopment Agency would have to rely on private developers to provide the bulk of the needed units.

Unable to rely on the Housing Authority for its 1,500-1,800 units, the Agency had to find its own sites and subsidization funds, neither of which was in abundant supply. And the Agency could not plead lack of support from the Housing Authority or HUD, since the November 9, 1970 agreement explicitly stated that failure of other agencies to assist in the production of the requisite units would in no way relieve the Agency of its responsibility.

HUD solved a good part of the money problem by committing funds from its federal rent supplement program. (These are 30-40 year contracts HUD enters into with private developers to lower market rents to public housing levels; they differ from public housing subsidies, which are given to local housing authorities to construct their own low-rent housing.) By February, 1972, HUD had made initial rent supplement grants for 362 units. Another grant, for 463 units, was made February, 1972, at the same time HUD rejected the Agency's revised relocation plan because of its reliance on temporary rather than permanent subsidies. (According to the February 27, 1972 *Examiner*, "HUD's unexpected decision to bail out The City came after weeks of behind-the-

---

† The cutoff wiped out an 800-unit authorization previously given by HUD (only some of which could have counted for the Agency's quota, since most units were programmed prior to April 30, 1970). According to the November 14, 1971 *Sunday Examiner & Chronicle*, "Official reasons given by HUD area director James Price are alleged bad management practices by the San Francisco Housing Authority and failure to produce housing swiftly and at reasonable cost. Unofficially, some political observers insist the allegations are a cover up for a Nixon Administration policy decision to reduce the federal deficit prior to next year's presidential elections."

scenes dickering with prominent Republicans, including former Mayor George Christopher, pitching in to get the Yerba Buena stalemate off dead center.") And in September, 1972, HUD made a final rent supplement grant, for 350 units. (This grant was announced by the White House, through Presidential assistant John Ehrlichman,[19] a somewhat unusual procedure which, along with a visit to San Francisco by President Nixon that same month and related stories floating around at the time, gave rise to rumors that the Nixon Administration and Mayor Alioto had made a deal for the latter to remain "neutral" during the 1972 Presidential campaign.[20])

TOOR had earlier sought to have supplementary funds HUD was granting to build Yerba Buena Center diverted to provide the 1,500-1,800 replacement housing units. The Redevelopment Agency had requested from HUD an additional $4.3 million to continue the YBC project. (Actually, the Agency had filed for an increase of $14.7 million in their federal loan for YBC to cover increased costs, but HUD was willing to grant only $4.3 million, due to budgetary cutbacks.) In a motion submitted in March, 1972, and heard two months later, TOOR asked Judge Weigel to enjoin HUD from allocating the moneys to the Redevelopment Agency and order them instead to transfer these funds to insure production of the housing units agreed to in the November 9, 1970 decree. As part of its motion, TOOR asked the court to compel SFRA to lay out a plan, with specific sites and developers, for completion of these units by the November, 1973 deadline; and to require that at least 1,000 of these units be rehabilitated housing within the YBC area, since there was no possibility of the Agency obtaining sites anyplace else at this late date.

Attorneys Amanda Hawes and Sidney Wolinsky argued that the additional HUD moneys being allocated to YBC should go for replacement housing because of the Agency's poor performance to date in meeting its obligations and HUD's November, 1971 cutoff of public housing funds for San Francisco. They pointed out that $4.3 million would renovate 750 low-rent units, about half the Agency's quota. On July 11, 1972, Judge Weigel handed down his ruling on TOOR's motion, refusing to redirect HUD's additional YBC grant or enjoin the project again. However, Weigel's reason for denying TOOR's motion was that YBC was in effect already halted by a combination of restrictions HUD had already placed on the project and an injunction issued two weeks before by Supreme Court Justice William Douglas in an unrelated suit on environmental aspects of the project (see page 156).

As to SFRA's ability to furnish the required housing, the court, while giving the Agency the benefit of the doubt, noted that:

[A] large body of. . .evidence is both uncontroverted and impressive in supporting plaintiffs' claim that defendant San Francisco Redevelopment Agency is

The Legal Battle

*failing in its obligations for provision of low-cost housing. . . .[T]he evidence
presently before the court raises serious questions as to whether defendant San
Francisco Redevelopment Agency will be able to meet its legal obligations by its
own voluntary deadline date of November 9, 1973.*[21]

Noting the short time left to complete the housing, the court ordered
the Agency to submit quarterly progress reports. Judge Weigel's ruling
also took account of previous Agency deceptions and stipulated that no
housing unit would be acceptable to fill the Agency's quota if "it had
been the subject of any written plan, proposal, or study" before April
30, 1970, thus sharpening the consent decree's definition of eligible
housing. With respect to creating replacement housing by rehabilitating substandard units, the court ruled that only units permanently
converted from high-rent to low-rent status through subsidies would
be eligible.

One of the Agency's strategies with respect to the November, 1970
decree was to allow and encourage depopulation of the YBC area. It
could then maintain that providing units for people no longer there
was absurd, and therefore it should be released from its full replacement housing commitment. With virtually no one moving into the
neighborhood, the combination of "voluntary" moveouts, sickness and
death were reducing the area's population rapidly. (The Agency was
reliably reported to have included a "mortality factor" in its relocation
planning, and the Arthur D. Little study of Agency relocation files for
the 1972 period suggest the reality of such calculations.[22] Of the 654
relocated persons for whom records were available, 53, or eight percent, were listed as "deceased," and another 38, or six percent, were
listed as in a hospital or convalescent home. Over one-sixth of official
relocatees were listed as "location unknown," and it may be assumed
that a proportion of these also died or were institutionalized.) Exact
interim population figures are not available, but through a combination of all factors the original population had dropped to about 1,300
by late 1970, and to about 700 (120 of whom were in the Central
Blocks) by late 1972. In the lonely, hostile surroundings created by the
Agency's clearance and hotel management activities, TOOR found it
increasingly difficult to convince people to stay in the area.

The Agency was constantly reminding the court and the public of
how few people remained in the area, a stance designed to place pressure on the residents, TOOR, their attorneys and the court. The
Agency's tactic was to try to convince the general public that a handful
of persons was selfishly standing in the way of a major redevelopment
project of benefit to the entire city. But Judge Weigel was not to be
diverted by this ploy. In his July, 11, 1972 ruling with respect to HUD's
supplementary YBC grant, he noted:

Housing Progress(?)

Defendant Agency urges that there has been a reduction in the number of families and individuals who continue to reside in the Yerba Buena area. That is true. But it is immaterial. The commitment was made to comply with the law in the light of an over-all shortage of such housing throughout the city of San Francisco. Defendant cannot get rid of its obligation to provide a minimum of 1,500 units of new or rehabilitated low-cost housing by getting rid of some of those who need it.

The court also took due note of the somewhat disingenuous use of these figures by the Agency, in its footnote to the above statement, which read: "The evidence also shows that defendant San Francisco Redevelopment Agency has not been unwilling to contribute to the rate of attrition."

In addition to the Agency's money problem was the more difficult problem of finding sites for the units. Given the high cost of land for new construction, the length of time it takes to construct new housing, and problems of locational suitability and acceptance by the surrounding neighborhood, the Agency opted to meet its commitment primarily through rehabilitation. (Several new housing developments were set into motion, however, including two high-rise buildings near the Clementina Towers public housing project, sponsored by the Salvation Army and St. Patrick's Church, and a converted industrial building in the Mission district sponsored by the St. Vincent de Paul Society.) But the defects inherent in the rehab approach were cogently pointed out by TOOR attorney Amanda Hawes when the Redevelopment Agency, following receipt of its second rent supplement grant, announced it was looking for 463 transient hotel rooms suitable for conversion to permanent housing:

[Attorney Hawes] accused the city and the Redevelopment Agency of wanting to "continue to play musical chairs."

Old hotels would be rehabilitated, she said, and their permanent guests forced to move elsewhere to make way for Yerba Buena residents. No one, however, would look after the interests of the set of guests forced to move to make way for rehabilitation.

"It is really a crime to displace these people," she said, "because they are often as old and poor as the people in the Yerba Buena area."[23]

Consistent with its opposition to "superpriority" in public housing, TOOR was not about to solve its problems by climbing over the backs of other poor people. Judge Weigel, in his July 11, 1972 ruling on TOOR's motion, placed stringent limitations on any further Agency attempts to play "musical chairs" with poor people's housing.

The problem of obtaining suitable sites related, of course, to what part of the city the YBC relocatees were moved to. The only substantial supply of residential hotels suitable for rehabilitation were either in the

The Legal Battle

YBC area itself or across Market Street, in the Tenderloin. The reaction of the Agency and its supporters to TOOR's proposal to rehabilitate several South of Market hotels for permanent low-rent use was vitriolic, as described on pages 119-21. The Tenderloin was opposed not only by TOOR—because of its high crime rate, hills, and high restaurant prices—but by many supporters of YBC as well, who did not want such persons in the downtown area at all. In fact, Werner Lewin, vice-president and general manager of the Hilton Hotel Corporation, made strenuous attempts to keep the YBC relocatees away from his Hilton Hotel by trying to block the SFRA from using the nearby Ramona Hotel as a replacement housing resource. The Hilton even threatened the Agency with legal action over its proposed use of the Ramona. In a letter to Mayor Alioto, dated August 10, 1972, Lewin stated: "We believe that the relocation of Yerba Buena residents in the Ramona would have a very adverse effect on our guests, a great many of whom will pass the Ramona a number of times daily to catch cable cars, to shop in Union Square, and to visit other parts of our fine city. . . . The neighborhood and our hotel cannot afford any additional adverse influences."† A "blight" South of Market, an "adverse influence" North of Market, the old men living on the Yerba Buena Center site would be eliminated from the downtown, and possibly from the city altogether, if the city's economic leaders were to have their way.

Pressed by TOOR, HUD and the federal court, the Redevelopment Agency began to realize that it would indeed have to produce the promised units. The changes within the Redevelopment Agency and in the Agency's relationship to City Hall that occurred after Justin Herman's death in late 1971 (see pages 190-92) doubtless were an additional factor in lessening the Agency's intransigence on the housing issue. But so much time had been lost in the interim that it was clear the Agency would not meet its three-year deadline. The *Examiner's* urban affairs writer, a firm supporter of YBC and SFRA, wrote on February 8, 1972, "As things stand now, these 1,500 housing units will never be provided within the three-year limit set by the court." It was not until the following September that the Agency was able to find a sufficient number of vacant hotel rooms, acceptable to HUD, to begin to use the rent supplement moneys the federal government had made available.

But more subsidy money was needed than the federal government

---

† This pressure by the Hilton came to light when the owner of the Ramona filed a $4.3 million damage suit against the Hilton and several other defendants, charging pressure to prevent sale and renovation of the Ramona. The suit was later dropped and a compromise was reached, under which the Redevelopment Agency promised that future tenants for the Ramona would be "screened." See *San Francisco Chronicle*, January 12 and February 7, 1973.

had offered; and in August, 1972, in the first of the quarterly progress reports Judge Weigel had ordered, the city introduced the idea of using local funds, raised via the hotel tax (see page 52), to subsidize replacement units for YBC residents. This fitting notion—requiring hotel users and owners to bear some of the financial burdens caused by a project designed to benefit them—eventually became the core of the plan that was finally to break the TOOR litigation stalemate (see Chapter VII).

Blaming the Victims (and Others)

The Redevelopment Agency's attempts throughout the YBC battle to create the image that the project was being held up by malcontents and publicity-seeking lawyers served to mask the truth: that the Agency itself was responsible for the delays by ignoring federal relocation requirements at the outset and then stalling and reneging on its promise to rectify the housing shortage and the relocation inequities it had created.

The Agency and its supporters waged a constant campaign to discredit TOOR, its attorneys, and even the court. An example was the fatal fire in November, 1971, at the St. James Hotel on Third Street in the YBC area. The hotel was owned by Benjamin Blumenthal, a man with heavy political connections in San Francisco. In 1969 the St. James had been cited for no less than 18 housing code violations, including an absence of sprinklers in the halls and stairways and illegal cooking in rooms. Just months prior to the fire a major controversy had arisen over Blumenthal's appointment to the Housing Authority board by Mayor Alioto, due to his alleged widespread ownership of slum properties. Angry protests followed from the Public Housing Tenants Association, the NAACP and the Family Service Agency, including a sit-in in Alioto's office and a threatened city-wide public housing rent strike. These protests did not move either the mayor or Board of Supervisors, who confirmed the appointment unanimously. However, the protests continued, and three weeks after the Supervisors' approval Blumenthal decided to decline the position.

Out of the St. James Hotel fire came a rash of charges against TOOR by the Redevelopment Agency. The Agency issued press releases blaming TOOR for the loss of life because it had initiated litigation that kept the Agency from moving families out of "slum firetraps." TOOR responded by pointing out that it had urged rehabilitation of the St. James, but the Agency instead had given Blumenthal special treatment and allowed him to retain ownership of the St. James while other hotels in the area were purchased, and either demolished or managed, by the Agency. According to the chief of the city's Bureau of Building Inspection, "If they had taken care of the cooking facilities, the fire ought not

The Legal Battle

have started. If they had installed sprinklers, the fire would never have gotten out of the room."[24] The Redevelopment Agency had let the "firetrap" remain to accommodate a local political influential, who kept on changing his plans for the building's future, but never made any improvements.

The St. James was not the only fatal hotel fire in the surrounding area. In February, 1972, there was a fire at the Sherman Hotel on Eleventh Street, killing two persons; and in May, 1972, a woman was burned to death in the Jefferson Hotel in the Tenderloin. Unlike the St. James fire, no Agency press releases came from these incidents, possibly because both hotels had been on relocation lists for displacees from YBC.

Many other instances of "blaming the victim" were to be found as well. Project delays and resulting expenses were all attributed to TOOR. These sums ranged from $7,000 a month to keep hotels open for remaining residents (who were protected by court orders), to $7,000 a day for increased interest and administrative costs, to $1 million per month due to construction cost inflation. Responsibility inevitably was assigned to TOOR's persistence in pressing its claims, not to the Agency's adamance in resisting the court's, and later HUD's, findings and orders. As a letter to the *Chronicle* noted, however, rather than blaming citizens protecting their rights for wasting public funds,

The commissioners of the Redevelopment Agency owe the people of San Francisco an explanation for the squandering of this great amount of money, for their non-compliance with the Court's order and their own agreement over a period of more than 14 months, and from a legal standpoint, owe the city an accounting for the waste and losses and frustrations involved.[25]

Another situation arose during the summer of 1972 over the Redevelopment Agency's alleged inability to give relocation payments to former YBC residents. These payments, available under the 1970 Uniform Relocation Act, provide up to $1,000 per year for four years for displaced persons forced to pay higher rents than in their previous housing. In July, the Agency issued a public statement which termed "criminal" and "sickening" the Agency's inability to make these payments because of the court's injunction.[26] Again TOOR had to respond, this time pointing out that the Agency was trying to use relocation payments as bribes to force residents to relocate into substandard housing outside the project area; TOOR (along with HUD and the federal court) also noted that such payments were no permanent solution, since subsidies would end after four years and people would still be left without decent places to live. TOOR further observed that persons leaving voluntarily during the injunction period would be eligible to receive these payments at a later date.

Blaming the Victims (and others)

Personal attacks were also leveled against the attorneys, and even against Judge Weigel. TOOR's attorneys were repeatedly attacked as "ideologues" and "outside Berkeley agitators," even though SFNLAF is located and operates exclusively in San Francisco. The only basis for these charges was that all three attorneys live in Berkeley and that the Housing Law Center is located there. A particularly strong attack on attorney Wolinsky and Judge Weigel came from the San Francisco Building and Construction Trades Council, whose primary interest was securing construction jobs for its members. In March, 1972, the BCTC passed a resolution saying that Wolinsky "lives high in the Berkeley Hills by night and is a radical chic poverty lawyer by day," responsible for "an endless stream of obstructionist lawsuits." And the same resolution characterized Judge Weigel as "an accommodating federal judge. . .who lives in one of the most luxurious highrise Russian Hill penthouses and has never had to stand in an unemployment line."[27]

What was undoubtedly the most bizarre attempt to intimidate the court came in January, 1972, when the Redevelopment Agency filed a motion in U. S. District Court, asking that Judge Weigel remove himself from the Yerba Buena case on the grounds of bias and prejudice and being "overwrought and extremely emotional" in his rulings. According to the January 21, 1972 *Chronicle*, "Court observers could recall no other such accusation filed in U. S. District Court here over the last 15 years." The action seemed a coordinated attempt on the part of elements in the city's power structure to eliminate the principal hurdle to continuation of the project, and was reminiscent of the Agency's earlier attempt in the summer of 1970 to bring what it hoped would be a friendly judge into the case during Judge Weigel's absence from the country (see pages 129-30). Members of the redevelopment booster club had prepared the ground for the Agency's legal maneuver over the previous two weeks. The *Examiner's* contribution was a January 6, 1972 editorial that fairly whined:

HOW MUCH LONGER must the city of San Francisco put up with the dictatorial decisions on community affairs of U. S. District Judge Stanley Weigel? . . .

Weigel long has been a central figure in the semi-disastrous delays suffered by the $350 million Yerba Buena redevelopment project. This week he imposed costly new restraints.

What now? How long, oh lord? . . .

Weigel and the foundation [SFNLAF] refuse to give proper recognition to the Redevelopment Agency's humane and efficient program to relocate residents displaced by Yerba Buena. . . .

Is there no way to get this crucial issue out of Weigel's court?†

† The *Examiner* apparently had had a change of heart about the judge. A

The Legal Battle

A few days later (January 11, 1972), radio station KCBS chimed in editorially: "Judge Weigel's continued resistance regarding a removal of the injunction strikes us as poor judgment." And the same day, Redevelopment Agency board member Stanley Jensen, president of the local Machinists Union, charged that Weigel was biased and accused him of "taking a righteous attitude of doing all right and nothing wrong."[28] The charges against Weigel, a liberal Republican appointed by President John F. Kennedy, were also tied to his recent ruling ordering the integration of San Francisco's schools by busing. Supervisor Peter Tamaras, whose family-owned hotel supply business services most of the downtown hotels, accused Judge Weigel of being "dictatorial and biased" and of "doing a great disservice to the city. . .by the harmful political decisions he has made. . . . Except for Judge Weigel and a handful of dissidents, most people approve of the Yerba Buena project."† Tamaras, noting that Weigel's children attended all-white private schools, offered the following analysis: "Quite an irony. Maybe he feels guilty about it, but he shouldn't get his therapy by halting the Yerba Buena Center and ordering cross-town busing."

Judge Weigel's response was to ask the Chief Judge of the Northern District of California to review the case. In early February, 1972, Chief Judge Oliver J. Carter rejected the Agency's charges and returned the case to Judge Weigel, terming some of the bias charges "incredible." Judge Carter noted that in November, 1970, the Agency had voluntarily signed a consent decree and even had expressed appreciation to Judge Weigel. "Clearly, when they thought the cards were with them they enjoyed the game," noted Carter's opinion. Commenting on the fact that remarks made by Judge Weigel in September of 1970 were cited by the Agency as proof of prejudice, Judge Carter noted: "For the defendants to have sat back for this long and now attempt to pick through the record and allege that prejudice was evidenced 15 months ago strikes this court as incredible." Discarding another claim that there was prejudice in Judge Weigel's remark that the Agency wanted to "throw out tenants, using federal funds to do it," Judge Carter said, "It appears to me that is merely a colorful way of describing the Agency's actual function."[29] The Agency appealed Judge Carter's ruling, but the appeal was denied by the Ninth Circuit Court of Appeals without a hearing. (The *Examiner* pressed the issue nonetheless; in a March 2, 1972 editorial it urged "self-disqualification" on Judge

---

feature article on Weigel in the July 11, 1971 paper concluded about him: "Regarded as firm, fair, concerned with the individual rights of criminals, he seems the personification of the idealized federal judge."

† *San Francisco Examiner*, January 25, 1972, and *San Francisco Chronicle*, January 25, 1972. Tamaras was immediately criticized by the Bar Association of San Francisco for his remarks (see *San Francisco Chronicle*, January 27, 1972.)

Blaming the Victims (and others)

Weigel, Judge Carter's ruling notwithstanding, out of "concern for the judicial system's all-important image in the eyes of the public.")

The blatant attempt by the Agency and its constituency to intimidate the federal court did arouse considerable resentment in the legal community. Among many criticisms of the "get Weigel" drive was the following perceptive letter by two Legal Services attorneys:

By his outrageous attack on Federal Judge Stanley Weigel, Supervisor Tamaras has dramatically revealed—perhaps unwittingly—a fundamental assumption of the San Francisco power elite. That assumption, simply stated, is that the judiciary itself is so integral a part of the Establishment that its primary duty is to rule in favor of the dominant business and political interests.

Under this view, judges are not to treat elderly hotel residents the same way they do real estate developers. . . . And whatever happens, judges are not actually to give judgment to the poor—even if such a decision is legally correct—if that decision would create "tremendous suffering to the city's tourist and convention industry". . . .

But now for the real irony. People like Tamaras—outspoken "law and order" types—would surely admonish black parents or the elderly poor not to "take the law into their own hands" but rather to proceed "within the system," i.e., through the courts. (They'll lose in the courts, get it?) But when they do go to court and then actually WIN, all hell breaks loose and the cat is out of the bag at last. For

Karen Gottstein

TOOR Attorneys Amanda Hawes, J. Anthony Kline and Sidney Wolinsky

The Legal Battle

what judges in San Francisco are REALLY supposed to be faithful to–in the Tamaras view–is not the Constitution of the United States but rather financial interests like "the city's tourist and convention industries."[30]

More Lawsuits

While the TOOR lawsuit was the principal legal action challenging the Yerba Buena project, several other suits were also filed, each undertaken independent of the TOOR-SFNLAF strategy. These suits had primarily to do with the environmental impact of YBC and the financing plan for the project.

In January, 1972, six conservation groups, including the Sierra Club, filed suit in federal court, claiming that YBC and two other Bay Area renewal projects in Oakland and Berkeley violated the National Environmental Policy Act of 1969 in not filing detailed environmental impact statements with HUD. The suit asked that all three projects be enjoined until such statements were filed. The environmental concerns about YBC were outlined in a letter to the *Examiner* (July 27, 1972) by the president of San Francisco Tomorrow, one of the plaintiff organizations:

The project's most objectionable feature, in our view, stemmed from the enormous impact that its thousands of visiting users, to say nothing of their automobiles, would have upon The City.

. . .Why so many parking stalls, particularly in view of the fact that the project will be served by two BART stations? What is to stop the publicly developed portions of the project from encouraging the construction of still more stalls by nearby private developers?

What is to prevent the multitudes of incoming tourists and conventioneers from further clogging the streets of San Francisco with their automobiles as they move to and from the project and to various other points throughout The City?. . .

Some of the issues raised in our case concern: the serious earthquake hazards that will be presented by extensive high-rise in an area of The City that is most vulnerable to tremors and now has no high-rise; the enormous sewage disposal problems that the Yerba Buena project would create for the already overloaded North Point Sewage Disposal Facility (which discharges "treated" sewage into the Bay).

Also, the visual impact of concentrated high-rise in one of the few remaining downtown areas with unimpaired views; the impact on traffic flow, air quality and population densities; and the negative impact of Yerba Buena on the BART system.

Although the plaintiffs' motion for preliminary injunction was denied by both the U. S. District Court and the Ninth Circuit Court of Appeals, in June, 1972, Supreme Court Justice William Douglas granted a stay of the Circuit Court ruling and ordered the case back to that court for full hearing, in the interim enjoining all physical activities in connection with the three projects. In January, 1973, the Ninth Circuit affirmed the District Court's ruling that the National Environmental Policy Act did not apply to YBC, since federal funds were contracted for in 1966, before enactment of the statute. (The provisions of the Act were, however, held applicable for the Berkeley project—the Oakland project had earlier been withdrawn from the suit.) The plaintiffs decided not to appeal the case to the Supreme Court when HUD, in order to avoid the delays such an appeal might entail, offered to produce an environmental impact statement for Yerba Buena Center.[31]

A related but more complex suit involving both environmental and financing issues was brought in state court by conservationist-businessman Alvin Duskin in January, 1972. Duskin's suit challenges the project for failure to comply with the provisions of the California Environmental Quality Act, as well as for illegalities in the financing plan—specifically, circumvention of the State Constitution with respect to the proposed issuance of lease revenue bonds by the Redevelopment Agency for construction of the Central Blocks public facilities (see page 162) and use of tax-increment financing to repay the bonds (see pages 167-68). (The city has since commissioned an environmental impact report for Yerba Buena Center, which was carried out by Arthur D. Little, Inc. and URS Research Company. This report was approved by the Board of Supervisors in September, 1973.) The Duskin suit, as of this writing, is still pending (see pages 202-03).

A third suit, filed in state court by a local attorney named Gerald Wright, similarly challenges the basic financing plan approved for Yerba Buena Center because the city, through its leasing agreement with the Redevelopment Agency for the public facilities, is obligated to back up with its own funds any deficiency in the amount of projected revenue needed to pay off the Agency's revenue bonds. This arrangement, Wright as well as Duskin maintains, is in effect a general obligation bond issue and therefore illegally circumvents the constitutional requirement that such bonds be submitted to the voters and receive a two-thirds approval. (Wright's suit also charges an illegal conflict of interest by Supervisor Robert Mendelsohn, who was both chairman of the Supervisors' Finance Committee, which approved the YBC financing plan, and also was employed by Lawrence Halprin and Associates, landscape architects for the Yerba Buena Center project.) Wright's suit, although filed nearly two years ago, still has not been answered by the city. The project cannot advance to the construction stage until both his and Duskin's suits are settled, because bonds cannot be sold with litigation pending over the legality of the bond issue itself.

6. Economic Magic or Economic Folly

Bob Fitch

**[The YBC financing plan is] a document
that is so preposterous that it would
constitute prima facie evidence of fraud
if utilized in a private transaction.**
Gerald A. Wright, attorney, 1973

**I really had no idea
what was in the [financing] plan . . .
Once a project reaches the financial stage
it becomes almost unstoppable.**
Member of San Francisco
Board of Supervisors, 1972

Yerba Buena Center's role as the blockbusting wedge to expand the city's financial district southward across Market Street (outlined in Chapter I) provided the driving force behind the project. To sell the public, however, it was held out as a project that would increase the city's tax base, create employment and enhance convention and tourist business—with concomitant economic benefits for all. The land was being put to a "higher and better use," in the jargon of the planners. The claims of YBC proponents at times sounded like the pitches of old-time carnival hucksters peddling snake-oil, in this case a cure-all for the ills of a city. But in fact the economic arguments supporting YBC turn out upon examination to be at best tenuous, at worst spurious. Whatever economic benefits do result will accrue to a small group of investors, corporations and businesses. The general public, as well as the people who previously occupied the land, will be picking up the bills for years to come.

Fiscal Gymnastics

Although Yerba Buena Center clearly involves an enormous investment of public and private funds, there is little public understanding of how the project will affect the city economically. In the confusing world of financing and planning projections, the word of the Redevelopment Agency, City Hall, and their consultants is accepted at face value.

The price tag for YBC has been a matter of constant, and not entirely unintentional confusion. Official documents and press accounts have labeled its cost as anywhere from $34 million to $400 million. The wide disparities in these figures are in part a function of whether they refer to the Central Blocks or the entire project; the public facilities, private facilities, or both; the federal subsidy, combined federal and local contributions, or total public and private investment. The date of the figure is also a factor: whether it was put forward in the 1950s, early 1960s, late 1960s, or early 1970s in turn reflected differences in the

Economic Magic or Economic Folly

content of the plan as well as cost increases due to inflation. The figure cited also has often been influenced by the need to sell the project to the public: if the aim was to obtain support based on the number of construction jobs that would result or the projected increase in the city's tax base, higher figures were called for; if the subject was the amount of the bond issue needed to float the project, then estimates were scaled down as far as possible.

The federal government as of mid-1973 had provided some $45 million in urban renewal subsidies to cover planning, land acquisition and clearance, relocation of residents and businesses, administration, and related costs for the entire YBC project (excluding federal subsidies for replacement housing required as a result of the TOOR litigation).†

Although the costs of acquiring, clearing and otherwise preparing an urban renewal site by statute must be shared by the federal and local governments on a two-thirds to one-third basis, in fact the city of San Francisco makes no direct cash contribution to YBC under this formula. Urban renewal law permits a locality to pay its share of a renewal project by crediting expenditures for related public facilities. These expenditures often come from the regular city budget and in many cases would be or might have been spent anyway. For example, a portion of BART expenditures was credited as a local project cost because it was to serve YBC.

Like most successful local urban renewal administrators, Justin Herman prided himself in his ability to so juggle the use of these expenditures that the city never had to put its own cash directly into its renewal program; thus the federal renewal grant was regarded as "free" money. Furthermore, local expenditures exceeding the required local share for any one renewal project can be applied to other projects with insufficient local expenditures. This practice—sometimes known as the "credits shell game"—created an intricate web of interdependence between YBC and other renewal projects. The Redevelopment Agency is claiming nearly $49 million in local urban renewal

† This figure may be increased through future requests to HUD for supplementary funds to complete the project, based on unanticipated costs or cost increases. "Amendatories" of this type are quite common in urban renewal projects, and more cynical observers of the renewal process have suggested that some local administrators intentionally underestimate costs at the time of their first request to HUD for a loan and grant contract, in order to increase the likelihood of HUD approving the project, knowing that once HUD is "hooked," it will be hard to turn down subsequent requests for increases in project funds. The Redevelopment Agency has already estimated that completion of the YBC project will require an additional $7.6 million in HUD grants. (See letter dated July 9, 1973, from Mayor Joseph Alioto to James T. Lynn, Secretary of HUD.)

credits for YBC, $27 million of which is in excess of what is needed for the project. Three San Francisco projects—Western Addition A-2, India Basin and Hunters Point—directly depend on excess YBC credits for continued financing.† HUD must approve these credits, and local redevelopment agencies often try to get away with as much as they can in making such claims, only to have HUD pare down these figures. HUD regulations on what facilities (or portions thereof) are eligible for urban renewal credits are imprecise and often somewhat arbitrary.•

Land acquired and cleared under the urban renewal program must by law be disposed of at its "fair market value." In the case of Yerba Buena Center, the developer of the Central Blocks facilities—the convention center, sports arena, parking garages, heating plant and pedestrian concourse—will be the city itself (contrary to Justin Herman's original plan; this change is described in detail in Chapter VII). Therefore, the city must come up with the money to buy this land—$14 million. The city has, rather ingeniously, included these land costs in the bond issue it must float to construct the facilities. How these bonds will be paid off, then, becomes the crucial question—since all local costs for Yerba Buena Center have essentially been folded into this single financing instrument.

Federal loans permit a renewal project to proceed fairly far along before the local contribution is needed. Therefore, the city did not have to devise a financing plan for YBC until most of the other pieces were firmly in place. This permitted the Agency to avoid raising and discussing critical financial aspects of the project as part of the initial approvals process; and it created pressure on the Board of Supervisors to approve whatever financing plan the Agency devised to implement the project the Board had previously approved.

Several financing plans have been proposed over the life of the

---

† At an earlier time, the direction of dependency was reversed. In early 1962, in an effort to pressure the city into sponsoring a parking facility beneath the Japanese Cultural and Trade Center in the Western Addition A-1 project area, Justin Herman warned that "the South-of-Market redevelopment project will collapse unless the city agrees to sponsor the garage," and announced he would not spend the $600,000 planning grant for YBC until the garage plans had been approved. See *San Francisco Examiner*, March 30, 1962, and September 13, 1962. The garage was eventually built and has consistently run at a deficit.

• A small portion of the exhibit hall construction cost is being claimed, but none of the arena costs. The major credit elements are the parking garage, central pedestrian concourse, and general site improvements such as utility relocation, lighting, street widening and sewers. See "Yerba Buena Center Public Facilities: A Description of the Scope, Character, Financing, and Leasing Plans for the Public Facilities," submitted by Thomas J. Mellon, Chief Administrative Officer, March 6, 1972, pp. J-1 — J-3.

Economic Magic or Economic Folly

project. Their common objective has been to avoid financing through a general obligation bond issue, which is backed by the city's full faith and credit and which by law has to come before the voters and receive a two-thirds approval. The City Fathers simply did not want to risk such a vote since there is a high probability that the people of San Francisco would reject bearing the cost of YBC. As the *Examiner* stated on April 28, 1971, ". . .[W]inning voter approval for the project would be a near miracle. . . ."† The Board of Supervisors in March of 1972 finally approved a YBC financing plan which does not require general obligation bonds. One Supervisor stated when interviewed, "Most people in this city don't know much about Yerba Buena Center. . . .I am disturbed something this big is not going on the ballot." The Supervisors held barely perfunctory hearings on the plan before passing it unanimously.● One Supervisor explained:

When the financing plan came up before the Board, I asked for a two-week delay because we had no time to study the proposal.

But I voted "yes" on the plan finally because of the recommendation of the Finance Committee. But I really had no idea what was in the plan. . . .Once a project reaches the financial stage it becomes almost unstoppable.

Another Supervisor remarked, "If you really want me to tell you, we have very little control over the Redevelopment Agency."

The March, 1972 plan calls for the Redevelopment Agency to issue up to $225 million in lease revenue bonds to pay for construction and other development costs. Once the public facilities are completed, the Agency will then lease the sites and facilities to the City of San Francisco for a rent sufficient to amortize the bonds and "cover any additional expenses which may be incurred by the Agency."[1] When the bonds are paid off after 35 years, title to the public facilities will be transferred to the City. The financing agreement obligates the City to pay SFRA the stipulated rent (i.e., the full debt repayment costs) and

---

† The last time the voters had been consulted about a bond issue for a convention center, in 1948, they voted it down 149,000 to 137,000. The proposal was for a $15 million bond issue to construct a 200,000 square foot underground exhibition space, a 20,000 seat arena and other facilities, to be located west of the Civic Center, on a site that now is a freeway.

● Needless to say, the Redevelopment Agency board had earlier provided no forum for discussing the wisdom and implications of this financing plan either. According to the March 15, 1972 *Chronicle*:

"The Redevelopment Agency's decision to go $219 million into debt was without public discussion or question. The matter appeared as 19th on a routine and uncontroversial agenda. . . .

Agency executive director Robert Rumsey explained with a few sentences the outline of the agreement and asked if there were any questions. There were none and the proposal was moved, seconded and passed unanimously in a minute or less."

any other unexpected costs—whether or not projected revenues from the facilities it rents and other sources meet the amount of the rent.†

The public facilities' cost is estimated at $219 million, $142 million of which is for construction. The remainder is for funded interest (a special fund to pay debt service prior to the opening of revenue-producing facilities), land costs, architectural and engineering fees, consultants, administration, and other miscellaneous items. Taking into account interest payments on the bonds, the total long-term cost of the public facilities in YBC will be around $500 million—a staggering figure and well over twice their announced cost. (By way of comparison, San Francisco's entire municipal budget for fiscal year 1973-1974 was $648 million.)

The YBC facilities are terribly expensive compared with similar developments elsewhere. Construction cost for the sports arena alone will be $42 million, whereas in 1966 the Oakland Arena and Coliseum —together far larger than that planned for YBC—cost only $21.5 million. The per parking stall construction cost is estimated at $11,000, compared with the $6-8,000 per stall usually considered a high cost figure for downtown parking structures.

One of the more amazing aspects of these financial schemes is the way in which early cost estimates are dwarfed by subsequent figures, once the project has been approved. In 1965, for example, the *Chronicle* (August 25) reported that the two most expensive elements of the public facilities—the convention center and sports arena—would cost only $25 million. Yet according to the March, 1972 financing plan, their combined construction cost will be $102 million (exclusive of interest, land, design and administrative costs). As recently as the summer of 1971, when it looked as if a bond issue might have to be placed on the ballot to finance the YBC public facilities (see page 187), the amount of that issue was scheduled to be $118 million; thus, in the brief eight months between that time and passage of the 1972 financing plan, the stated cost of these facilities shot up $100 million, nearly 100 percent!

Perhaps most disturbing about this escalation is the equanimity with which those who govern the city regard these leaps, and the ease with which they assent to whatever the Redevelopment Agency deems required to bring YBC to fruition. During the Board of Supervisors' brief

---

†The courts must still sustain this financing scheme against the lawsuits described on page 157. The supporting document for the financing plan cited in the note to page 161 was described by one of the attorneys challenging the plan as a "document that is so preposterous that it would constitute prima facie evidence of fraud if utilized in a private transaction." (Letter dated April 30, 1973, from Gerald A. Wright to Friends of Yerba Buena Center, c/o William Brinton, Esq.)

Economic Magic or Economic Folly

consideration of the YBC financing plan, prior to giving its unanimous approval, virtually no one raised the basic questions of why the whole thing is going to cost so much, and who is responsible for misleading the public and their representatives about the true costs of the project.

The financing plan rests on extremely tenuous income estimates. These estimates are based on the assumption that the bonds can be sold at a six percent interest rate—which will require annual repayments of $14.5 million—even though a memorandum from the city's Budget Analyst suggested that a seven to seven and one-half percent interest rate is more likely. It is unclear what will happen if the litigation controversy delays the project much further. Construction costs are said to inflate by eight to ten percent annually, or as much as $14 million.† Any substantial delays in opening the facilities will require an increase in the bonding limit and alteration of the underlying financing plan. At the time of the Board of Supervisors hearings the exhibition hall and the sports arena were scheduled to open in the summer of 1976; it is now clear that this deadline cannot possibly be met.

Most questionable is whether revenues from YBC will fully cover the debt payments assumed by the city. These revenues are to come from four sources:

● Private land rents: the amount the private developer will pay annually for the right to develop and sub-lease the private sites in the Central Blocks.

● Income from the public facilities: about half this amount is expected to come from the 1,850-car public parking garage, one-fourth from the sports arena, and one-fourth from a ticket tax on all public events at the arena. (The exhibit hall is not expected to produce any net revenues.)

● Hotel tax allocation: One-third of the city's hotel tax revenue (see page 52) is now assigned to YBC development.

● Property tax increment: all property tax revenue from privately owned land in the entire project area, beyond what the city received in 1965 (before passage of the YBC plan), will be placed in a special fund to pay off the YBC bonds.

Total annual income from all four sources projected for 1976 (the sports arena and exhibit hall completion date), and for 1982 (the project's overall completion date), is as follows:

	1976	1982
Private Land Rents	$ 500,000	$ 600,000
Public Facilities	3,600,000	3,600,000
Hotel Tax	1,800,000	2,000,000
Property Tax	6,800,000	10,300,000
Total	**$12,700,000**	**$16,500,000**

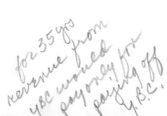

Fiscal Gymnastics

These are the income projections designed to cover the estimated $14.5 million annual debt payments. Thus, Yerba Buena Center is planned to run at a loss for the first few years, and not until 1979 or 1980 produce an increase over debt service needs. The Redevelopment Agency has acknowledged that this interim deficit may run as high as $9 million, and this will have to come from the city's general funds.[2] Should the interest rate turn out to be seven percent, as the city's Budget Analyst minimally predicts, the required annual payments will be around $16.6 million. The interim deficit will be correspondingly larger and the projected income would never be sufficient to meet debt payments. (Another revealing perspective on the annual debt service required for the YBC bonds lies in comparing it with property taxes now budgeted for some key city departments. The YBC bonds will require $14-16 million; the city property taxes budgeted for the entire municipal public transit system are $22 million, for public health $21 million, for recreation and parks $13 million, and for public works $9 million.[3])

A closer look at the projected revenues from the public facilities shows how shaky the grounds are on which the YBC financing plan stands. The exhibition hall-convention center is expected to produce no net revenue at all; in fact it is likely to operate at a substantial loss, as do almost all large-city convention facilities. San Francisco's current convention facilities in the Civic Auditorium and Brooks Hall operate at a $200,000 annual deficit. In the competitive world of convention business, rents on facilities cannot be raised beyond the prevailing rate—or the city risks losing conventions. YBC will probably result in an excess capacity of exhibition space which will drive rental charges down in other local facilities.

The sports arena is projected to bring in an annual net revenue of $817,000.[•] Yet this figure is also deceptive, as it is based on the assumption that the Bay Area's professional basketball team, the Golden State Warriors, and hockey team, the California Golden Seals, will play al-

---

†A 1974 HUD study (cited in footnote 31, Chapter 5) indicates (at p. 130) that inflation has already pushed construction costs to $163 million from the $142 million figure in the financing plan approved by the Board of Supervisors, with a corresponding increase in other development costs.

•The new Nassau County (N. Y.) Coliseum, a 16,000-seat arena completed in 1972, which draws on a population of 2 ½ million, lost over $1 million in its first 21 months of operation, although it has both professional basketball and hockey, as well as ice-shows, rock concerts and other events. Its 1972 deficit will cost the average homeowner $2 in the 1974 budget. See George Vecsey, "Spotlight Still on Politics at the Nassau Coliseum", *New York Times*, October 29, 1973.

Economic Magic or Economic Folly

most all home games in the new arena.† As of now both teams play their home games in the Oakland Arena, a new but slightly smaller facility. Neither team has made any commitment to move to San Francisco; probably the best San Francisco could hope for is that both clubs would share Oakland and San Francisco as their "home city", playing half their home games in each.• Even this prediction may be overly optimistic. The owner of the Seals, Charles O. Finley, sold the team to the National Hockey League in February, 1974; given Finley's claim of a $2.5 million loss over the previous three years and his earlier desire to move the team to Indianapolis, it is possible the hockey franchise may be moved out of the Bay Area entirely. In addition, neither team breaks attendance records. In their 1972-1973 season the Warriors averaged 6,000 persons per home game, the Seals 5,300, in the Oakland Arena, which has a capacity of 12,000. (The world of sports has many unanticipated adversities that could affect project revenues. The City lost a good deal from the baseball strike at the beginning of the 1972 season. As described in the April 5, 1972 *Chronicle*, the city lost rental fees for Candlestick Park, the $.50 per ticket tax revenue —$22,500 on opening day alone—the $.25 per car parking tax from the 6,400-car parking lot, and the $.90 per car net revenue from the parking fee. Much of this revenue was specifically earmarked to pay off the bonds issued for renovation of the stadium.)

Any shortfalls in the projected use of the arena and convention center will have multiplier effects, making the whole operation more of

---

† Assumptions and "promises" of this nature are promiscuously made. In the November, 1972 elections the voters of Santa Clara County, 40 miles south of San Francisco, approved a measure directing the County Supervisors to develop a plan for a new sports arena; one of the arguments used by proponents of the arena was that it would attract the Warriors and Seals to play many of their home games in the new facility. See "New Arena for Santa Clara," *San Francisco Chronicle*, November 9, 1972, and "Seals, Warriors to San Jose?," *San Francisco Examiner*, November 9, 1972. (However, when the Santa Clara Supervisors the following year asked the voters to approve an arena financing plan that would have raised the tax rate, the proposal was overwhelmingly defeated.)

• Several professional sports teams now play their home games in more than one city: the Kansas City-Omaha Kings of the National Basketball Association, the Carolina Cougars of the American Basketball Association, etc.

The city's last attempt to bring a major league sports team to San Francisco (the successful attraction of the New York Giants in the late 1950s) through construction of a new stadium produced one of its major scandals, in many ways paralleling the YBC story: circumvention of the voters, underestimation and understatement of the true costs of the project, assignment of tax levies specially to debt retirement, and ultimate reliance on the city's general fund and the property tax to pick up the pieces. See Burton J. Wolfe, "The Candlestick Swindle," *San Francisco Bay Guardian*, May 14, 1968.

a risk. Thus, the arena is scheduled to produce another $843,000 annually in ticket taxes for debt service (over and above profits from rental fees for facilities and concessions); but if the projected use is less than anticipated, revenues from ticket taxes as well as from rentals will be down. The parking garage is supposed to bring in $1.9 million annually in net revenue, all of which is earmarked to pay off the bonds. Should the arena not be used as projected, garage revenues too will fall. Additionally, revenue projections for the 1,850-car YBC public garage may be inflated in assuming that it will be used as intensively as the nearby 2,000-stall Fifth and Mission garage, when the latter's rates are considerably lower and it is not operating at full capacity.

The $2 million projected hotel tax revenue is fairly certain, although to label it "income" from YBC, as the Redevelopment Agency does, is somewhat disingenuous. This $2 million is already being collected by the city, and from hotels all over the city which for the most part were built years before YBC. As attorney Gerald Wright observes about this mislabeling, "Surely, if the Board of Supervisors were rash enough to allocate a specific portion of property tax revenues—say, $16,000,000 annually—to YBC, the Agency would not thereupon contend that such an allocation constituted 'income' from the project."[4] In fact, there are opportunity costs in assigning the hotel tax (an attractive revenue source because it is paid by relatively well-to-do outsiders†) to one use to the exclusion of others, which the Agency does not acknowledge.

The central component of the financing plan—accounting for three-fifths of all projected revenue—is the property tax increment. The Agency's fiscal projections assume a 718 percent increase in assessments between 1965 and 1978,[5] a figure which strikes knowledgeable observers as highly optimistic. In addition, there may be some tendency to "go easy" in setting assessment values on these properties and granting abatements,• in order to encourage development and because of the political connections of developers. The tax increment projections also assume that all the private sites will be completed between 1976 and 1982, even though 15 of the 18 sites in the periphery

---

† Ironically, a portion of this tax, albeit small, is paid by former and current low-income transient residents of YBC hotels. The tax is levied on any hotel room which rents for more than $2 a day and is occupied for less than a 30-day period.

• In 1973, 42 owners of buildings valued at $1 million or more asked the city's Assessment Appeals Board to lower the taxable value of their properties. Included in the list were the I. Magnin department store, the Metropolitan Life Insurance building, the Mark Hopkins Hotel, the Shell Oil building, and, most notably, two urban renewal developments, Golden Gateway Center and the Japanese Cultural Center (in the Western Addition project.) The decreased assessments asked for on these two renewal developments alone

Economic Magic or Economic Folly

were still unsold by 1973 and developers may yet change their plans, particularly if the litigation discussed on pages 156-57 or other delays persist. Should this happen, tax revenues will undoubtedly be less than projected and the deficit already planned may last more than three to four years.

Beyond these possibilities, it is clear that YBC will actually make demands on the city's general fund which have not entered into the Agency's calculations or public presentations. About $1.3 million in site improvements in the YBC area is being paid for directly out of the city's regular departmental budgets. Further, no estimates are given of what it will cost to provide the redeveloped YBC area with increased police, fire, street-cleaning and other city services that a convention-sports-office complex will require. All of these services are paid for out of the city's general tax revenues. (According to one estimate, in 1970 the city's downtown district contributed $5 million less in taxes than the amount it cost to provide the area with city services.[6])

Finally, tax increment financing in effect robs the public schools and other taxing districts of needed revenue. Of the city's 1973 $12.59 tax rate, $5.36, or 43 percent, goes to: the San Francisco Unified School District ($4.03), the Community College District ($0.66), BART ($0.65), and the Bay Area Pollution Control District ($0.02).[7] The financing plan for YBC sequesters the entire tax revenue produced by this land; schools, public transit and air pollution control thus are shut off from needed revenue sources.[•]

From all indications, revenue projections for Yerba Buena Center have been outrageously inflated. With the City's open-ended legal

---

amounted to $5.4 million. (See "Big Building Owners Ask Tax Break," *San Francisco Chronicle*, September 19, 1973.)

This apparently is an annual ritual. The September 21, 1972 *Chronicle* reported that "owners of 50 pieces of property in San Francisco worth $1 million or more have applied at City Hall for reductions in their property taxes." Most prominent among that year's supplicants were many of the city's major hotels: Ben Swig's Fairmont, the Sheraton-Palace, the Travelodge, the Jack Tar, the Townehouse, and the Drake Wiltshire, which together applied for a $10.3 million reduction in their assessed valuations.

• A bill (AB 321) was introduced in the California Legislature in 1972 to prohibit the use of the tax allocation mechanism for non-residential urban renewal projects, in order to prevent the situation where local and school district governments dependent on property taxes to provide basic health, education and welfare services are in effect required to contribute to commercial enterprises. The bill failed, largely as a result of opposition by local redevelopment agencies, and was not reintroduced in 1973. (Letters to author, dated March 21, 1972, and June 25, 1973, from Robert H. Frank, Committee Consultant, Select Committee on Housing and Urban Affairs, California Legislature.)

commitment to back the SFRA's lease revenue bonds, the taxpayers are clearly going to be paying the tab.† As one of the attorneys challenging the financing plan correctly observes, "If one assumed the worst, in terms of ultimate construction costs and interest charges, one could easily estimate that YBC's annual cost to the City might be on the order of $25,000,000 or more."[8] And it should be clearly understood that the city is not merely "guaranteeing" the financial solvency of the project. It is paying for the project, primarily through the property and hotel taxes it collects which have been assigned to YBC. Shortly after the Board of Supervisors passed the YBC financing plan, Supervisors Quentin Kopp and Dianne Feinstein introduced a resolution saying that the general property tax (beyond the stipulated tax increment fund) could not be used to pay off the YBC bonds—formalizing a commitment the Redevelopment Agency had made verbally. But when the city's Budget Analyst informed the Board that a restriction of this type would make the interest rate on the bonds prohibitively expensive, the Board unanimously voted (8-0, three having "managed to absent themselves from the room when it came time to vote") for a substitute resolution which in effect says that the costs of these bonds may be borne by the property tax.[9]

These realities differ sharply from claims by public supporters of YBC who have steadfastly maintained that it "will not cost the taxpayers of this city one cent."• Sticking the taxpayers with the bill for huge projects of this sort which fall short of the promises made about

---

† "The way these things are managed, when Yerba Buena is completed . . . the project will be neatly divided into parts. The parts that make money will have come into private ownership. 'We' shall have retained, with the canny business sense for which 'we' are famous, the parts that lose money. That's 'our' plan. . . .

"The people who have been doing the Yerba Buena things do know what they want, they have been asked, and they know how to get their wishes. Moreover, they know how to get us to pay for what they want and we don't. It is why they are rich." Dick Nolan, "Whose Yerba Buena?", *San Francisco Examiner*, January 16, 1974.

• See, for example, Justin Herman's statement quoted in the October 23, 1970 *Daily Commercial News*: ". . . [T]he financing can be done without resort to property taxes, assuming a city lease guarantee, which the agency is prepared to back up with any rental income"; and his statement quoted in the October 22, 1970 *Examiner*: "The public facilities will be financed solely through revenue bonds and with funds committed by the Board of Supervisors from the hotel tax."

Although the average taxpayer will bear the burden of paying off the bonds, it is the wealth-holders who will purchase these bonds and who will benefit from their tax-exempt status, which provides one of the greatest loopholes in the federal income tax system. Over their life the YBC bonds will generate

Economic Magic or Economic Folly

them is a common phenomenon, moreover, as exemplified in a recent *Fortune* study of stadium complexes:

Most. . .are financed with bonds issued by state, county or city governments that are supposed to be paid off by revenues derived from the project. But in practice these revenue bonds almost always turn out to load an open-ended general obligation upon the taxpayer. . . .

To drum up public support, the advocates of a stadium generally understate the probable costs, which invariably balloon as construction proceeds. They also overstate probable revenues by anticipating multiple uses for the structure . . . that in actuality dwindle to a few. The stadium's recurring deficits prove to be much higher than promised and the taxpayer discovers that civic pride has been compromised by special interests, blind boosterism, and inept planning.[10]

Perhaps the most blatant fallacy in the YBC financing plan is use of tax increment financing as the principal source of revenue. This destroys one of the basic economic justifications given for the project: that it will increase the city's tax base and provide more revenue for the city. If increased tax revenues from YBC are fed back into paying off its bonds, then nothing is available to the city to pay for improved municipal services or to reduce the general tax rate. (This deprivation will be occurring at a time when the city already is in deep financial troubles. According to the April 8, 1974 *Chronicle*, the City Controller has announced that the city will take in $50 million less in 1974-1975 than it did in the previous fiscal year, due to a sharp decline in state welfare support and federal revenue-sharing funds.) By contrast, in the Oakland City Center renewal project a substantial portion of the tax increment revenues will be used to develop 300 units of low-rent replacement housing, should federal funds be unavailable. This arrangement resulted from pressures by an organization of displaced residents and their attorneys; the litigation and consequent delays across the Bay in Yerba Buena Center were a powerful, if implicit, "persuader" in negotiating with Oakland officials.

---

some $200-250 million in tax-exempt interest income to bond-holders (depending on the actual interest rate). The beneficiaries of state and local bond interest income (and hence of the tax shelter they provide) are persons in very high income brackets. In 1971, 80 percent of the total interest received from such bonds went to persons with annual incomes of $50,000 or more. For this tax group, the marginal tax rate averages 54 percent, and "because a dollar of exemption means a loss in tax revenue equal to 54 cents, taxpayers who do not purchase municipal bonds must subsidize those who do by making up for the lost revenue from the exemption." See David J. and Attiat F. Ott, "The Tax Subsidy through Exemption of State and Local Bond Interest" in *The Economics of Federal Subsidy Programs*, A Compendium of Papers Submitted to the Joint Economic Committee, Congress of the United States, Part 3, "Tax Subsidies," July 15, 1972, pp. 305-316.

Rather than derive any tax revenues from the Yerba Buena development, the city will lose tax money in four other important ways:

• To the extent that some of the private office development to take place in YBC would have occurred elsewhere in the city, sequestering these property tax revenues robs the city treasury of funds that otherwise would have accrued to it.[11]

• Increased vacancies in older office buildings, caused by tenants moving to newer YBC quarters, will result in lower assessments on these buildings and hence lower tax revenues for the city. (The owners of these older buildings will suffer financial losses as well.) Relocation of the garment and apparel industry into the new apparel mart is a prime example of this process. As the Arthur D. Little report notes, "already there are indications that vacancies [in office buildings] are on the rise, especially in older buildings. This could result in financial distress for older buildings and, carried to the extreme, eventual abandonment."[12] A newspaper account from late 1972 describes extensive concessions—two-three months' free rent, extensive redecorating, etc.—as an inducement to rent space not only in old San Francisco office buildings, but in buildings constructed just five years ago; the 6.7% vacancy rate for office space was predicted to rise well above 7%.[13]

• The city's general fund will lose for 35 years (until the bonds are paid off) the annual revenue it would have received from the properties in the Yerba Buena area above the 1965 level, revenues which would have increased over the years due to rising property values and tax rates.

• Tax revenues in the YBC area decreased markedly after 1965, as the Redevelopment Agency's land acquisition and clearance activities removed properties from the tax rolls. This "fallow" period between the clearance of the project area and completion of construction, which will last at least until 1976 if not beyond, has cost the city millions of dollars in foregone tax revenues. During the 12-year period 1965-1976 the difference between actual tax revenue from land in the Yerba Buena area and estimated revenue had there been no YBC project amounts to $5.6 million.[14] The true extent of this loss shows up as even greater when the yearly loss is compounded to account for the interest the city would have earned had it received the lost revenues. Using a six and one-half percent interest rate, the present value of the estimated tax loss from Yerba Buena area is $7.8 million.

Convention City

San Francisco is a highly attractive city—a 1967 Gallup national survey ranked it as the city Americans desired most to visit. As such, it receives a disproportionate share of conventions and trade shows. One

Economic Magic or Economic Folly

of the principal arguments for building Yerba Buena Center has been that better convention facilities will bring more conventions, that conventions are good for business, and that what is good for business is good for San Francisco. Yet there has been little hard evidence to support this proposition, and what evidence exists comes from the convention industry itself—through its organ, the Convention and Visitors Bureau.

The YBC exhibition hall is being built in the hope of attracting new convention business from three groups: those that have avoided San Francisco because of inadequate facilities, those that have outgrown or shortly will outgrow the city's current facilities, and those that now cannot be accommodated because existing facilities are already booked. But just how much new convention business YBC will generate is little more than speculation. The recent Arthur D. Little report asserts:

It is very difficult to estimate the net new conventions and consumer shows that would come to San Francisco as a result of YBC's existence. To date, a thoroughgoing market analysis concerning San Francisco's market share of the tourism and convention industry in the United States has not been completed.[15]

As the general manager of the Convention and Visitors Bureau himself admits, "hard information is a little tricky to come by."

Tricky or not, the Bureau and the Redevelopment Agency's consultants have assumed that the average annual growth rate in San Francisco's convention industry during the 1960s—six per cent—will continue through 1985, producing an increase in the number of conventions from 397 in 1960, to 646 in 1970, to 950 in 1975, to 1,250 in 1980, to 1,550 in 1985![16] No basis is given for these assumptions, and this averaging and projection game totally disregards the fact that from 1966 to 1970 the number of conventions coming to San Francisco actually dropped from 688 to 646. The CVB has even put together elaborate listings showing bookings for the new exhibition hall through the 1980s amounting to some $300 million. How much of this is business which would merely switch its present San Francisco base to the new center, the Bureau cannot or will not say. But the Arthur D. Little report notes that ". . .a significant portion of the conventions and show activity which will utilize Yerba Buena will be conventions and shows which could have utilized the existing Brooks Hall facility."[17] The conclusion of one of the Agency's own consultants was that:

. . .*the new facility [YBC] could probably attract one or two very large national conventions per year which do not now consider San Francisco as a location. It is unlikely that this number of new conventions of large scale would be materially exceeded because of new facilities, since the number of such events in the country is extremely limited, and the number which rotate to the West Coast is even smaller.*[18]

The Convention and Visitors Bureau itself acknowledges that "the heart of the convention business" is the smaller conventions, which find present meeting facilities adequate to their needs. In 1968 only 15 of the city's 740 conventions required exhibition or meeting space larger than that already available in San Francisco's hotels (although these 15 represented a far larger proportion of delegates).[19] The Hilton alone has 60,000 square feet of space for exhibits and other convention needs. Even some very large conventions require only hotel meeting facilities. For example, the American Bar Association, with 12,000 persons, held its 1972 annual convention in several hotels and had no need of the city's formal convention facilities.

While the Convention and Visitors Bureau is constantly releasing "scare stories" about some major conventions threatening not to return to San Francisco unless YBC is built, or others threatening to cancel bookings unless ground is broken or the lawsuits settled by a certain date, these tales find little verification outside the CVB.† Since the CVB and many national organizations would like to see YBC built to provide better facilities, it is clearly in their mutual interest to make such claims—especially since they are not picking up the bill. The ease with which convention center backers can secure assentive response for their ventures is described by an experienced New York City convention official, in opposing plans for a new YBC-like exhibition hall in that city:

You, of course, perhaps have seen lists of shows who have indicated that if the convention center were built they would come to New York. To those of us who are sophisticated in the business, this falls in the category of the "Playground Syndrome". Every manager in the world when asked by questionnaire whether he would like to have a convention center in New York will respond in the affirmative. It simply gives him another playground, another place for bargaining, an opportunity to use more leverage in dealing with the Coliseum [New York City's major existing exhibition facility] and after all a new playground costs him nothing. He is not in any way committed to it on a lease and these lists are meaningless and cannot be translated in any way into dollars.[20]

Direct attempts to verify the CVB scare stories via telephone interviews with the organizations named (carried out as part of this study) produced some curious results. For example, although the Convention and Visitors Bureau has publicly announced that the American Chemical Society is one of several major groups that "will not come to San Francisco without the Yerba Buena facility",[21] ACS officials revealed

---

†A typical CVB claim (by its vice-president for conventions), duly propagated by the media, is the following lead paragraph from the September 11, 1973 *Chronicle*:

"San Francisco stands to lose some $56 million from 22 major conventions if Yerba Buena Center is not completed by 1977, it was charged here today."

Economic Magic or Economic Folly

that the Society has meetings scheduled for 1976 and 1980 and that Brooks Hall facilities are adequate to their needs. Another major convention that will be lost to the city, according to the CVB, is the American Dental Association. The Bureau's claim, parroted in a September 4, 1973 *Examiner* editorial entitled "Yerba Buena Foes at Work,"† was that "if Yerba Buena's facilities. . .aren't ready by then [1977], some of the bigger conventions that bring thousands of visitors, including the American Dental Association with 15,000, have served [*sic*] notice of cancellation." Again, phone interviews with Association officials indicated that the group, which operates on an eight-year cycle and was last in San Francisco in 1972, is not scheduled to return to the city until 1980 in any case, and that YBC is not a major factor in their decision whether to return.

While it must be conceded the city would gain *some* convention activity with a modern, larger exhibition facility, the basic question of *how much* new business YBC would bring has by no means been satisfactorily answered. Constructing the exhibition hall alone will cost $63.5 million, almost double that amount when construction bond interest is added, and higher still if the 1972 cost estimates must be raised further at the time actual construction begins. No convincing evidence exists that enough new business will be generated to justify this massive expenditure of public funds.

In any case, a substantial portion of the bookings for the YBC convention facility would be shows drawn away from the city's existing Brooks Hall-Civic Auditorium complex. It is anticipated that nearly two-thirds of the shows currently booked for this complex for the years 1977-1980 will be lost to YBC.[22] These facilities were renovated and modernized in 1960 through a $7.6 million general obligation bond issue, which will not be fully retired until 1980. In 1971 the city's net loss from these facilities was $175,000, which can be expected to increase by at least $100-150,000 as users move over to YBC. This will cause an even larger drain on the city's treasury, which the taxpayers will have to make up. An additional, smaller loss to the city will be the reduction in parking tax revenue from decreased use of the Civic Center underground parking facility.

---

†The *Examiner* editorial was an example of the daily papers' rapid editorial response to any threat to the YBC project (see pages 68-71). Just the week before, Richard Goldman, an influential San Francisco businessman and former member of the Public Utilities Commission, had held a small private luncheon to introduce to key supporters of Yerba Buena Center and some members of the press Howard Sloane, managing director of the New York Coliseum. Sloane offered some negative observations about the consequences of constructing new complexes of this sort, and the *Examiner* rushed to put down this "doomsayer" editorially.

But the Brooks Hall complex is not the only nearby convention facility from which YBC will divert business. It can be assumed that the Oakland Arena and Coliseum and the Cow Palace will also lose trade shows (as well as sports events) to YBC. If the city's projections about use of the YBC sports arena turn out to be correct, Oakland will lose some 80 event-days per year—about half its present usage.[23] The Oakland facility, built in 1966 and only 18 minutes from downtown San Francisco by BART, now loses half a million dollars annually, which YBC can be expected to increase. Thus, federal urban renewal funds are being used to subsidize a wasteful competition between adjacent cities. The number of conventions and trade shows is finite: a recent survey indicated that if every city in the United States with 50,000 square feet or more of convention and exhibition space divided the convention trade equally, each city would end up with no more than six bookings a year.[24] City after city keeps building bigger and better convention facilities to attract this business,† although whichever city "wins" a competition of this sort will do so only by inflicting costs on other cities and their populations.

Broader questions can also be raised about attempts to buttress the city's economy through tourism, conventions and the entertainment business. "Tourism is San Francisco's largest industry," the Convention and Visitors Bureau is fond of proclaiming. In homage to current ecological concerns, the Bureau's vice-president for conventions, Robert F. Begley, recently rhapsodized, "Tourism, the smokeless in-

---

† Both New York City and Washington are in the throes of convention center controversies. For the New York story, see Nicholas Pileggi, "How Things Get Done in New York: A Case History", *New York*, February 18, 1974, pp. 58-68; and Jack Newfield, "Seven reasons not to build the West Side convention center", *The Village Voice*, September 13, 1973. Six of the seven reasons given by Newfield apply to YBC as well: that a convention center has a lower priority than meeting more pressing city needs; that it will not bring much new convention business to the city; that conflict of interest exists among proponents of the center (particularly hotel owners); that the center will produce air pollution problems; that an adequate environmental impact report has not been filed; and that it will destroy a neighborhood. The Washington situation is discussed in Sam Smith, "Through Mt. Vernon Square with bonds and boondoggle", *D. C. Gazette*, November, 1973. The planned Eisenhower Convention Center will inflict damage on Washington's Chinatown area; will dislocate jobs and businesses; will add to air pollution and traffic congestion; is supported by superficial impact, feasibility and site selection studies; has had insufficient public hearings; and is being pushed by the large banks, which are interested in the bond issue the center will require (fourteen District of Columbia banks gave an unsecured 1% interest rate loan to the District government for initial convention center planning, and the chairman of the Riggs Bank, leader of the consortium, was appointed to head the non-profit corporation which will offer tax exempt bonds for the center.)

Economic Magic or Economic Folly

dustry, does not dissipate our natural resources, nor does it desecrate
·,ur natural environment".[25] But tourism is notoriously susceptible to
fluctuation according to the up's and down's of the general economy.
As Mayor Alioto noted in his Introduction to the 1971 Annual Report
of the Convention and Visitors Bureau:

> *San Francisco's convention and tourist industry. . .is suffering from the pres-
> sures of a national recession and unchecked inflation. This [year's] decline [in
> tourism and convention attendance] is by no means exclusively a San Francisco
> phenomenon. People all across the country are simply spending less and travel-
> ing less as they feel the incredible economic squeeze caused by the recession-
> inflation cycle.*

A more recent blow to the industry is the energy crisis. According to
a travel organization executive quoted in the February 19, 1974
Chronicle: "Quite simply, without adequate transportation, the tourism
industry is stopped dead in its tracks."[26]

It is a commonly accepted economic principle that diversity builds
strength, and if the Convention and Visitors Bureau's optimism proves
justified, a major impact of YBC may be to weaken the city's economic
base by decreasing diversity and enlarging dependence on a highly
unstable industry. *Examiner* columnist Dick Nolan notes, "One of the
things that is alarming about [the city's concern with declining tourism]
is the fact that it is alarming. It suggests how heavily we have come to
depend on what used to be an economic sideline. It is another indicator
of how far out of balance San Francisco has become—as a direct result
of the design enforced by our movers and shakers."[27] As one local
industry official put it, "If you cut off tourism to San Francisco, you can
imagine what the unemployment rate would be. It would be fantastic."†

Moreover, in their desire to remake the city the movers and shakers
may be destroying the very character of San Francisco that has made it
"everybody's favorite city." A study of the tourist trade concluded that
the things visitors liked most about San Francisco were its atmosphere,

---

† Jerry Carroll, "Tourist Industry Faces a Shaky Future," *San Francisco
Chronicle*, February 19, 1974. The vulnerability of tourism to unpredictable
events is one of the industry's most salient characteristics. For example, the
recent racial violence and other forms of disorder have affected the Virgin
Islands' tourism business markedly. (See Earl Caldwell, "Violence Hurting St.
Croix Tourism", *New York Times*, October 13, 1973, which also notes the following: "Although tourism is the principle [sic] industry on Saint Croix, it involves
few Crucians. Most of the hotels, restaurants and clubs are operated by
whites. . . Through the years the Crucians have shunned the service jobs that
have been offered. Instead, they have preferred to work in government and
have accepted unemployment rather than to submit themselves to positions
such as waiters, housekeepers and janitors in hotels and restaurants.")

views, sightseeing, ethnic communities, and the like—the exact opposite of what is being created by large-scale high-rise construction of the
type that will characterize Yerba Buena Center.†[28] In a column entitled
"The Urban Insult" (February 4, 1974), the *Chronicle's* Charles McCabe
wrote of this worship of tourism:

> *Our notions of what is wrong and what is right in urban life are so mis-*
> *directed that a reasonable man could not be faulted for believing the Devil*
> *himself has been called in as planning director.*
>
> *If the purpose of San Francisco is to pleasure and profit the likes of Mr. Ben*
> *Swig and Mr. Henri Lewin and our other hotel magnates (and try and get dear*
> *Joe Alioto to give you a No on that one!) then we are doing a great job.*
>
> *Tourists, who are supposed to be our greatest economic asset, are becoming an*
> *environmental abomination. . . .*
>
> *I've only been a resident since 1955; but I've watched a real city turn plastic*
> *in that time. The new downtown hotels are structures precisely designed to*
> *debauch a metropolis. They are ugly, and they are wasteful of both space and*
> *amenity. . . .*

Another, less important consideration is that convention business
—which has been labeled "wholesale tourist trade"—may, due to the
economics and psychology of expense accounts and credit cards, raise
already high hotel and restaurant prices, and thus discourage family-
type tourism (and restaurant dining by local residents as well). In short,
San Francisco's process of Manhattanization may cost the city its draw-
ing power, and its retaining power as well, as the Redevelopment
Agency continues to act to defeat its own motto, "Omnes Habitare in
Urbe Volunt Sancti Francisci" (Everyone Wants to Live in the City of
San Francisco.)

The approach to conventioneering and tourism embodied in the
YBC project and similar centers across the country—creation of a special, protected zone unrelated to the rest of the city—demonstrates an
official set of values that ignores the city's most pressing problems.
Yerba Buena Center will be a self-contained convention-tourist complex, within which the representatives of the business and professional
community can convene, safe from the dangers and problems of the
urban society outside, which continues to deteriorate precisely because
of that pattern of expenditure and building by the city which favors a
haven for conventioneers over much needed housing and services for
its own citizens. Here again, the cities are serving the wealthy and
powerful, while neglecting the basic needs of their people.

---

† In a fitting symbol, the Convention and Visitors Bureau has its offices in
Fox Plaza, a 29-story office, parking and residential tower built in 1967 on the
site of the Fox Theater, one of San Francisco's true architectural gems.

Economic Magic or Economic Folly

White Collars for Blue

Taken together, the jobs and economic activity being destroyed by
Yerba Buena Center and those it is creating are markedly hastening
the drain of blue-collar employment from the city and thus hastening
the conversion of San Francisco into the administrative headquarters
of the West Coast and Pacific Basin.

Although public officials, construction unions, and corporate and
financial interests constantly stress that YBC will create construction
and office jobs, they discount the 723 businesses and 7,600 jobs located
on the site in 1963. The work force then consisted primarily of small
proprietors, skilled, semi-skilled and unskilled workers in diversified
light manufacturing, specialized printing, publishing, warehousing,
transient hotels, small cafes and groceries, parking lots, second-hand
stores, pawnshops, and a variety of other commercial and service institutions. The average age of these businesses was 20 years, and at the
time of a 1963 Redevelopment Agency survey fully 90 percent of all
businesses stated they planned to remain at their location.[29] The ad-
vantages of the area were its central location, access to freeways, ties to
the local market and pedestrian traffic, and low rent.

With respect to what has become of these businesses and jobs, a
survey undertaken as part of this study indicates a pattern of business
relocation similar to that in other cities experiencing redevelopment:
larger businesses with regional markets and some risk capital often
moved out of the city altogether and were able to improve their conditions; marginal and highly localized businesses, often operated by elderly or minority group owners, rarely survived displacement.† The
latter group had neither time nor resources to search for another site
or start their businesses over again, and were dependent on familiar
customers and the good will they had built up over the years. Perhaps
hardest for these people was the lengthy period of uncertainty and
reduced business during the planning period of the late 1950s and
1960s, as the neighborhood deteriorated and their clientele moved
away. Many businesses that did relocate reported lower incomes and

---

† A sample of 60 relocated businesses was surveyed and interviewed during late 1971. Prof. Roger Crawford of the Departments of Geography and
Urban Studies at San Francisco State University supervised the study and
analyzed the results. The interviewers were Michelle Gallagher, Denise Mar-
tinez, Wayne Merbach and Toby Michelson. For a review of business relocation
experience under the urban renewal program, see Basil Zimmer, *Rebuilding
Cities: The Effects of Displacement and Relocation on Small Business* (Chicago:
Quadrangle Books, 1964), and Brian J. L. Berry, Sandra J. Parsons, and
Rutherford H. Platt, *The Impact of Urban Renewal on Small Business: The Hyde
Park-Kenwood Case* (Chicago: Center for Urban Studies, University of Chicago,
1968).

higher rents, and in not all cases were they fully reimbursed for moving costs.† In all, the project probably caused the loss of several thousand jobs, particularly blue-collar jobs, along with several hundred small businesses.•

With respect to the new economic activity YBC is expected to generate, job claims have varied at different times and according to different claimants; but it is generally put forth that YBC will create some 8,000 to 10,000 person-years of construction work, and approximately 20,000 permanent jobs, the latter relating to the convention facilities, hotels and offices. The Arthur D. Little report, however, projects that only 3,600 jobs will be directly created by the YBC project; another 5,100 permanent jobs will be created indirectly, only some of which will be located in San Francisco.[30] One important fact generally hidden in the barrage of statistics designed to evoke public support for YBC is that only 400 jobs will be generated by the exhibit hall and sports arena, the two central facilities of the Center; well over 90% of all employment in YBC will be in the office buildings.[31]

The majority of office jobs will be white-collar and will go to white, middle-class, suburban commuters. In the years 1958-1969 the number of jobs held by commuters in San Francisco's central business district rose by 38 percent, while the number of jobs held by San Franciscans rose by only one percent.[32] Well over 90 percent of all new white-collar jobs in San Francisco are going to commuters.[33]

The lower level convention center and hotel jobs will go primarily to the city's Black, Chicano, Latino and Asian population, as busboys,

---

† Not until the Uniform Relocation Act, which did not come into effect until 1971, was there statutory provision for reimbursement of all actual moving expenses for businesses, without a maximum. Up until that point, the urban renewal statutes contained a $3,000 maximum, with the possibility of higher amounts if certified exceptions were granted. For businesses that cease to exist, the owner may now receive a "going out of business" payment of up to $10,000. However, as with residential relocatees, the existence of statutory compensation provisions by no means signifies that all eligible businesses apply for or are granted these sums.

• A HUD study that became available just as this book was going to press provides additional data on businesses in the YBC area. Of the 135 business concerns relocated from January, 1971, through June, 1973, 45 (33%) ceased to exist, and 27 (20%) relocated outside the city. The highest proportions of businesses relocating outside the city were in the manufacturing and business/personal services categories, and fully 95% of all "mom and pop" stores went out of business. HUD anticipates that the remaining YBC businesses will generally follow these patterns. See "Environmental Impact Statement for Yerba Buena Center" (review draft), prepared by Department of Housing and Urban Development, Region IX, February, 1974, Appendix L2 and Section IV (D) (2).

Economic Magic or Economic Folly

dishwashers, bellhops, cooks, maintenance personnel, and other roles associated with servicing and cleaning up after conventioneers and visitors. While three-fifths of the hotel and restaurant jobs in the city are held by minority workers, the higher paying and more prestigious positions—waiters, headwaiters, bartenders, etc.—are held almost exclusively by whites. In March, 1973, the Federal Equal Employment Opportunities Commission brought suit in federal court against the San Francisco and East Bay locals of the Bartenders International Union for alleged racial discrimination, charges leveled by the Commission as far back as 1967.[34] And in the same month a federal suit was brought by the Employment Law Center against the Waiters' and Dairy Lunchmen's Union and several hotels and restaurants charging racial discrimination in the hiring and assignment of waiters; the local named as defendant has only 25 Blacks among its 3,000 members.[35]

Thus, jobs created by YBC will maintain and perpetuate existing racist employment patterns.† The construction jobs are relatively short-term and to a large extent will go to out-of-towners;• these jobs rarely provide new opportunities for the unemployed workers who suffer from the exodus of manufacturing and trade jobs. Nonwhites also will find few opportunities for construction employment, save as laborers and hod-carriers.

In sum, Yerba Buena Center is hurting blue-collar skilled and unskilled workers and small proprietors; is providing office jobs for middle-class commuters; and will give some employment to the city's lower income racial minorities, but only through maintaining and perpetuating the existing racist job hierarchy.

Some Fallacies of Urban Redevelopment

The official line on Yerba Buena Center—that it will enhance the

---

† That this is of no particular concern to at least some supporters of YBC was evidenced by a remark made by Robert Sullivan, General Manager of the Convention and Visitors Bureau, at a panel discussion held at Stanford University on November 6, 1973: "A lot of people prefer to be busboys and waiters because it fits their life style."

• The HUD study cited in the footnote to page 179 states (at page 173) that only an estimated 33% of the construction labor force is San Francisco residents.

In August, 1973, the Employment Law Center, on behalf of four minority action groups, filed suit in Superior Court to force the city to implement a 1932 City Charter provision giving job preference on public works projects to city residents, following two years of unsuccessful negotiations with city officials who, according to the plaintiffs, simply refuse to enforce the law. Among the defendants named were the Redevelopment Agency and the City's Chief Administrative Officer. (See "A Suit to Force More S. F. Hiring," *San Francisco Chronicle*, August 22, 1973.)

Some Fallacies of Urban Redevelopment

city's tax base and clear a slum—glosses over some important hidden costs, falling mainly on the city's lower income population. In most redevelopment cost-benefit analyses, increases in assessed valuations are usually designated as a benefit. It is assumed by redevelopment proponents that any increase in land value benefits the community as a whole because it indicates that the land is being put to a "higher" (more efficient) use. SFRA reports proclaimed that after redevelopment the assessed value of buildings would be 10-12 times the assessed value of the land, whereas before redevelopment it was only 1.24 times the assessed land value.[36] For large commercial enterprises and speculative landholders such increases are welcome. New and bigger buildings imply more profits (even if they do involve increased real estate taxes). But for users and owners of residential land, as well as small businesses, these increased values tend to be harmful, because of resultant higher rents and taxes. And as land values rise, the possibility of constructing and rehabilitating low- and moderate-income housing is dimmed. High land values lead to the intensive, often high-rise, development which destroys existing uses. For example, in the Mission District, a low- to moderate-rent Latino area, land value increases precipitated by construction of the Bay Area Rapid Transit line and neighborhood stations are causing replacement of existing homes, stores, and community institutions by more profitable uses, and consequently destroying a cohesive ethnic neighborhood.[37]

"Slum clearance" is virtually a synonym for urban renewal. One of the central canons of the program is that it will remove slums and thereby eliminate their costs to society. According to the pseudo-clinical language of public pronouncements, the aim of Yerba Buena Center is to "cure" the "social maladjustment" and "undesirable environment" through clearance of the area and relocation of its residents.[38] But the social problems that produce and are produced by "slum environments"—apart from the issue of how that term may be legitimately defined—do not disappear with the physical destruction of the site labeled "slum" or "blighted." Urban renewal may merely be moving the bump along the carpet, by shifting the population and problems to another area of the city.† Displacement caused by YBC resulted in increased overcrowding and deterioration in the area around Sixth Street, just to the west of the project, and now one of the most run-down, depressing and dangerous areas in the entire city. According to a recent report commissioned by the Redevelopment

---

†". . . Slum clearance projects themselves generate effects that are adding impetus to a process that results in the cumulative development of blight in the older, low-rent neighborhoods outside clearance areas." Claude Gruen, "Urban Renewal's Role in the Genesis of Tomorrow's Slums," *Land Economics*, August, 1963, pp. 285-291.

Economic Magic or Economic Folly

Agency itself:

> *Perhaps the most profound impact of the proposed [YBC] project will be the intensification of a population shift into nearby blighted areas. The people involved are mainly single, older men, including the "skid row" transient, drinking population from the Third Street area that has shifted westward in the past several years. Redevelopment has not meant rehabilitation for this group. It has meant a clustering around Sixth Street north of Harrison, and this can be expected to increase . . . . The data indicate that by sheer concentration of the economically indigent there is an acceleration of the "skid-row" phenomenon in three districts of San Francisco . . . South of Market, Downtown [the Tenderloin], and the Mission . . . . Relocation activities, public or private, may eliminate the low-income and/or minority population from a given area, but could well create an "instant, blighted, skid-row" environment in these three districts.*[39]

Nor is it likely that relocation of residents reduces the costs of the welfare and social services they require. In fact, relocation may actually increase these public costs, as the disruption of social networks, particularly among the elderly, can lead to a need for greater medical and psychological treatment, social services and welfare support.[40] As noted in Chapter IV, many of the costs of "slum clearance" are borne by the displacees themselves in the forms of higher rents and personal suffering. If the $36 per person average monthly rent increase shown in the Arthur D. Little study (see page 116) holds true for the displaced population as a whole, the total added rent bill caused by Yerba Buena Center relocation will be around $1 million per year. Although a portion of this amount is offset—for a few years at least—by relocation payments to some of the displacees, an enormous private bill still is forced on people who can least afford it. (This is not something unique to San Francisco. Anthony Downs has calculated that on a national basis households displaced by urban renewal and highway projects will each have imposed on them uncompensated costs ranging from $812 to $1,194; since the median income of these displaced households is about $4,000, "the average uncompensated loss which each is compelled to suffer amounts to confiscation of from 20 to 30 percent of one year's income."[41]) Rather than "slum clearance," the YBC project has brought about "slum transference," and in the process has imposed enormous costs on those living in the area.

While the urban renewal process is intended to correct market imperfections through supposedly neutral public intervention and investment, detailed economic analysis makes it clear that there are winners and losers in the process.

The methods the Agency and City have used to calculate and adver-

Some Fallacies of Urban Redevelopment

tise the potential of Yerba Buena Center represent a peculiar form of cost-benefit analysis. The issue as posed by the Redevelopment Agency was whether the project's aggregate benefits, narrowly defined, precisely quantified, and confidently predicted, were greater than its budgeted costs; this methodology represents a comparison of revenues and expenditures rather than of real benefits and costs. Costs difficult to calculate or express in quantitative terms (e.g., social costs) have simply been ignored. Benefits have been calculated through long-term projections based on inadequate or tenuous premises. Despite the tentative nature of these projections, they were offered to the public and to the public's elected representatives as if the predicted future were guaranteed. The Agency and the City consciously suppressed known or likely negative effects and the gossamery quality of their projections.

Nowhere in the entire process has there been anything which resembles rational public decision-making. Assuming that jobs, economic growth, and municipal revenue are the underlying problems requiring public intervention, the question of how these problems could best be solved was never posed. The Agency believes without question that projects beneficial to business interests benefit the whole economy of San Francisco and therefore all the people of San Francisco. In reality, however, the aggregate benefits are private benefits, and will accrue to a small, select segment of the city's elite "public," while the costs of the project will fall on those least able to bear them and most in need of the kind of assistance which truly public programs might bring to them, under a very different set of conditions.

Yerba Buena Center demonstrates that public intervention does not per se "improve" the usage of a piece of land, but often, and certainly in this case, is used to take from the have-not's and give to the have's.

The general public is as much a victim of the YBC project as is TOOR. Yet the Redevelopment Agency and the City sought to avoid having to secure direct public approval of the project by opting for a financing mechanism that allegedly allows circumventing the voters. The necessity for explaining the impact of the project and justifying it publicly was therefore considerably diminished. The average citizen of San Francisco is somewhat mystified by what YBC means and only dimly aware of its future impact on his welfare. It is because the victims of the "positive" building phase of YBC are more diffuse than the victims of the preparatory destruction-displacement process, and because the damages will take place over the long-term future rather than in an immediate, easily recognized form, that little protest and organization have arisen over the construction of YBC, compared with what has happened vis a vis its destructive phase.

7. The Final Solution?

> It's a moral issue.
> The City shouldn't ask its guests
> to pay for indigents to be relocated.
> Underwriting the Convention Center
> is another story.
> Irving Baldwin, Hotel Employers Association, 1972

TOOR's stand-tough position on the replacement housing and relocation rights won in federal court in November, 1970, finally compelled the Redevelopment Agency and City Hall to take serious steps to meet their statutorily and judicially imposed obligations. Yet the response was slow; and in the interim the residents, protected by court orders and HUD's belated administrative supervision, were still holding the Central Blocks hostage. With intense pressures building to break ground for the convention center complex, the city was forced to make further concessions in order to rid itself of the seemingly immovable obstacle presented by TOOR and its lawsuit. This partial capitulation to TOOR came in mid-1973. It stemmed from changes precipitated by two events occurring nearly two years prior: the shift of control over the YBC public facilities from the Redevelopment Agency to City Hall; and Justin Herman's death.

The Palace Revolt

When Yerba Buena Center was approved by the Board of Supervisors in 1966, the interests behind the renewal scheme left its planning and execution in the hands of Redevelopment Agency Director M. Justin Herman and his staff. But the delays caused by TOOR's successful lawsuit and Herman's obvious intransigence in the face of this legal obstacle began to implant serious doubts among the City Fathers as to the Agency's handling of the YBC project. The instigator of these concerns was Thomas Mellon, the city's Chief Administrative Officer, for whom, according to the March 23, 1973 *San Francisco Progress*, "mandatory retirement was waived . . . to allow him to see the Yerba Buena Convention Center through." In early 1971, Mellon suddenly announced the existence of possible illegalities and conflicts of interest in the public facilities financing plan the Agency had first proposed, plus serious defects in the design for the YBC exhibition hall. What ensued was a struggle that in a few short months removed power over

The Final Solution?

the YBC public facilities development from the Redevelopment Agency and their private developers and placed it in the hands of the City Hall and its convention industry supporters.

 Mellon's job as Chief Administrative Officer, as well as his personal stature among local business and political figures, put him right at the heart of the developing YBC controversy. The CAO's role is to serve as grand coordinator for the City's administrative and bureaucratic apparatus; it is an extremely powerful post, particularly since its holder in effect has life tenure. Mellon, appinted by Mayor John Shelley in 1963 after heading "Republicans for Shelley," was a successful businessman and former head of the Chamber of Commerce and the Police Commission. He is known as an extremely hard worker, sits on innumerable civic and governmental bodies, knows everyone of influence in the city, and has well-honed abilities to "wheel and deal." He is also responsible for annually allocating half the hotel tax receipts assigned to the City's Publicity and Advertising Fund (over $2 million), which has been termed "the last pot of sugar in San Francisco politics." In short, he is an extraordinarily powerful man in city government, probably second only to the mayor, and in some areas more influential than the mayor.

Mellon's intervention in the YBC project began shortly after the Redevelopment Agency had announced selection of its developer for the Central Blocks area, and was triggered by the Hotel Employers Association and the Convention and Visitors Bureau. Both groups were worried about possible delays in constructing the convention facilities, given the overbuilding of new luxury hotels in the city (see page 54), and were also anxious to create a superior functional design, one better able to compete with other new centers around the country. Richard Swig had himself appointed head of a joint committee formed by the HEA and CVB to review plans for the Center. When the Agency showed them the detailed plans for the convention hall, Swig's group raised a great hue over the design, objecting to the idea of an underground facility and to many specific design features, including inadequate ceiling heights, insufficient distance between supporting pillars, and too few meeting rooms. Swig and the hotelmen took their complaints directly to Mayor Alioto, who agreed there were real design problems. Alioto also realized his powerful hotel and convention supporters had to be pacified, and therefore assigned Mellon to arbitrate the dispute. After a series of discussions convened by Mellon, the Swig group agreed to accept an underground facility (since moving it above ground would cause serious additional delays) in exchange for an agreement to meet their other design objections. All of this was done through City Hall, completely bypassing both Herman and his developers, a move which antagonized him considerably. The Swigs' role in financing Mayor Alioto's election in 1967 (see page 59) to be repeated in his successful 1971 reelection campaign, gave Richard Swig more leverage at City Hall than he could have had with Herman and the Redevelopment Agency.

More serious intervention was Mellon's publicly voiced criticisms of the Redevelopment Agency's original plans for financing the YBC public facilities. As noted earlier, the Agency financing plan devised by Herman and Albert Schlesinger was an amalgam of political and economic considerations. The goal was to put together a scheme which, while not necessarily least costly, would provide the most rapid, flexible and politically acceptable method of raising funds and exercising control over their use. Schlesinger's plan was developed originally for the Dillingham Corporation and later transferred to the successful bidder, Arcon-Pacific. It called for tax-exempt bonds, backed by the city's hotel tax, to be issued by nonprofit corporations Schlesinger and his partners would establish. Schlesinger/Arcon-Pacific would then receive substantial developer's fees (over $5 million) for building the public facilities and would negotiate a fee with a general contractor rather than submit the project to competitive bidding. Mellon's criticisms, supported by the City Attorney, concerned the legality and propriety of these arrangements. His financial cautiousness derived in part from recent experience with the expansion of Candlestick Park, where costs had ballooned to such an extent that the city was forced to impose an admissions tax of 50 cents per ticket and add a half percent to the hotel tax in order to guarantee the bonds which financed construction.

YBC Financial arrangement

Mellon accompanied his critique of the Agency's YBC financing arrangements with a suggestion that the project's public and private segments be split and that the public facilities be built by the City and funded through a general obligation bond issue, to be submitted to the voters the coming November. Mellon moved ahead with his plans and won the approval of the City's Capital Improvements Advisory Committee (which he chairs) for a $118 million bond issue to appear on the November municipal elections ballot.

But Mellon's motivations in denouncing the proposed YBC financing plan were not limited to those proclaimed publicly. At issue was a more fundamental power struggle between himself and Herman. The

The Final Solution?

Redevelopment Agency's entire operation and the economic and political control being amassed by this quasi-independent "government within a government"† were a distinct threat to Mellon's own empire. In making this fight, Mellon was undertaking what the April 29, 1971 *Examiner* termed a "political power play" as the leader of a group within the city administration seeking to clip Justin Herman's wings. ("Empire-building" charges against Herman had begun almost as soon as he took over his job. In early 1961 he was involved in well publicized battles with the City Attorney and Controller over whether the Agency's support staff—attorneys, accountants, etc.—were to be employed by and responsible to the Agency or City Hall. Herman even went so far as to bring a lawsuit against the City Attorney to gain possession of some land acquisition files related to the Agency's eminent domain activities.) Herman's initial reaction to the Chief Administrative Officer's attack was to label it Mellon's "vendetta."[1] As the April 28, 1971 *Examiner* noted, "Mellon is reported to be upset over the fact that such vital parts of his City Hall empire like the Department of Public Works and the City Architect's office would be bypassed entirely in the Yerba Buena deal."

Mellon's intervention brought mixed reactions from Mayor Alioto. On the one hand, he did not want to tangle with Mellon and thereby create political waves among his administration's backers. The mayor probably agreed with Mellon that there were numerous problems surrounding Herman's handling of YBC and that the Agency's intransigence on the housing issue might keep the project stalled in litigation for years to come. Alioto was primarily concerned with getting YBC built, and getting it built as fast as possible. On the other hand, the last thing in the world he wanted was a general obligation bond issue on the ballot, and in this he sided with the Redevelopment Agency. Mayor Alioto averted a confrontation between the Chief Administrative Officer and the Redevelopment Agency through a series of meetings involving both Mellon and Herman. In these, the hotel owners' mild rebellion was useful as a tool to manipulate both men. According to the April 28, 1971 *Examiner* account of Alioto's strategy:

[H]e's determined to defeat any move that might endanger or even delay the construction of the convention complex.

That became clear yesterday as the Mayor summoned the pick of The City's hotelmen and businessmen to his office for a meeting . . . to mobilize the business

---

† See memorandum dated December 18, 1967, from T. J. Kent, Jr., Deputy for Development, to Mayor John F. Shelley: "In important ways, the Redevelopment Agency has become a government within a government. It already has too broad a range of responsibilities for effective control to be exercised by the Mayor and Board of Supervisors."

*community to battle, if necessary, for the Yerba Buena Center. Mellon was out of
town as the Mayor called the closed meeting . . . .*

*[S]ome of the top hotelmen attending the session appeared not entirely to
grasp the full impact of the big City Hall intrigue in which they were called to
participate . . . . Trying at all cost to avert a showdown with Mellon, et al., the
Mayor was obviously laying the groundwork for assuring support for rapid
construction of the convention center–with whatever financing method brings
fastest results.*

Mellon was brought to realize that a general obligation bond issue
would be defeated, probably spelling an end to the entire project. In
order to pacify the Chief Administrative Officer and still his objections
to the Central Blocks financing and development plan, Mellon himself
was put in charge of developing the public facilities, and his office
authorized to devise with the Redevelopment Agency a new financing
plan (the March, 1972 plan described on pages 162-71). The hotelmen for their part got a new design for the exhibition hall. The designs
were redrawn to provide for more widely spaced columns and other
improvements, following a nationwide tour of convention facilities in
August, 1971, by representatives of the Redevelopment Agency, the
Chamber of Commerce, the Downtown Association, labor unions and
the hotel industry, organized and led by Richard Swig.

When the dust cleared from this internal squabble, the City Administration under Mellon and Mayor Alioto emerged as the developer
of the YBC public facilities; the Redevelopment Agency had been
pushed into the background, with the developer it had chosen—
Schlesinger/Arcon-Pacific—holding only a part of the project, the private sites in the Central Blocks.† The key members of the Agency's
YBC administrative staff continued working on the project, but were
now responsible to Mellon.•

Shortly after this palace revolt, Justin Herman died. And with his
death, the role and power of the San Francisco Redevelopment Agency
were further diminished.

---

† The March, 1972 financing plan calls for Schlesinger/Arcon-Pacific to
receive $516,000 as reimbursement for the studies and plans they had pre-
pared for the public facilities.
    • The Agency's long-term project director for YBC, John Dykstra, left
public service in early 1974, to become executive vice-president of a corporate
development consortium, to be called—Pacific Rim Associates. The group will
provide construction, architecture, engineering and management "packaging"
to foreign real estate firms wishing to invest in this country. According to the
February 10, 1974 *Sunday Examiner & Chronicle*, "Several of the firms that
created the new combine are long acquainted with Dykstra because of their
participation in various San Francisco redevelopment projects."

The Final Solution?

End of an Era

M. Justin Herman suffered a heart attack and died on August 30, 1971, at the age of 62. Many ascribed his demise in large part to the stresses and disappointments caused by the undermining of his authority and control. At the time, he and his Agency were under constant pressure from City Hall to make concessions regarding relocation housing for South of Market residents so that the project could get underway. Herman was adamant in his opposition to such concessions, as well as to the design changes demanded by the hotel owners and convention-tourist industry. Reportedly, his heart attack came while he was at work in his Golden Gateway apartment, drafting a memorandum to the Mayor explaining why he would never agree to a change in the YBC plan. "Hours before," the August 31, 1971 *Examiner* reported, "he'd mapped strategy against efforts aimed at radically changing the design of his latest monument-to-be, the convention center in the Yerba Buena complex South of Market. With a showdown scheduled in the Mayor's office this morning, Herman told his colleagues: 'One more design change and I'll quit.' " In a later interview, *Examiner* urban affairs writer Donald Canter asserted: "One of the greatest weaknesses of M. Justin Herman was that he used to brag that he always won every battle." The stalled YBC project and the continuing successful opposition from South of Market residents presented Herman his first major defeat as head of San Francisco's redevelopment efforts. Indeed, YBC had become so problematic that the City Fathers were moving to take the whole matter out of Herman's hands and place the responsibility elsewhere.

During his dozen years in San Francisco Herman had shaped the Redevelopment Agency into a powerful force to carry out the city's redevelopment master plan. His successes earned him and the Agency pretty much of a free hand in pursuing their work. The *National Journal* probably best summarized Herman's career, characterizing him as:

> . . . one of the great urban renewal grantsmen of the 1950's and 1960's . . . . In pushing through his program, Herman brusquely overrode opposition from minority groups and small merchants in areas to be redeveloped. He was one of the men responsible for getting urban renewal named "the federal bulldozer" and "Negro removal" . . . . [A HUD official said] "Herman could move rapidly on renewal—demolition or construction—because he was absolutely confident that he was doing what the power structure wanted insofar as the poor and the minorities were concerned . . . . That's why San Francisco has mostly luxury housing and business district projects—that's what white, middle-class planners and businessmen envision as ideal urban renewal . . . . Also, with Herman in control, San Francisco renewal never got slowed down by all this citizen participation business that tormented other cities."[2]

Yet ironically, according to one intimate, "Justin was always stunned that he—as a liberal New Dealer—could be regarded as an enemy."

In choosing a successor to Herman, Mayor Alioto was determined to further the transfer of control over the YBC Central Blocks development from the Agency to City Hall in order to move the project ahead. A supercompetent, inflexible director was no longer what the City Administration wanted. In December, 1971, following the brief interim reign of an acting executive director, Mayor Alioto announced the appointment of Robert Rumsey, an assistant director of SFRA and a long time associate of Herman. (An amusing sidelight to this announcement was the lack of any pretense as to where real, as opposed to nominal, power in the Agency would lie in the future. Although the Agency's quasi-autonomous five-man board is responsible for hiring and firing its executive director, the choice of Rumsey was announced at a press conference by Mayor Alioto, "who said he assumes the decision will be made official at next Tuesday's meeting of the Agency's directors."[3]) Rumsey presented a sharp contrast to Herman's energy and charisma. Appointed at the same time were three assistant directors to serve as a "new management team," one of whom had been Mayor Alioto's former campaign manager.

While the Redevelopment Agency continues to play a central function in the Yerba Buena Center project, its role has considerably diminished over the past two years. The stringent national cutbacks in the urban renewal program announced by the Nixon Administration in January, 1973, provided a further major blow to the fortunes of the Agency, which was forced to reduce its staff by 25 percent and shift into low gear on several of its projects.[4]

The decline in the Redevelopment Agency's role and power was triggered by the TOOR lawsuit. Not only did the suit delay the Agency in carrying out the YBC project, but the battle over Yerba Buena Center reduced the Agency's general credibility and the public's confidence in its ability to get things done. To an extent an institutional strategy had been part of the lawyers' thinking from the outset. The TOOR case represented not only protection of individual and class rights, law reform, and raising of public consciousness about housing and relocation issues; it was an attempt to place a roadblock in front of a governmental apparatus which had been captured by enemies of those whose rights the OEO Legal Services program was established to protect. The Agency's redevelopment program and its political alliances were having a devastating impact on the city's poor, and together with future projects which the Agency was likely to undertake—in the South of Market, the Tenderloin, Chinatown and the port area—might totally eliminate poor and minority residents from downtown San Francisco. The TOOR suit was undertaken in part

The Final Solution?

to stop this juggernaut—and to an extent succeeded.

The Settlement Pact

While City Hall's takeover of the YBC public facilities and Justin Herman's death laid the groundwork for a final solution to the TOOR lawsuit, there was little noticeable movement on the replacement housing issue until the fall of 1972. With the Board of Supervisors' March, 1972 approval of the substitute public facilities financing plan devised by Mellon and the Redevelopment Agency, and the new difficulties that HUD and other lawsuits were creating for the project (see pages 143-45), it was obvious that new moves would have to be made to meet the November, 1973 deadline set by the consent decree.

It now seemed possible for the Agency to locate a sufficient number of hotels suitable and available for renovation as permanent low-income housing; however, the problem of subsidy funds was more difficult, given the federal government's January, 1973 moratorium on housing programs and the extensive rent supplement aid already given by HUD in the rehousing of YBC residents (see page 146). In August, 1972, the City proposed subsidizing the additional units needed to fill its quota by imposing an increase in the hotel tax. This tax, then a five and one-half percent surcharge added to transient hotel rates, had already been raised from three percent to five percent in 1967 to create a special fund to help pay YBC development costs. The City proposed an additional one-half percent increase, projected to generate about $375,000 annually. This money in part would provide debt service payments on a bond issue the Agency proposed for purchasing and rehabilitating some 350 low-rent units, and in part would lower the rents in 353 additional units of moderate-income housing approved for or under construction.† These 700-plus units it was felt would insure the Agency's meeting its commitment to the federal court with a margin of safety, since a substantial number of the 1,359 units the Agency already had scheduled (only 425 of which, by its own figures, were under construction or already built) were being challenged by TOOR as ineligible to meet the Agency's quota.

Although an increase in the hotel tax was a politically sensitive matter

---

† A variant of this notion—assessing beneficiaries of the YBC project to provide housing subsidies for displacees—had been proposed in early 1972 by *Examiner* writer Donald Canter. Canter's plan was to add a one-cent per-square-foot per-month surcharge on office and commercial space rentals, which he estimated would produce over $500,000 a year to create a housing subsidy fund. He argued that the Redevelopment Agency already required that builders spend one percent of their total development costs for works of art. See "City Faces Paying for Yerba Buena", *San Francisco Examiner*, February 8, 1972.

and elicited great anguish from the hotel industry (which, in a grand-stand play, even threatened to challenge the legality of the hotel tax altogether), the Board of Supervisors approved the half percent increase in October, 1972. However, the opposition of the hotelmen and other representatives of the convention industry was effective to the extent that the Supervisors, in an effort to mollify these powerful interests, gave in to their "demand" that a portion of any new hotel tax revenues—approximately $100,000—be given to the Convention and Visitors Bureau, increasing their annual allocation from the city to nearly $1 million. As the September 28, 1972 *Chronicle* noted, "Before approving the half cent increase in the hotel tax, members of the [Finance] committee attempted to pacify unhappy hotel operators by moving to provide more funds for advertising the city as a convention and tourist attraction."†

But even this new infusion of funds did not solve the problem. TOOR continued to challenge before Judge Weigel both the validity of the Agency's re-revised, HUD-approved relocation plan and the eligibility of replacement housing units the Agency listed for the federal court in its mandatory quarterly reports (see page 148). Substantial numbers of these units, TOOR claimed (with evidence), either had been programmed prior to April 30, 1970, or already were occupied by non-transient low-income residents, contrary to Judge Weigel's guidelines. The City's urgent need was to get on with the actual construction of the project, as inflation kept pushing development costs higher and hotel owners and other convention industry figures kept pressing for the new exhibition facility. Continued delay might even endanger the project altogether. A further consideration was that three privately sponsored housing developments containing 422 units outside the YBC area were almost ready for occupancy. About a third of these were reserved for YBC displacees, but if not occupied within a certain time would be filled by other applicants. The loss of these units could jeopardize the Agency's YBC relocation plan and cause HUD to withdraw its approval.

---

† The Supervisors' special treatment of the hotel owners was noted by a representative of the city's cultural groups (also recipients of subsidies from the hotel tax), who stated to the Finance Committee: "You didn't ask me or the other taxpayers if you could impose a sewer or property tax on us. . . . Why do you have to ask the hotel owners' permission in order to tax their guests?" Use of the hotel tax primarily to assist the hotel industry is a far cry from the principles put forth editorially by the *Chronicle* (January 17, 1962) to govern allocation of these revenues, at the time the tax was introduced:

"The first principle, we should say, is that this revenue belongs to all the people of San Francisco, to be disposed of in the broad general interest and not in the limited interests of the proprietors of the 1,158 hotels and motels who collect it from their customers and pay it over to the city."

The Final Solution?

In January, 1973, William Coblentz, a local attorney influential in state Democratic circles, a University of California Regent, and a political advisor to Mayor Alioto, undertook to bring the parties together and arrange a settlement that would induce TOOR to abandon its lawsuit. This course was prompted by the calculation that TOOR, through further legal actions and appeals, could delay the project nearly two full years past the November, 1973 deadline of the consent decree—which the Agency could not meet in any case—even if it lost every step of the way (an unlikely assumption, since up to that point TOOR had won in court at almost every point).

After several weeks of behind-the-scenes negotiations between TOOR, its attorneys and the Redevelopment Agency staff, a tentative agreement was fashioned: in essence it called for the Agency and City to construct some 400 units of new housing (over and above the previous 1500-1800 unit commitment) on four sites in or adjacent to the project area, in return for which TOOR would dismiss its lawsuit. This figure represented a considerable compromise with the demand for 1,000 units in the project area, which TOOR had made in mid-December at a meeting in Mayor Alioto's office of all litigating parties. The meeting, initiated by the Chamber of Commerce, was called to discuss settlement of the TOOR case and other suits.

Following the tentative agreement, Mayor Alioto began to play his political cards by publicly expressing concern that the Agency staff had conceded too much to TOOR; this was immediately echoed by the Redevelopment Agency commissioners (appointed by the Mayor). Within the Agency staff, too, some tensions arose between the "hawks," who wanted to maintain Justin Herman's old position of not giving an inch, and the "doves," who felt it was prudent to make concessions to TOOR. Alioto requested that the Board of Supervisors hold hearings on the proposed settlement package. The mayor clearly wanted the Board to take some responsibility for the settlement, which not only contained a major concession in allowing replacement housing to be built in the project area, but also called for still another increase in the city's hotel tax, from six to six and one-half percent, to pay for this housing. The mayor's strategy, and later the Board's, was to use the compromise agreement TOOR and the Agency staff had worked out as a starting point for wrenching additional concessions and whittling down TOOR's gains even further. In a novel proceeding, the full Board of Supervisors held a hearing in late April, 1973, on a tentative agreement not yet approved by the parties involved and therefore not calling for any action by the Board.

The key element in this hearing was the hotel tax. The hotel owners were livid at the prospect of a second increase within the span of a few months. Irving Baldwin, testifying for the Hotel Employers Association, decried the proposed tax increase as "immoral." "Why should visitors be forced to solve the problems of indigents in San Francisco?" he reasoned to the Board, with respect to a project that was demolishing thousands of low-rent housing units and displacing thousands of low-income people to create a convention center. Baldwin's ethical sensibilities had also been offended the previous October, when the hotel tax was increased from five and one-half to six percent. As the October 6, 1972 *San Francisco Progress* quoted him: "It's a moral issue. The City shouldn't ask its guests to pay for indigents to be relocated. Underwriting the Convention Center is another story." But it was not morality that decided the issue; rather, it was the raw political and financial muscle the hotel owners and the convention industry exerted in the political arena. As the April 24, 1972 *Examiner* observed:

When it became known that another half cent increase in the hotel tax was proposed to help finance this housing, the hotel industry revolted. With five Supervisors up for reelection in November, the reaction to the hotel industry's stand was predictable. Feverish behind-the-scenes dickering then resulted in a complicated financial counter offer that excluded any hotel tax increase. . . . In what observers considered a show of allegiance to the Mayor, labor leaders joined the hotel industry in demanding that Yerba Buena be built but without any additional burden on the hotel tax. [The presidents of the San Francisco Labor Council and Building and Construction Trades Council testified against the increase.]

Although the Board of Supervisors refused to support the hotel tax increase and the agreement worked out by TOOR and the Redevelopment Agency staff, they did fashion what amounted to a counter-offer. The settlement package originally proposed offered some $670,000 annually to subsidize YBC replacement housing—$270,000 from the one-half percent increase approved the previous October,† plus approximately $400,000 from the new one-half percent increase. The Supervisors' scaled-down offer amounted to roughly $400,000 annually in housing construction and rent subsidies: the $270,000, plus $100,000 which the Convention and Visitors Bureau agreed to "donate" (the sum the city gave the CVB in exchange for its "allowing" the hotel tax increase to go through), plus $30,000 which CAO Thomas Mellon "discovered" was available through juggling his allocation of the tax. This $400,000, assigned for 35 years to subsidize YBC replacement housing, amounted to $14 million, substantially less than the $20 million value of the package which TOOR and the SFRA staff had originally negotiated ($670,000 a year, but for only 30 years).

---

†This money was no longer needed to provide the 1,500 units required under the November, 1970 consent decree, due to the availability of the federal rent supplement moneys (see pages 146-47).

The Final Solution?

The Board postponed the matter for a week to allow TOOR and the Agency to meet once again and discuss TOOR's response to the Supervisors' counter-offer. What finally emerged was a compromise between the original and revised proposals: $500,000 annually ($17.5 million over 35 years), based on the assumption that the one-half percent of the hotel tax assigned to YBC replacement housing will increase in value over the years. Although no specific number of units is included in the agreement, it is generally believed that this amount will permit the Agency to float lease revenue bonds that will support construction and subsidization of approximately 400 units.

On May 15, 1973, in the lobby of the Milner Hotel, TOOR and the Redevelopment Agency put their signatures to an agreement, the essence of which is that the Agency will produce the aforementioned 400 low-rent units within the project area in exchange for TOOR's dropping its lawsuit. The 41-page document sets forth a series of detailed steps to be taken by TOOR and various city agencies, each of which triggers a subsequent step. The agreement is roughly as follows:

Immediately upon signing the agreement, the Agency is permitted to contact the approximately 120 remaining Central Blocks residents in order to persuade them to move to one of three new or newly rehabilitated buildings just being completed (one in the Tenderloin, one South of Market, a third in the Mission district). Rents for those electing to move to one of these units can be no higher than 21.4 percent of gross income for individuals, 20 percent for families. (Not all Central Blocks residents will be eligible for these units, however; two of the three developments are confined to the elderly [62 years and over] and disabled, and all have an income limitation of $4,800 per year, which means that a small number of YBC residents with higher incomes will be ineligible for these units.†) The Agency will have no eviction powers, however, until the Board of Supervisors, Redevelopment Agency, and Planning Commission take several steps: amendment of the hotel tax ordinance to assign revenues to TOOR's replacement housing; amendment of the YBC redevelopment plan to devote three small sites on the southern border of the project to housing; and acquisition of a fourth housing site outside the project boundaries. The Agency can begin eviction proceedings against the remaining residents of the Central Blocks after the first of these steps is taken but cannot actually displace residents until the second and third steps have been taken. Relocation must, of course, be in accord with HUD standards for hous-

---

† According to Table E-26 of the Arthur D. Little report on Yerba Buena relocation (see footnote 23, Chapter IV), about ten percent of all YBC displacees had incomes over $4,800 per year. No income distribution is available solely for the Central Blocks residents remaining at the time the agreement was signed.

The TOOR Housing Sites

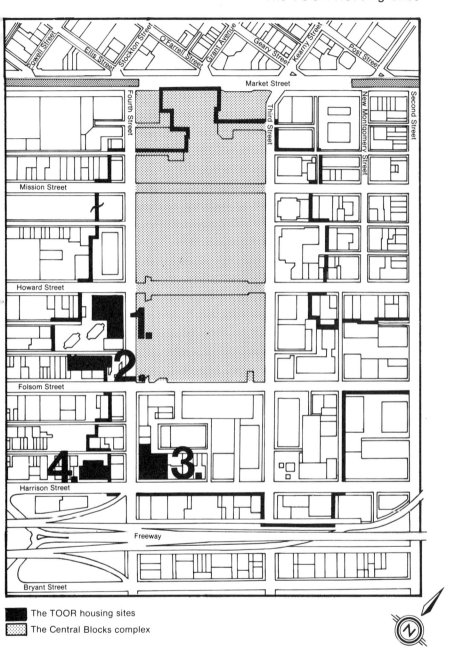

The TOOR housing sites

The Central Blocks complex

The Final Solution?

ing quality and ability to pay, and, as before, any resident who feels he is being displaced to housing that does not meet these standards may appeal to the Relocation Appeals Board (see pages 140-42). The Board's operation, however, will be governed by procedures which will produce speedy disposition of any cases brought before it. All displacees, from the Central Blocks and other areas, will have the absolute right to interim housing, at rents no higher than they presently are paying, in any of four hotels in the YBC area which the Agency will maintain until such time as the 400 replacement units are completed, and all present—and former—YBC residents will have first priority on these 400 units.

An important element of the agreement is the continuation of TOOR in a new incarnation as the no-profit, community-based housing sponsor for the 400 units (this was one of the provisions to which Mayor Alioto and the Redevelopment Agency originally had strongest objections). The Tenants and Owners Development Corporation (TODCo) will be assigned responsibility for selecting the architect for the replacement housing (from a panel of five first chosen by the city); working with the architect to prepare the architectural program, preliminary plans and working drawings for the four housing sites; reviewing construction cost estimates and developing rent schedules and subsidy estimates; participating in preparation of the financing program for the replacement housing; and assisting in the eventual management of the housing. From the money raised by the Redevelopment Agency revenue bonds for replacement housing, $50,000 will annually go to TODCo, and it is likely that Peter Mendelsohn, TOOR's chairman, Stephen Dutton, TOOR's former community organizer, and others active in the four-year struggle will play important roles in the development of the housing they fought to bring about. Formal designation of TODCo as sponsor for the 400 units will not be delayed, since eviction proceedings against YBC residents living outside the Central Blocks cannot begin until this is done.†

With respect to the 1,500 units•of replacement housing which the Agency committed itself to in its November 9, 1970 consent decree, the

---

† On the other hand, voluntary displacement may occur with the proper inducements. The London-based Taylor Woodrow Company made a private relocation payment of $6,000, to be used as a down-payment on a house, to the last remaining resident of the site on which the company plans to construct a $10 million office building. (See "A typically British 'cheerio'," *San Francisco Sunday Examiner & Chronicle*, October 21, 1973.)

• The agreement refers to the Agency's "1,500 unit low-income housing program." It is now apparent that the Agency will be giving YBC displacees priority in at least 300 units, thereby making applicable the lower figure of the 1,500-1,800 unit range referred to in the November 9, 1970 consent decree.

agreement allows the Agency an extra year (until November 9, 1974) to complete these units and provides that in the interim TOOR will waive any objections to the Agency's program for producing these units. In exhibit D of the agreement the Agency lists 15 developments containing a total of 1,667 units, which are to constitute fulfillment of the consent decree.†

TOOR's half of the bargain is, of course, what the city had sought for nearly four years: dismissal of its lawsuit with prejudice (i.e., without possibility of reinstituting it). The agreement requires TOOR's attorneys to move for dismissal in federal court within two days after the hotel tax ordinance is amended; this is a precondition to the sale of Central Blocks construction bonds. The agreement also provides that complaints about alleged breaches can be brought in federal court, dismissal of the suit notwithstanding, and under court rules such complaints would almost certainly be assigned to Judge Weigel. (This was another provision that rankled Mayor Alioto and the Redevelopment Agency, who wanted to sever all ties with Judge Weigel; but TOOR insisted on retaining some recourse to the judge who had provided protection of the residents' rights for over three years and without whom they most likely would never have reached the stage of signing such an agreement.)

At the Agency's insistence, the agreement includes an important "fail-safe" clause: the Agency is not required to issue its replacement housing bonds until its public facilities bonds have been sold. Thus, anything that interferes with the financing of the Central Blocks facilities will also prevent construction of the replacement housing that was TOOR's big victory in this final settlement. TOOR is even required "to use its best efforts to assist in settling all legal actions which currently or in the future interfere with execution of activities leading to the prompt completion of the public facilities, low-income housing, and private development scheduled for construction in the YBC Project Area." The subject of this provision is clearly the various lawsuits still pending on financing and environmental aspects of the project.

The agreement thus insures that from this point on TOOR will be as much pro-YBC as the Agency. As proof of this loyalty, the attempts by conservationist-businessman Alvin Duskin to stop the YBC project entirely, through his lawsuit and a signature drive to place the issue on the November, 1973 ballot, were publicly denounced by TOOR's at-

---

† According to the Agency's quarterly reports to Judge Weigel, 72 of these units, located in hotels scheduled for rehabilitation, were occupied by non-transient, i.e., permanent, residents. Since these residents had to move out to facilitate rehabilitation, it appears that the Agency is still attempting to relocate its YBC displacees by displacing residents outside the YBC area. This is more of the "musical chairs" process which TOOR had vigorously objected to.

The Final Solution?

torney Anthony Kline as "sheer insanity."† And the *Examiner's* May 15, 1973 account of the press conference at which the final agreement was signed noted:

> [*TOOR chairman Peter*] *Mendelsohn also vowed TOOR will do everything to make sure that the agreement is carried out and vowed to oppose anyone who might try to sabotage the deal.*
>
> *Asked to clarify this statement Mendelsohn said he was referring to Alvin Duskin's newly formed Friends of Yerba Buena organization which has announced it will start an initiative campaign to place on the ballot a measure that would veto construction of the convention complex.*
>
> *"They're not the friends of Yerba Buena," Mendelsohn said, adding that no TOOR member will sign the initiative.*

The heavy play given by the newspapers to TOOR's conversion and their effusive praise for its gains in this agreement—particularly striking when contrasted with previous attitudes toward TOOR—may also be part of the campaign to bring public pressure to bear on Duskin et al. to drop their anti-YBC efforts. A *Chronicle* editorial on May 17, 1973, two days after the agreement was signed, approvingly cited Kline's blast at Duskin and characterized the Duskin-Brinton effort to stop YBC as being undertaken "for no good reason except it doesn't fit their personal anti-convention center concepts." The May 1, 1973 *Examiner* spoke of TOOR's "stunning victory over City Hall"; the May 16, 1973 *Chronicle* wrote of TOOR's "highly effective young legal team"; and the May 15, 1973 *Examiner* noted "the fact that the ceremony [signing of the agreement] was held in a Skid Row hotel rather than in the offices of the Redevelopment Agency left no doubt as to who emerged as the victor."

---

† See *San Francisco Progress*, April 27, 1973. During the spring of 1973 Duskin and his attorney, William Brinton, a former member of the City Planning Commission, were promoting an alternate plan to use the YBC site for low- and middle-income housing, a cultural center, health complex and manufacturing, with no parking; they proposed to finance this plan through the hotel tax and federal revenue-sharing funds. However, their organization, Friends of Yerba Buena, failed to collect a sufficient number of signatures to get their initiative petition on the November, 1973 ballot (see "Yerba Buena Vote Petition Falls Short," *San Francisco Sunday Examiner & Chronicle*, August 26, 1973). While TOOR might have agreed with Duskin's proposal four years ago, they feel pushing such a plan at a time when they have won a major victory would clearly be against their interests. (See Carol Kroot, "Duskin YBC plan rapped," *San Francisco Progress*, June 13, 1973). Another practical problem is that several million dollars in architectural and engineering fees have already been spent for the present YBC plan. Duskin had previously produced two well publicized and extremely controversial "anti-highrise" initiatives, in 1971 and 1972, each receiving about 40 percent of the vote.

The Settlement Pact

In sum then, the agreement provides for ending the TOOR litigation in exchange for a commitment by the Redevelopment Agency and the city to provide about 400 units of permanent new low-income housing within the YBC project area itself (above the 1,500-1,800 units the Agency already is committed to provide elsewhere in the city). On July 19, 1973, Judge Weigel gave his approval to the agreement and dismissed the TOOR lawsuit with prejudice. As noted, the agreement is for the most part self-enforcing, in that it is in each party's interest to take or allow to be taken certain steps so as to proceed to a subsequent step.†
Should either party fail to meet its obligations, the matter likely will come before Judge Weigel again, for violation of contract. How Judge Weigel would deal with such a breach is an intriguing question; both parties to the dispute, and the court, would probably be highly reluctant to reopen this legal can of worms.

The only issue remaining before the court is legal fees for TOOR's attorneys. The attorneys filed a motion to have the court award them fees for the time they put into the case since leaving their previous OEO-funded Legal Services offices. On January 30, 1974, Judge Weigel ordered the SFRA to pay these fees. According to the January 31, 1974 *Chronicle*:

> *The amount of the attorney's fee is to be worked out between lawyers for the agency and for Public Advocates, Inc. . . .*
> *The money will not go to the individual lawyers who handled the lengthy case, but will go to the firm, which has been partially financed by the Ford Foundation.*

TOOR and its attorneys feel that important principles are involved in the fees issue, as well as the future ability of low-income groups and their advocates to carry on protracted fights to secure their legal rights. Attorneys J. Anthony Kline and Sidney Wolinsky, who helped found Public Advocates, Inc., are seeking ways to put these public interest law firms on a permanent, self-sustaining basis, and court-awarded attor-

---

† By February, 1974, the following positive steps had been taken to implement the TOOR-Redevelopment Agency agreement: the necessary changes had been made in the YBC redevelopment plan to permit replacement housing on three sites; the fourth site, outside the original project area, had been approved by the Planning Commission, and the Redevelopment Agency was in the process of acquiring the site; the hotel tax had been amended to redirect revenues as called for in the agreement; the Relocation Appeals Board had been established to adjudicate any grievances regarding the Agency's resumed displacement activities; and the Agency had signed an agreement with TODCo. TODCo has already selected its architect for the 400 units from the panel of five submitted by the City—Robert Herman, who, amusingly, turns out to be Justin Herman's cousin.

The Final Solution

neys fees in public service cases seem the most promising avenue.[5] They likely will ask fees in the $200,000-250,000 range, and if they and the Agency cannot agree on a sum, the matter will come before Judge Weigel again for a ruling. Kline and Wolinsky note that the agency spent $120,000 of public funds to hire special counsel to fight the TOOR suit (see page 139), and that shortly after TOOR filed its suit, Justin Herman threatened to "paralyze" Wolinsky's San Francisco Neighborhood Legal Assistance Foundation by inundating it with so many legal motions and papers that it would be unable to do any other work. In the years that followed, literally thousands of hours of the Foundation's and Housing Law Center's time, and later Public Advocates', were spent in attempting to force the San Francisco Redevelopment Agency to obey the law. It is unclear who ultimately will pick up the bill for any fees the Agency must pay to TOOR's attorneys, since the Agency has no money of its own. It may be able to secure a grant from HUD, but this is unlikely. More likely, the city will have to pay these costs, possibly from the general fund—which would place still another burden on the taxpayers for the city's mishandling of the YBC project.

Although the TOOR suit is out of the way and TOOR is now an ally, the two other lawsuits pending continue to hold up the project. The claims by Alvin Duskin and attorney Gerald Wright that the public facilities financing plan is illegal will prevent sale of the Agency's bond issue; therefore an early settlement would certainly be in the City's interest. The City still has not filed a reply brief to Wright's suit although it was brought two years ago.

In November, 1973, however, the Redevelopment Agency filed a counter-suit asking the Superior Court to validate its proposed financing plan. (Herb Caen's November 30, 1973 *Chronicle* column notes: "To fight and hopefully dispose of the two suits still roadblocking Yerba Buena Center, the Agency has hired the gilt-edged supercharged law firm of Orrick, Herrington, Rowley and Sutcliffe. . . The firm's fee [will be] 'more than $50,000 but less than $100,000,' according to Agency sources. . .") A month later the Agency announced, and the papers printed, that "Yerba Buena Foes Dwindle to 1—Duskin" (January 7, 1974 *Examiner* headline), claiming that since Gerald Wright had failed to answer the Agency's summons, his suit would be dismissed. Wright indeed had not answered the summons; several weeks later, however, when the Agency troubled to contact him, he pointed out that the summons was illegal, since it gave only 27 days' notice whereas the law clearly stipulates 30 days are required. The Agency has quietly renewed its summons, but Wright maintains that it cannot dispose of his suit in this manner, and must instead respond to his original suit. The future of these matters is unclear, but to date the Agency's track record in court and on legal matters generally has been such as to lead one to place little faith in its posture of self-assurance.

Both Duskin and Wright would agree to dismiss their suits in exchange for well publicized full disclosure hearings before the Board of Supervisors on all aspects of the financing plan, followed by a public vote on the project itself. The City, however, is unlikely to agree to such terms; rather, it is likely to supplement its legal efforts against Wright and Duskin with a publicity campaign designed to pressure the two men into dropping their opposition, by depicting them as loners and cranks.†

For TOOR the final settlement was a significant advance over the gains promised in federal court in November, 1970; but it came as a result of nearly three frustrating years of struggle to realize these gains, and was still short of what the community wanted and firmly believed would have been a just solution. Only 600-700 units of housing—the 400 units from the settlement pact plus the Clementina Towers public housing project built as part of the original redevelopment plan—will be constructed in the area to replace the 4,000 units removed by the YBC project. It will be at least three years before the 400 units gained in the final agreement are available for occupancy; and as Pete Mendelsohn notes, "My people are old people and they can't afford any more delay."[6] TOOR also feels that two of the four sites (3 and 4 on page 197) are inferior locations, since their proximity to industry and the elevated freeway and their remoteness from the residential and commercial concentrations in the South of Market area may result in a poor living environment for those who move there. Completion of the 1,500-1,800 units is still at least one to two years off. And large numbers of people living at the Milner and other Central Blocks hotels will have to move to temporary, and in many cases inferior, dwellings on the project site until their new units are available.

But for TOOR this was, in the words of organizer Stephen Dutton, "our last best hope." Time was working against them as well as against the Redevelopment Agency. The area's population was fading fast; the "unthinkable"—abandoning the project altogether—at that point might have left the residents with no relocation or rehousing rights at all, since the remaining hotels would have been sold to private developers. And everyone wanted to see some end—even a compromise victory—to four years of exhausting and time-consuming battle.

---

† In his remarks to the Board of Supervisors at the ceremony initiating its 1974 legislative session, Mayor Alioto "also managed to slam attorney William Brinton. . .by referring to Brinton as Alvin Duskin's 'free lawyer, who seems to be doing it (suing to halt the Yerba Buena redevelopment project) on a malicious basis.' " (*San Francisco Examiner*, January 9, 1974).

8. A Reckoning and a Strategy for the Future

A lot of people prefer
to be busboys and waiters
because it fits their life style.
Robert Sullivan, General Manager,
Convention and Visitors Bureau, 1973

For nearly four years, a relatively small organization of powerless and obscure people managed to stall construction of a massive downtown redevelopment project against the full array of San Francisco's political and financial power. The City Fathers held steadfastly that nothing illegal or wrongful was occurring in the displacement and relocation of South of Market residents, and that complainants were only a small group of selfish troublemakers backed by publicity-seeking attorneys. But by holding on to their land, by insisting that government adhere to its own laws protecting their rights, and by making their plight a nagging and embarrassing public issue, they forced the City Fathers to make a deal with them.

Without the fight waged by South of Market residents and their lawyers, both the relocatees and the city's housing supply would clearly have suffered far more than they did. Now some 2,000 units of low-rent housing will come into being that otherwise would never have been produced—assuming the Redevelopment Agency does not continue to renege and delay on its own commitments. Production of these units probably will also provide the added benefit of decreasing inflationary pressures on the city's low-rent housing market as a whole. This rate of production is far in excess of what the city had been producing for low-income households (from 1963 to 1969, the San Francisco Housing Authority built not a single unit of family public housing and only 110 units for the elderly).† But these will replace only

---

† It is worth noting that guidelines for future redevelopment projects which stress housing and community participation goals were passed by the San Francisco Planning Commission in late 1971, and in all probability were heavily influenced by the YBC experience. The five specific guidelines, which presumably are to form the basis for Planning Commission approval or disapproval of any future renewal projects in San Francisco, are: construction or rehabilitation of moderate- and low-income housing should be the major purpose; prior planning activities should have been undertaken with the affected

A Strategy for the Future

half the 4,000 units demolished for the YBC project, of which probably ten percent were not in substandard condition to begin with. Perhaps as many as one-third of the YBC residents will eventually improve their housing conditions, either by moving to replacement housing units as they become available or through improved Agency relocation practices prompted by the lawsuit, HUD pressure and the general publicity given the Agency's misfeasance. Several hundred residents were permitted to remain in their preferred, familiar surroundings for a few more years—even if in poorly managed Agency-owned hotels and a depressing, uncertain environment. And, of course, those who stayed with the fight to the end had the satisfaction of seeing their persistence pay off in concrete benefits.

But singular and exhilarating as this victory may have been, the fact is that for the vast majority of the 4,000 residents (and 700 businesses) originally on the site, Yerba Buena Center was, overall, a disaster. Most have been dispersed throughout San Francisco or outside the city altogether; have lost the social networks and sense of community they felt in the South of Market area; are paying considerably higher rents and other living costs; and in all too many cases still are in substandard housing and run-down neighborhoods. Furthermore, a great many of these people can expect to have to move again in a few short years, as market forces and other public projects spurred by YBC create of them a permanent population of displacees; the plight of these DP's may be the most distressing form of disruption to be caused by Yerba Buena. Even those who will reap gains from the settlement package must for the most part wait several years to enjoy their benefits. And given the Agency's poor performance on its previous commitments of YBC replacement housing and its insensitive, even hostile attitudes toward South of Market residents, it is by no means unrealistic to raise the specter of an Agency failure to follow through on time, or at all, on the agreement which cost TOOR the only real weapon it had, possession of the Central Blocks. This is the stark reality of the Yerba Buena resistance; and yet the residents of South of Market have won far more than virtually any other victims of downtown redevelopment.

The experience in South of Market demonstrates that through organized resistance and the political power that arises from a firm,

---

community; minimal displacement of residents and businesses should be involved; projects should be small in size and consistent with the scale and character of the area (except where a non-residential area is being converted into a new residential community); and redevelopment should be used only where normal private actions cannot be expected to achieve renewal of the area or provide new housing. YBC, by contrast, violates four, if not five, of these precepts. See San Francisco Department of City Plannning, "Recommended Guidelines for Future Redevelopment Projects", September 16, 1971.

united stance, communities being decimated by "public action" are capable of at least delaying and interfering with this process until concessions are granted. Throughout the controversy TOOR refused to compromise on the legal obligations of the Redevelopment Agency and the City of San Francisco to provide displaced South of Market residents with decent, safe, sanitary housing at rents they could afford; at the same time they advanced political demands for rehousing in the same part of the city. When they found they could not deal with the Redevelopment Agency the residents lost little time in taking their case to the courts. Although a great many residents—pressured by the Redevelopment Agency, fearful of being left out in the cold, and understandably skeptical of their organization's ability to beat City Hall—moved from the area in the midst of the battle, TOOR throughout the entire struggle was virtually free of internal divisions and the usually successful attempts at cooption by the city which have undermined so many other community protests. Community leaders were not "neutralized" by accepting paid positions with city agencies, or bought off by finding themselves appinted to meaningless commissions and committees, bestowed with honorary titles and brought into contact with the rich and powerful. TOOR's leaders and spokesmen were not, as in so many other community struggles, politicians, businessmen or ministers. Middle-class or aspiring middle-class leaders, whether from inside or outside the community, are bound to waver when faced by strong opposition from City Hall and powerful economic interests with which they have social and financial ties.

The only significant rift in the TOOR resistance came precisely as the result of a conflict between the community and the outsiders to whom it had to turn for assistance. Residents and their lawyers disagreed over the settlement their lawyers proposed and which both the Redevelopment Agency and the court were pressing them to accept. The residents, unlike the lawyers, recognized clearly and immediately that the settlement did not guarantee protection of their rights and welfare. This important incident highlights some of the critical weaknesses in dependence on outside support by a community engaged in struggle. While the lawyers and the litigation strategy, and other outside planning and design assistance, were crucial to TOOR's success in fighting the YBC project, there can be no substitute for internal organizational strength. Too great a dependence on attorneys and other outsiders—many of whom are somewhat transient, since they frequently move on to different career opportunities, locations and projects—can place the people of the community in a secondary position. When a community of poor people places its faith in outside professionals, it becomes dependent on individuals from a different

A Strategy for the Future

social class who have their own agendas, reference groups, priorities and styles. Unless the community is able to exercise full policy control over its legal and other outside technical assistants, these class differences may generate damaging conflicts in approach, goals and commitment that may compromise its struggle. Outside surrogates simply are not and cannot be as involved personally as those whose lives are affected. They cannot say, as does Peter Mendelsohn, "You live it 24 hours a day . . . . You can't help it because that's your life they're playing with."

This conflict applies generally to litigation as a strategy for social change. While in TOOR's case the physical limitations of its constituency ruled out more militant forms of protest and opposition and virtually dictated primary reliance on a litigation strategy, a community that has a choice of strategies may be at a real disadvantage in placing its fate in the hands of a court. In the courtroom, ground rules and the pace of the proceedings are imposed, the community cannot participate directly, and the scene is dominated by judges and lawyers and their mode of action. Litigation is a painfully slow process, as the progress of the TOOR suit from November, 1969, to July, 1973, demonstrates.† And for displacees in their sixties, seventies, and eighties the adage "justice delayed is justice denied" rings sadly true. Judges, on the whole, derive from the same class and reflect the same interests as most public officials and the local economic elite, and may therefore be reluctant to intervene drastically in a public project involving numerous resources and commitments and solidly backed by the local power structure. When a dispute arises between propertied interests and the

---

†In the analogous Hamtramck, Michigan lawsuit (see note to page 136), the tortoise-like pace of litigation is equally evident. There, a suit was brought in the fall of 1968 charging that the city's urban renewal program was in effect a plan of "Negro removal." A federal court agreed with the plaintiffs and in November, 1971, ordered both parties to submit plans for rectifying the wrongs perpetrated by the city. Not until March, 1973, did the court issue its final order, directing the city to build 530 new units of housing for Black and elderly residents who have already been displaced, and to insure that future and past displacees have full access to and priority in available vacancies throughout the city. The ruling, characterized by the mayor of this heavily Polish city as "an earth-shattering decision which affects every commmunity in the continental United States", will be appealed (see *New York Times*, April 4 and 8, 1973.) If the District Court decision is upheld by the Sixth Circuit Court of Appeals, implementation of the plan could begin around the beginning of 1975; however, it is expected that HUD, which is appealing the decision along with the city of Hamtramck, will take the case to the Supreme Court if necessary (letter dated December 28, 1973, from Michael J. Barnhart, Esq., Center for Urban Law and Housing, Detroit.) This would result in substantial additional delay.

poor, as it did in Yerba Buena, the courts, even if they sympathize with and support the legal position of the less powerful parties, tend to take a middle ground to avoid a sweeping ruling that would substantially and perhaps permanently damage these powerful interests. In this case, the federal court went to great lengths to avoid ruling on TOOR's motions to enjoin the project, and afterwards to terminate as rapidly as possible the injunction it finally did issue. The court used its powers and influence to encourage bargaining and a settlement between TOOR and the Redevelopment Agency; but that negotiation process, carried on between parties of vastly unequal power and backing, was bound to produce an agreement compromising TOOR's rights and claims. The resultant agreement not only offered inadequate benefits; it even failed to guarantee that they would be delivered. In such unequal confrontations true judicial protection is tendered only when the court is willing to make compliance with the law a precondition for continuation of the project. Applied to YBC, this approach would have forced the city of San Francisco to come up with replacement housing before the court would allow work on the Central Blocks complex to continue. Without this kind of judicial protection, the result is what befell South of Market—the literal destruction of a neighborhood; dispersal of its population (either under overt pressure by the public agency or because the agency's past and continuing actions have made the area dangerous and undesirable); and a settlement that falls far short of meeting the housing needs of former or remaining residents. As a recent *Yale Law Journal* article concludes:

> . . .[*T*]*he courts must intervene decisively and promptly in the relocation process, or judicial safeguards will serve little purpose. Denial of injunctive relief is likely to render the case moot; enforcement of the relocation assurances becomes difficult; and any later victory for the plaintiffs is a paper one.*†

† Peter W. Sly, "In the Path of Progress: Federal Highway Relocation Assurances," Note, 82 *Yale Law Journal*, (1972), p. 399. A good example of this phenomenon and the limitations of the litigation approach is contained in one of the leading cases regarding highway displacement, *Concerned Citizens for the Preservation of Clarksville v. Volpe* (No. 30286, 5th Cir., June 9, 1971), where a group of Black and Mexican-American families sought to halt a federal-aid highway through their section of Austin, Texas, based largely on their claim of inadequate relocation housing. The Fifth Circuit Court of Appeals, in upholding the lower court's decision against the plaintiffs, noted that it based its affirmance on the fact that all of the area's residents had been relocated by the time the case was argued on appeal. When the displacing agency is not enjoined at the outset, it will proceed expeditiously to move families and demolish buildings, and as the Fifth Circuit noted, "there must come a point in time when even the most grievous wrong is sadly beyond the power of equity to rectify."

A Strategy for the Future

In assessing the import and replicability of TOOR's strategy and successes, it should be borne in mind, too, that the elements of its case were near optimal: a sympathetic and steadfast federal judge, an excellent fact situation, and a team of exceptionally talented and tenacious attorneys. (The necessity for prodigious effort and time investment, plus high quality legal papers and courtroom work, cannot be over-emphasized; few legal services offices are able to furnish these resources, yet it is unlikely that results such as those obtained in the Yerba Buena suit can be secured with lesser talents and time commitments.) If the power of "the law" to remedy injustice and bring about rapid and real social change is so severely circumscribed in a situation as promising as the Yerba Buena litigation, any community engaging in this type of struggle would be well advised to limit its expectations. A further atypical characteristic of the Yerba Buena case is that virtually all displacees were white. Had the project uprooted several thousand nonwhite residents—far more typical of urban renewal displacement—the problems of finding and producing replacement housing would have been vastly more difficult.[1]

If projects such as Yerba Buena Center are to be successfully fought in the future, then, much more than landmark litigation will be necessary. Community organization and political power are essential. An interesting and important comparison is the successful long-term fight in the Boston area against continued construction of the highway system, which began as a series of neighborhood-based protests, these eventually linking to form a metropolitan anti-highway coalition. These activities, aided considerably by advocate planners and community organizers, led to a governor-ordered moratorium on all new highway construction in the Boston area and to a comprehensive restudy of the area's transportation needs and alternative ways of meeting them. Eventually most of the $400 million highway system was stopped. No lawsuit was ever filed as part of this effort, and the few lawyers who played a role acted mainly as community organizers and lobbyists with the state legislature.†

---

† For further information about this extraordinary effort, see Alan Lupo, Frank Colcord, and Edmund P. Fowler, *Rites of Way: The Politics of Transportation in Boston and the U. S. City* (Boston: Little, Brown, 1971); Stephen C. Lockwood, "The Boston Transportation Plannning Review: A Case Study in Community/Technical Interaction," *Planners Notebook*, Vol. 2, No. 4, August, 1972; Kenneth J. Geiser, Jr., *Urban Transportation Decision Making: Political Processes of Urban Freeway Controversies* (Cambridge, Mass.: MIT Urban Systems Laboratory, 1970); and Gordon Fellman, in association with Barbara Brandt, *The Deceived Majority: Politics and Protest in Middle America* (New Brunswick, N. J.: Transaction Books, 1973). Fellman and Brandt observe, however, that the professional advocate planners, in the initial stages of the protest at least, showed some of the same biases and proclivities that lawyers have been accused

A Strategy for the Future

TOOR, on the other hand, was not able to put together a political force strong enough to win more than a compromise victory. A central weakness was its inability to gain widespread support in other parts of the city. Yerba Buena Center is part of an overall scheme for redeveloping the city that already has victimized thousands of people in other neighborhoods of San Francisco. The dynamics of this process are such that TOOR was isolated from related and nearby groups and struggles.

Urban redevelopment pits the poor against one another. Residents of one renewal area hoping to secure low-rent housing are forced to support projects elsewhere in the city which destroy such housing, because, in a version of the "domino theory," the system of renewal financing makes all of a city's projects mutually interdependent. "Superpriority" for admission to public housing is offered one group of displacees, but at the expense of others already on waiting lists and equally in need of decent housing. The city's leaders cynically manipulate the public by presenting it with the choice of retaining housing for the ill-housed or providing jobs for the unemployed, playing off one disadvantaged group against another—when both might be helped. (The January 31, 1972 *Examiner* editorial, for example, entitled "Attention Minorities," begins, "Jobs for at least 12,000 minority workers are at stake in Yerba Buena Center," and ends, "Tell them [Redevelopment Agency, HUD, TOOR, Mayor Alioto, Judge Weigel] enough is enough. Tell them you want those minority jobs filled. Tell them you want Yerba Buena back on the track."†)

It is clear that no single struggle can in itself bring power to those in our society who traditionally have had none. Perhaps the most important lesson from the Yerba Buena experience is that abuses against the poor and powerless, such as those perpetrated by the city's redevelopment program, cannot be fought successfully by isolated communities. Community organizations must cease competing with other disadvantaged groups for limited funds and programs and unite in a struggle to increase the amount of available funds and to change the distribution

---

of: "Thus, while the organization-class allies [the professional advocate planners] had a key role in helping Middle American citizens of Brookline and Elm Streets keep away the Inner Belt, they did so by taking over the battle and waging it on their own terms, without actively involving the neighborhood people." (p. 131)

† This editorial was placed on the *Examiner's* front page, a gambit the paper rarely uses in its weekday editions. The coda "Tell them enough is enough. Tell them you want Yerba Buena back on the track" repeated verbatim the ending to the *Examiner's* January 17, 1972 editorial (also front page). This attempt to over-kill was doubtless related to the disqualification move against Judge Weigel initiated at this same time (see pages 153-56).

A Strategy for the Future

of resources and power in our cities.

"From a perspective broader than TOOR's interests and demands, the Yerba Buena Center project illustrates the failure of what is in theory democratic, representative, responsible local government." The project was conceived by and for the men who control the economic and political life of the city, and was carried out by a public agency representing their will. This involved no large-scale secret conspiracy but was a confluence of powerful and influential people acting in their class interest. The results of this elitist decision-making process are that the costs and benefits of a project presumably designed for the public good are distributed in a highly regressive manner: those who benefit most are a small group of the economically and politically powerful, while the costs, financial and psychosocial, are borne by a far larger group of people with the fewest resources and the greatest need for government assistance. The probable costs to the larger public are minimized or ignored. Most risks are passed on to the average tax-payer. And the elected officials who promote such decisions will in all probability not be around to take responsibility for the bill.

Nowhere has there been an honest and full presentation of the pro's and con's of the project. The failure of public decision-making is perhaps best revealed in the city's use of every maneuver possible to avoid bringing the project and the bond issue it requires to a popular vote.† The Redevelopment Agency, a public body, and the City Administration were outspoken advocates of the project and, as controllers and manipulators of the information, disseminated selected statistics and misleading arguments. The federal Department of Housing and Urban Development, which theoretically supervises urban renewal funds and agencies, played absolutely no role in overseeing the validity and wisdom of the project itself; its only function, and that belated and reluctant, was to provide occasional marginal protection to persons being relocated in violation of federal law. The Board of Supervisors, presumably repository and agent of the public will, abdicated completely to the technical judgments and positions of the Redevelopment Agency. The major newspapers, future beneficiaries of the project, virtually gushed editorial support and gave the public little analysis of the underlying issues.

---

† The nearest thing to a vote on the YBC project we have found is a small public opinion poll taken in early 1973 of attendees at an exhibition of YBC plans held at the San Francisco Art Commission Gallery, across the street from City Hall. The poll was taken by a high school student who was staffing the exhibit. Of 35 persons who responded, 23 (66%) expressed negative views about YBC, while 12 (34%) expressed positive views. (See letter dated April 2, 1973, to TOOR and the San Francisco Redevelopment Agency, from Kathy Connors, Wilderness School, Daly City, and accompanying survey results.)

In sum, it was an effective "snow job" by business and planning interests. At the same time, there was no one with the resources to examine alternative ways of meeting the city's needs for jobs, public facilities and revenue, or to advocate opposition to the project itself. (The more recent efforts to challenge the legality of the project's financing plan and possibly sink YBC altogether in favor of a different use for the site are late in the game. Further, they lack any base of community support; are being undertaken without a substantial community education and organizing effort; and, ironically, pit project opponents against one another—since such efforts are now a distinct threat to TOOR's own gains, wrenched from the city after so long a struggle.)

The slow process of planning and implementing a major redevelopment project of this sort—Yerba Buena Center dates back at least to 1961, and essentially to the mid-1950s—also hinders opposition. At what point exactly the opposition should take action, and what form it should take, are difficult questions. Redevelopment plans and commitments take shape and fall into place gradually, and millions of dollars may be spent in preliminary plans and designs. TOOR's lawsuit was too late to have brought about any fundamental change in the project itself—as opposed to winning gains for relocatees. Yet it probably could not have been brought any earlier in the planning and implementation process, and by the time it was brought eight years of preparatory work had already gone into the project.

An all-important question for the future is how community groups can and will participate in and organize around forthcoming government programs for urban redevelopment. It appears likely that urban programs will be developed more and more at the local (city, county, and state) level, financed by federal revenue sharing and bloc grants to local governments. This is in line with the current Administration's move away from the approach used over the past four decades of developing programs in Washington and financing them with categorical grants (e.g., HUD's funding of specific programs such as public housing, urban renewal, rent supplements, water and sewer improvements). While this implies a fundamental shift toward decentralizing government, the YBC saga reveals clearly that real control of these programs already is at the local level. The federal government did little but supply the urban renewal funds, applying only some very general standards for how they were and were not to be used. All the basic decisions about the use of these moneys were made by the local government and private power structure.

Nor is there reason to believe revenue-sharing and bloc grants will lead to eliminating programs like urban renewal and projects like Yerba Buena Center. The many special interests that have been in-

A Strategy for the Future

volved in promoting and profiting from urban renewal locally will function no differently in the future. Under the new federal revenue-sharing legislation, cities might undertake redevelopment even more freely since they would not have to make the matching local contribution now required. One recent analysis of the probable effects of federal revenue-sharing concludes:

Local governments will shift existing redevelopment activities. . . [toward] downtown central business district redevelopment projects for the advantage of commercial interests, which will be at the expense of residents of low-income housing and owners of small businesses condemned for the project.[2]

The March 9, 1973 *New York Times* adds:

Because local officials could use the funds pretty much as they wished and the federal emphasis on the needy is no longer in force, it is considered certain that there would be a shift away from assisting the poor.

Even existing housing and relocation rights would be thrown out the window in the urban redevelopment of the future. According to the February 13, 1974 *San Francisco Progress*:

. . .Mayor [Alioto] would seek "reforms" in state and federal grant procedures to free the City from spending guidelines such as those requiring minority employment or the relocation of persons left homeless by urban renewal programs.

Such "reforms" would leave the TOOR's of the future defenseless.

As urban population increases, as land becomes increasingly scarce and more valuable, and as economic control and coordination continue to centralize, corporate interests will be willing to risk even larger conflicts to put land to the uses they want. The "urban fortress" notion underlying Yerba Buena Center and similar projects across the country—and which, indeed, is coming to shape all our major cities—may become even more pervasive, further insulating and isolating from one another within the city various groups—rich, middle-class, poor, whites and nonwhites; and uses—residential, business, tourism, and recreation.

The YBC saga showed how hard it is for the poor and powerless to enter their objections, proposals and counter-plans into the planning process. Under revenue-sharing it is likely that community groups will find participation in this process even more difficult. The current inadequate level of neighborhood participation in both the urban renewal and model cities programs came largely as a result of pressures by community groups and their advocates on the federal government, and federal guidelines and mandates were strongly resisted by local governments.[3] With city-wide allocation of federal revenue-sharing funds, few low-income community groups will be able to compete effectively with the powerful economic and political interests pushing downtown development.

It must be recognized that the chances of developing a truly just participatory planning process within the existing framework of urban power and resource distribution are highly unlikely. There is obviously something profoundly wrong with a political system under which poor people get listened to not because they have something valuable to contribute, or their cause is just, but only when, and because, they threaten trouble. But that's the way the cookie seems to crumble. And if these are to be the rules of the game, the strategy for low-income communities living on "valuable" land slated for "higher and better" uses then must be to assert a right of turf—to stand firm on their home ground, putting forth plans and demands of their own. Only if there is no other choice should they surrender their land, and then only after extracting the maximum concessions form those who want that land. This principle applies to private as well as public development, although it may be far more difficult to carry out when government is not involved. (One of the implicit and explicit threats the Redevelopment Agency made to TOOR was that it would abandon the Yerba Buena project altogether and sell off the land to private interests to do with as they wished; this would have left TOOR with no rights or bargaining powers. An illustration of their fate should this happen had already been provided in the spring of 1971 when the Shell Oil Company purchased a 100-unit hotel just west of the project area and within a few months had evicted the residents, demolished the building and constructed a shiny new filling station. A brief, ineffective protest was mounted by TOOR and others, but the residents were out, with no homes, no relocation payments, no replacement housing. And the city lost one hundred units of low-rent housing as a result of an action taken by a private corporation to increase its profits. The costs of this private sector decision were to be borne by low-income persons forced to pay higher rents in a tighter housing market, and possibly by the taxpayers in subsidies to provide needed substitute low-rent housing.†)

A "right of turf" sharply clashes with free-market notions of private property and profit maximization. An owner of private property should not have the absolute right to buy up homes and businesses and displace their occupants in his quest for profits. Legal controls should

---

† The following letter, by Howard J. DeNike, appeared in the March 1, 1974 *San Francisco Chronicle*: "As I passed by the Shell service station at the corner of Sixth and Harrison streets and observed the 'Sorry No Gasoline' sign, I recalled, this time with new poignance, the fight waged by the 96 residents of the Joyce Hotel to prevent the destruction of their home in favor of the construction of that station. I conducted a survey of the number of stations within

A Strategy for the Future

exist on his ability to evict current occupants when this action imposes serious personal and social costs. And where the owner is permitted to evict his tenants and demolish his structure, he must be required to compensate the victims and the community for whatever costs his action has imposed.†

"BLIGHT"

A right of turf also clashes with the wide latitude given government's "public purpose" eminent domain powers in the Supreme Court's seminal 1954 *Berman v. Parker* decision (348 US 26) and with the promiscuous use of these powers over the past 25 years in the name of "blight removal" and urban redevelopment. As the leading social-legal history of urban redevelopment notes, "Finding blight merely means defining a neighborhood that cannot effectively fight back, but which is either an eyesore or is well-located for some particular construction that important interests wish to build. . . . Urban renewal takes sides; it uproots and evicts some for the benefit of others."[4] Development of organized political power at the community level, not in isolation but through alliance of like struggles, is the strategy that can bring the greatest gains to poor people. In the short run, dispossession from their homes and neighborhoods and the social and financial costs of dislocation they must bear can be reduced, and in the process meaningful victories and concessions can be wrought. In the long run, unified political struggle offers the only chance for reshaping public programs so as to place first priority on meeting the needs of the poor and powerless in our cities.

Without this kind of struggle, lower income groups face a dismal future in our cities. Projects such as Yerba Buena Center and BART, and their counterparts in other cities, not only displace the poor and

———

a five-block radius of the hotel site. There were 22 stations. Five of them were Shell stations, including one in the same block as the Joyce.

"I still see several of the old-timers who lived in the Joyce when I am walking downtown. Many of these people lived in that 'hotel' for years and years, several for more than 40. I am prompted to wonder what their feeling is when they see the Joyce's corner closed down tight. I dare say it is something more basic than a sense of irony."

†There are a few scattered examples of attempts to regulate displacement by private property owners. In April, 1973, the voters of Berkeley, California, passed a Neighborhood Preservation Ordinance which requires that private developers provide alternate housing for residents as a condition to obtaining a demolition permit (Ord. No. 4641). And under New York City's rent control ordinance, an owner who wishes to demolish his building or renovate it must pay displacement "bonuses" to any households thereby evicted. These bonuses, which vary according to the size of the dwelling unit, run as high as $750. Under some circumstances the owner may be compelled to pay his former tenant a rent supplement, to cover the gap between what the tenant was paying and his new rent, for 2-3 years.

fail to meet their needs; they squeeze the poor and middle-class alike economically, by placing on them the burden of paying for these projects, through sales taxes and property taxes (passed on to renters as well as owners), the two most regressive levies of all. The high and open-ended costs of these developments, if they do not bankrupt the cities themselves, will in any case drive moderate-income families out of the city. And they will further oppress the urban poor and may make of them a permanent underclass supporting a city that exists primarily to serve those who do not live there.

Ira Nowinski

Footnotes

Proposed YBC Sports Arena

SFRA

Chapter One

[1] BART Impact Studies Final Report Series, Part II, Vol. IV (Institute of Urban and Regional Development, University of California, Berkeley, June 29, 1973), p. 1.

[2] Wells Fargo Bank, N. A., Branch Expansion Department, *San Francisco, Central Business District: A Growth Study*, February, 1970, p. 22.

[3] Quoted in Paul Rupert, "Corporate Feast in the Pacific," *Pacific Research and World Empire Telegram*, Vol. I, No. 4, January-February-March, 1970. p. 3.

[4] *San Francisco 1970 Population Characteristics*, prepared by the San Francisco Department of City Planning, April, 1973, Table 11.

[5] See "Yerba Buena Center Public Facilities and Private Development, Environmental Impact Report" (draft), submitted to the City and County of San Francisco (Arthur D. Little, Inc. and URS Research Company, May, 1973), Table A-14 and Figure A-2.

[6] See, in general, Bruce Brugmann and Greggar Sletteland (eds.), *The Ultimate Highrise: San Francisco's Mad Rush Toward the Sky . . .* (San Francisco: San Francisco Bay Guardian Books, 1971).

[7] Burton H. Wolfe, "Must San Francisco Choke Itself to Death?", *San Francisco Bay Guardian*. June 18, 1968.

[8] See Les Shipnuck and Dan Feshbach, "Bay Area Council: Regional Powerhouse," *Pacific Research and World Empire Telegram*, Vol. IV, No. 1 (November-December, 1972), pp. 3-11.

[9] Quoted in Danny Beagle, Al Haber, and David Wellman, "Turf Power and the Tax Man," *Leviathan*, Vol. I, No. 2, April, 1969, p. 28.

[10] The Bay Area Council's rise in relation to penetration of the Pacific region is covered in a special study of the giant Bechtel Corporation. See Burton H. Wolfe, "BART—Steve Bechtel's $2 Billion Toy," *San Francisco Bay Guardian*, Vol. 7, No. 8, through February 14, 1973.

[11] R. A. Sundeen, "The San Francisco Bay Area Council: An Analysis of Non-Governmental Metropolitan Organization," masters thesis, University of California, Berkeley, 1963.

[12] *San Francisco News*, May 18, 1956.

[13] "Financiers Set on Redevelopment," *San Francisco Examiner*, January 18, 1957.

Footnotes

[14] "How Business Spurs a City's Revival," *Business Week*, September 9, 1961, pp. 87-92.

[15] *San Francisco Chronicle*, April 30, 1959.

[16] A privately printed biography, produced for his 75th birthday, is the source of much information on Swig's personal and financial history. See Walter Blum, *Benjamin H. Swig: The Measure of a Man* (San Francisco: 1968, Library of Congress Catalogue Card No. 68-57033).

[17] Marsha Berzon, "Yerba Buena: A case study in how SF Development went wrong—too little planning, too much Swig/SPUR/downtown muscle, no community participation, all edifice complex", *San Francisco Bay Guardian*, April 17, 1970.

[18] *San Francisco Examiner*, October 12, 1955.

[19] *San Francisco Chronicle*, October 25, 1955.

[20] Dick Nolan, "Showdown Nearing on the Swig Plan," *San Francisco Examiner*, November 27, 1955.

[21] *San Francisco Chronicle*, March 14, 1956.

Chapter Two

[1] Frederick M. Wirt, *Power in the City: Decision Making in San Francisco* (Berkeley and Los Angeles: University of California Press, forthcoming), p. 11.31 (page reference to draft copy).

[2] George Dorsey, *Christopher of San Francisco* (New York: Macmillan Co., 1962), p. 230.

[3] Alan Temko, "San Francisco Rebuilds Again," *Harpers Magazine*, April, 1960, p. 53.

[4] *San Francisco Examiner*, April 26 and April 27, 1956.

[5] See Nathaniel Lichfield, "Relocation: The Impact on Housing Welfare," *Journal of the American Institute of Planners*, August, 1961, pp. 199-203.

[6] For portraits of the few figures in the urban renewal game who rivaled Herman, see Jeanne Lowe, *Cities in a Race with Time* (New York: Random House, 1967), Ch. 2, "The Man Who Got Things Done for New York", pp. 45-109 (on Robert Moses); and Richard Schickel, "New York's Mr. Urban Renewal," *New York Times Magazine*, March 1, 1970 (on Edward Logue). See also Jewel Bellush and Murray Hausknecht, "Entrepreneurs and Urban Renewal: The New Men of Power," in Bellush and Hausknecht (eds.) *Urban Renewal: People, Politics and Planning* (New York: Doubleday, 1967), pp. 289-297. Further description of Herman may be found in William Lilley III, "Herman Death Ends an Era," *National Journal*, September 18, 1971, p. 1939.

[7] Dorothea Katzenstein, "Tom Mellon's 'Trickle Down' Policy," *San Francisco Bay Area Guardian*, July 5, 1972.

[8] *San Francisco Chronicle*, January 18, 1962.

[9] "Yerba Buena Center Public Facilities and Private Development," Environmental Impact Report (draft), submitted to the City and County of San Francisco (Arthur D. Little, Inc. and URS Research Company, May, 1973), Table A-48.

[10] "San Francisco's Empty Rooms," *Business Week*, March 17, 1973.

[11] *San Francisco Progress*, August 11, 1971.

[12] Interview quoted in John Emshwiller, "Yerba Buena: A New Colossus for San Francisco," paper submitted to Political Science 109 and Social Science 100BC, University of California, Berkeley, Spring, 1972.

[13] See "Shelley Not Happy with RA 'Dynasty'," *San Francisco Examiner*, September 15, 1966.

[14] *San Francisco Examiner*, September 8, 1967.

[15] *San Francisco Chronicle*, September 12, 1967.

[16] See, for example, the unpublished but widely circulated study by Francis Fury and Andrew Moss, *Moving Out the People* (San Francisco, 1970).

[17] *San Francisco Examiner*, September 9, 1967.

[18] Dick Nolan, "Showdown Nearing on the Swig Plan," *San Francisco Examiner*, November 27, 1955.

[19] Norman Melnick, "Alioto—Key Figure in the Arena," *San Francisco Examiner*, September 8, 1967.

[20] *San Francisco Examiner*, September 10, 1967.

[21] Frederick M. Wirt, *op. cit.* pp. 7.21-22 (page reference to draft copy.)

[22] *San Francisco Chronicle*, January 4, 1968.

[23] Quoted in *Wall Street Journal*, May 27, 1970.

[24] See Meister's lengthy and informative essay, "Labor Power," *San Francisco Bay Area Guardian*, December 23, 1970.

[25] Interview quoted in John Emshwiller, *op. cit.*, note 12, this chapter.

[26] For a critique of both papers and the Bay Area press in general, see William L. Rivers and David M. Rubin, *A Region's Press: Anatomy of Newspapers in the San Francisco Bay Area* (University of California, Berkeley, Institute of Governmental Studies, 1971).

[27] "'May God Punish You'—Threats to Skid Row Holdout," *San Francisco Chronicle*, May 19, 1971.

Chapter Three

[1] Quotes from Marsha Berzon, "Yerba Buena: A case study in how SF Development went wrong—too little planning, too much Swig/SPUR/ downtown muscle, no community participation, all edifice complex", *San Francisco Bay Guardian*, April 17, 1970, and interview quoted in John Emshwiller, "Yerba Buena: A New Colossus for San Francisco," paper submitted to Political Science 109 and Social Science 100BC, University of California, Berkeley, Spring, 1972.

[2] See "A War of Agencies: Planners v. Redevelopers," *San Francisco Examiner*, June 25, 1965.

[3] *San Francisco Chronicle*, December 3, 1965.

[4] See Marsha Berzon, "Redevelopment: Bulldozers for the Poor, Welfare for the Rich," *San Francisco Bay Guardian*, April 17, 1970.

[5] *San Francisco Chronicle*, August 25, 1965.

[6] "Yerba Buena Center Public Facilities and Private Development," Environmental Impact Report (draft), submitted to the City and County of San Francisco (Arthur D. Little, Inc. and URS Research Company, May, 1973), Table A-4.

[7] See *San Francisco Chronicle*, February 11, 1966.

Footnotes

[8] See, for example, Real Estate Research Corporation, *Land Utilization and Marketability Study* (Los Angeles, 1965: prepared for the San Francisco Redevelopment Agency); Roy Wenzlick & Co., *Land Utilization and Market Analysis* (St. Louis, 1963: prepared for the San Francisco Redevelopment Agency); Economic Research Associates, *Economic Performance of Public Facilities in Yerba Buena Center* (Los Angeles, February 9, 1970: prepared for the San Francisco Redevelopment Agency).

[9] For accounts of the manipulation of consultants' reports by public bodies seeking to construct stadium complexes, see Charles G. Burck, "It's Promoters vs. Taxpayers in the Superstadium Game," *Fortune*, March 1973, pp. 104-107, 178-182.

[10] For a general description of the Supervisors, their financial support, and their links to the business community, see data compiled in Bruce B. Brugmann and Greggar Sletteland (eds.), *The Ultimate Highrise: San Francisco's Mad Rush Toward the Sky* . . . (San Francisco: San Francisco Guardian Books, 1971), pp. 72-80.

[11] For a detailed discussion of HUD's role in YBC, see Richard LeGates, "Ca the Federal Welfare Bureaucracies Control Their Programs: The Case of HUD and Urban Renewal," *Urban Lawyer*, Spring, 1973, pp. 228-263.

[12] Blair Paltridge, "Yerba Buena redevelopment: Relocation without representation," *San Francisco Bay Guardian*, December 16, 1969.

[13] See also January 30, 1966 *Examiner* for statement by Robert Rumsey, the Agency's assistant director, that the plan for a convention center and arena will require a city bond issue.

[14] Leon E. Hickman, "Alcoa Looks at Urban Redevelopment," in J. Bellush and M. Hausknecht (eds.), *Urban Renewal: People, Politics and Planning* (New York: Doubleday Anchor, 1967), p. 270.

[16] *Duskin v. Alioto et al.*, Superior Court of the State of California for the City and County of San Francisco, No. 641-688, February 23, 1973, Defendant San Francisco Redevelopment Agency's Answers and Objections to Fourth Set of Interrogatories.

[17] See "Del Monte Gives Up on Yerba Buena," *San Francisco Chronicle*, August 9, 1973.

[18] *San Francisco Examiner*, January 4, 1966.

[19] See *San Francisco Chronicle* and *San Francisco Examiner*, December 29, 1965.

Chapter Four

[1] A more complete historical sketch of the South of Market area, from which this section was drawn, is provided in Alvin Averbach, "San Francisco's South of Market District, 1858-1958: The Emergence of a Skid Row," *California Historical Quarterly*, Fall, 1973, pp. 197-223. The interviews and written sources on which this historical overview is based are provided therein.

[2] "South of Market Turmoil: Rumors and Redevelopment Agency," *San Francisco Examiner*, September 15, 1965.

[3] See, for example, the editorial in the June 11, 1971 *Examiner*, "Just Who Lives in Yerba Buena?", quoted at page 71.

[4] "Relocation Survey Report: South of Market Redevelopment Project," prepared for San Francisco Redevelopment Agency, December, 1963 (San Francisco: E. M. Schaffran and Co.), Table 12, "Highlights."

[5] Relocation Survey Report," *op. cit.*, Appendix Table 7.

[6] This estimate was made by Supervisor Roger Boas. See *San Francisco Chronicle*, March 2, 1971.

[7] San Francisco Department of City Planning, *Issues in Housing, Housing Report II,* (July, 1969), p. 26.

[8] The reasoning and methodology underlying the "turnover game" are to be found in their highest form in the "Relocation Survey Report, Prepared for the San Francisco Redevelopment Agency" (San Francisco: E. M. Schaffran and Co., August, 1967).

[9] See "The Shame of San Francisco: An Analysis of San Francisco's Housing Crisis and Defects of San Francisco's Proposed 'Workable Program for Community Improvement,' " prepared by Citizens' Emergency Task for a Workable Housing Policy (n.d. [1969]).

[10] See the story on the Carmel Hotel (mistakenly identified as the "Carlton Hotel") in "Displaced Persons Face Hardships," *San Francisco Argonaut*, March 2, 1968.

[11] See "U. S. Blasts Hasty S. F. Slum Ax," *San Francisco Chronicle*, September 28, 1967.

[12] Affidavit of Peter Bender, filed in *TOOR v. HUD* in support of a motion for a temporary restraining order, November 23, 1969.

[13] Exhibit submitted in support of plaintiffs' successful motion for temporary restraining order against interfering with attorney-client relationship; motion heard in December, 1969, before federal Judge Stanley A. Weigel.

[14] See "Redevelopment Agency Hotels: They Talk of Beatings," *San Francisco Chronicle*, April 14, 1970.

[15] See *San Francisco Examiner*, October 6, 1970.

[16] See "Renewal Agency Gets a Talking To," *San Francisco Chronicle*, March 6, 1970.

[17] See "Furor in Pensioner's Hotel Slaying: Renewal Agency Security Issue," *San Francisco Chronicle*, December 16, 1970.

[18] "South O' Market Renewal Makes Little People Unhappy" (last of three-part series), *San Francisco Examiner*, September 18, 1965.

[19] See Carol Kroot, "George Woolf, 1889-1972," *San Francisco Bay Area Guardian*, July 5, 1972.

[20] See *San Francisco Examiner*, June 19, 1970.

[21] *San Francisco Progress*, September 1, 1972.

[22] See *San Francisco Chronicle*, March 7, 1973. (The Transbay terminal project has subsequently been abandoned, but may be revived.)

[23] "Yerba Buena Center Public Facilities and Private Development: Environmental Impact Report" (draft), submitted to the City and County of San Francisco (Arthur D. Little, Inc. and URS Research Company, May, 1973), p. S-21.

[24] See "Parks' to lure industry here," *San Francisco Progress*, June 22, 1973.

[25] See *San Francisco Chronicle*, March 31, 1972, and *San Francisco Progress*, February 25, 1972.

Footnotes

[26] Report to Court, by US Dept. of HUD, *TOOR v. HUD*, No. C-69 324 (N. D. Cal., filed August 24, 1971).

[27] On the importance of these local ties, see Marc Fried, "Grieving for a Lost Home" in Leonard Duhl (ed.) *The Urban Condition* (New York: Basic Books, 1963), pp. 151-172; and Marc Fried et al., *The World of the Urban Working Class* (Cambridge, Mass.: Harvard University Press, 1973).

[28] *San Francisco Chronicle*, February 23, 1972.

[29] *San Francisco Chronicle*, February 25, 1972.

Chapter Five

[1] Housing Act of 1949, Ch. 338, s. 105, as amended (see note to p. 98).

[2] See *Western Addition Community Organization v. Weaver*, 294 F. Supp. 433 (1968).

[3] For a review of judicial supervision of the urban renewal program before and after the WACO case, see Chester W. Hartman, "Relocation: Illusory Promises and No Relief," 57 *Virginia Law Review* (1971) at pp. 756-69.

[4] The general state of the San Francisco housing market was well analyzed in a 1969 publication by the Citizens Emergency Task Force for a Workable Housing Policy, entitled "The Shame of San Francisco: An Analysis of San Francisco's Housing Crisis and Defects of San Francisco's Proposed 'Workable Program for Community Improvement.' "

[5] See "Renewal Agency Gets a Talking To," *San Francisco Chronicle*, March 6, 1970.

[6] *Concerning the Court's Decision on Pending Motions*, statement accompanying *Findings and Conclusions on Motion for Preliminary Injunction; Orders on Motions for Dismissal and Summary Judgment*, No. C-69 324 (N. D. Cal. April 29, 1970).

[7] According to TOOR attorney Amanda Hawes, who took notes at this session.

[8] See G. William Domhoff, *Bohemian Grove and Other Retreats: A Study in Ruling Class Cohesiveness* (New York: Harper and Row, 1974).

[9] "Judge Voices Misgivings on Yerba Buena Housing", *San Francisco Examiner*, August 19, 1970.

[10] For a good discussion of these issues, see Gordon Fellman, in association with Barbara Brandt, *The Deceived Majority: Politics and Protest in Middle America* (New Brunswick, N. J.: Transaction Books, 1973). A parallel account of the conflicts between Legal Services attorneys and the community is contained in Harry Brill, *Why Organizers Fail: The Story of a Rent Strike* (Berkeley and Los Angeles: University of California Press, 1971), pp. 112-139. A general description of the practice of "poverty law" and its legal-social context may be found in Stephen Wexler, "Practicing Law for Poor People", 79 *Yale Law Journal*, May, 1970, pp. 1049-1067.

[11] *San Francisco Chronicle*, November 6, 1969.

[12] *San Francisco Examiner*, May 28, 1971.

[13] Interview reported in John Emshwiller, "Yerba Buena: A New Colossus for San Francisco", paper submitted to Political Science 109 and Social Science 100BC, University of California, Berkeley, Spring, 1972.

[14] *San Francisco Chronicle*, June 22, 1971.

[15] Report to the Court, by U. S. Dept. of HUD, *TOOR v. HUD*, No. C-69 324 (N. D. Cal., filed August 24, 1971).

[16] *San Francisco Chronicle*, August 25, 1971.

[17] Letter dated August 30, 1972, from James P. Jaquet, Program Manager, San Francisco Area Office of HUD, to Robert Rumsey, Executive Director, SFRA.

[18] Quoted in Herb Caen's column, *San Francisco Chronicle*, July 23, 1972.

[19] See *San Francisco Chronicle*, September 6, 1972.

[20] See "Weigel Told of 'Political Pressure' in Yerba Buena," *San Francisco Examiner*, October 18, 1972, and "New Yerba Buena Attack", *San Francisco Chronicle*, October 19, 1972.

[21] Memorandum and Order, *TOOR v. HUD*, No. C-69 324 SAW (N. D. Cal. July 11, 1972).

[22] See draft copy of the Arthur D. Little environmental impact study of Yerba Buena Center cited in the note to page 117, Part E, "Social and Displacement/Relocation Impacts," Table E-5.

[23] *San Francisco Chronicle*, February 29, 1972.

[24] *San Francisco Examiner*, November 3, 1971.

[25] Letter in January 31, 1972 *San Francisco Chronicle* from Kenneth F. Phillips, Director, National Housing and Economic Development Law Project, University of California, Berkeley.

[26] *San Francisco Chronicle*, July 4, 1972.

[27] *San Francisco Chronicle*, March 18, 1972.

[28] "Redeveloper Accuses Judge Weigel of Bias," *San Francisco Examiner*, January 12, 1972.

[29] *San Francisco Chronicle*, February 9, 1972, and *San Francisco Examiner*, February 8, 1972, and 338 F. Supp. 29 (1972).

[30] Letter from B. E. Bergesen, III and Kenneth Hecht, Youth Law Center and Employment Law Center, San Francisco. An edited version of their letter appeared in the January 27, 1972 *Examiner*.

[31] A draft version of this report, sent out to interested persons for review and comment, became available just as this book was going to press; it is titled "Draft Environmental Impact Statement for Yerba Buena Center Redevelopment Area, Project No. Calif. R-59," prepared by the Department of Housing and Urban Development, Region IX.

Chapter Six

[1] "Yerba Buena Center Public Facilities" (see note to page 161), Exhibit 1, "Financing Agreement," p. 9. Cost and revenue figures for YBC in the following pages are from this same source.

[2] "City Fund Use and Yerba Buena," *San Francisco Chronicle*, January 10, 1974.

[3] Letter from Gerald A. Wright, *op. cit.* note to page 163.

[4] Letter from Gerald A. Wright. *op. cit.*

[5] "Yerba Buena Center Public Facilities," *op. cit.*, Exhibit VI, Summary Table.

[6] For a general description of the economic effects of downtown development in San Francisco, see Bruce Brugmann and Greggar Sletteland (eds.), *The*

Footnotes

Ultimate Highrise: San Francisco's Mad Rush Toward the Sky. . . (San Francisco: San Francisco Bay Guardian Books, 1971), pp. 30-63, 217-222. A computation of the costs that private automobiles impose on the city is to be found in Douglas B. Lee, Jr., "The Costs of Private Auto Usage to the City of San Francisco" (Institute of Urban and Regional Development, University of California, Berkeley, April, 1972). The "definitive" study on the costs and benefits of highrise construction in San Francisco is currently being undertaken via a $200,000 HUD grant awarded to none other than SPUR.

[7] Tax Collector, City of San Francisco, "1973-1974 Important Tax Information".

[8] Letter from Gerald A. Wright, *op. cit.*

[9] Lee Wakefield, "Supervisors vote tax help for Yerba Buena," *San Francisco Progress*, January 18, 1974.

[10] Charles G. Burck, "It's Promoters vs. Taxpayers in the Superstadium Game," *Fortune*, March, 1973, pp. 104-107, 178-182.

[11] The Arthur D. Little report cited in the following footnote makes this point, too (at p. v), but may exaggerate how much of the future office demand YBC will absorb.

[12] Arthur D. Little, Inc. and URS Research Company, "Yerba Buena Center Public Facilities and Private Development, Environmental Impact Report" (draft), submitted to the City and County of San Francisco (May, 1973), p. V-B-27.

[13] Jack Miller, "Boom Forces Bargains in S. F. Office Rentals," *San Francisco Sunday Examiner & Chronicle*, December 3, 1972.

[14] The method of tax loss calculation is adopted from Edward J. Ford, Jr., "Benefit-Cost Analysis and Urban Renewal in the West End of Boston," unpublished doctoral dissertation, Graduate Program in Economics, Boston College, 1971.

[15] Arthur D. Little, *op. cit.*, p. V-A-80.

[16] Development Research Associates, *Transient Housing Study* (1970), prepared for the San Francisco Redevelopment Agency.

[17] Arthur D. Little, *op. cit.*, p. III-4.

[18] Economic Research Associates, "A Summary of the Economic Performance of Public Facilities in Yerba Buena Center," (1965), prepared for the Redevelopment Agency of the City and County of San Francisco.

[19] Arthur D. Little, *op. cit.*, p. V-A-81.

[20] "What Should We Ask Ourselves Regarding the Convention Center" (mimeo), remarks by Howard G. Sloane, Managing Director, N. Y. Coliseum, n. d. (1973). Sloane of course does not wish to have a competitive facility built, but he is one of the few convention insiders who will talk candidly about the facts and fictions of convention business.

[21] "S. F. Told of Lost Conventions," *San Francisco Chronicle*, September 11, 1973.

[22] Arthur D. Little, *op. cit.*, Tables A-42, A-43.

[23] For a good treatment of the dynamics and effects of intercity competition in the world of professional sports, see S. Prakash Sethi, *Up Against the Corporate Wall* (Englewood Cliffs, New Jersey: Prentice-Hall, 1971), "Corporate Decisions and Their Effects on Urban Communities—The Milwaukee Braves, Atlanta: Indiscriminate Moving of Sports Franchises," pp. 267-280.

[24] Reported in an interview with Robert Sullivan, General Manager, San Francisco Convention and Visitors Bureau.

[25] "S. F. Told of Lost Conventions," *San Francisco Chronicle*, September 11, 1973.

[26] See also "A 'Threat' to S. F. Tourism," *San Francisco Chronicle*, November 20, 1973, for remarks by Robert Sullivan, General Manager of the Convention and Visitors Bureau, regarding the impact of the energy crisis on the city.

[27] *San Francisco Examiner*, May 27, 1971.

[28] See H. H. Oestreich and D. J. Wassenaar, *San Francisco Convention and Visitor Study*, Part I (California State University, San Jose: Institute for Business and Economic Research, May, 1971).

[29] Marybeth Branaman, *South of Market Commercial and Industrial Survey* (San Francisco Redevelopment Agency, July, 1963), p. 6.

[30] Arthur D. Little, *op. cit.*, Table A-61 and p. v.

[31] *Ibid.*, Table A-65.

[32] *Ibid.*, Table A-5.

[33] Wells Fargo Bank, *San Francisco Business District: A Growth Study*, February, 1970, p. 11, Table I.

[34] See *San Francisco Chronicle*, March 30, 1973.

[35] See *James Gay et al. v. Waiters' and Dairy Lunchmen's Union, Local No. 30 et al.* (Civil Action No. C-73-0489 SC, March 28, 1973).

[36] *Redevelopment Plan for Yerba Buena Project Area D-1*, San Francisco Redevelopment Agency, December, 1965.

[37] See Marjorie Heins, *Strictly Ghetto Property* (Berkeley: Ramparts Press, 1972), pp. 73-84; and Kathy Treffinger, Jim Shoch and Dan Feshbach, "BART in the Mission: If High Rents Don't Get You The Bulldozers Will", *Common Sense*, vol. 1, no. 4, January 15, 1974.

[38] *Redevelopment Plan for Yerba Buena Project Area D-1*, *op. cit.*

[39] Arthur D. Little, *op. cit.* These words were among those deleted from the final draft (see note to page 116).

[40] See Marc Fried, "Grieving for a Lost Home" in Leonard Duhl (ed.), *The Urban Condition* (New York: Basic Books, 1963), pp. 151-172.

[41] Anthony Downs, *Urban Problems and Prospects* (Chicago: Markham, 1971), p. 223.

Chapter Seven

[1] *San Francisco Chronicle*, April 29, 1971.

[2] William Lilley, III, "Herman Death Ends An Era," *National Journal*, September 18, 1971.

[3] *San Francisco Chronicle*, December 4, 1971.

[4] See *San Francisco Chronicle*, March 7 and 8, 1973.

[5] See Peter E. Sitkin and J. Anthony Kline, "Financing Public Interest Litigation", 13 *Arizona Law Review* (1971), pp. 823-827.

[6] *San Francisco Examiner*, May 15, 1973.

Footnotes

Chapter Eight

¹ See, for example, "Sorry, It's Just Been Rented: Twelve Cases of Discrimination in San Francisco" (Human Rights Commission of San Francisco, June, 1973). Four of the case examples offered by the Human Rights Commission involve discrimination in downtown residential clubs, hotels, or furnished apartments.

²Richard T. LeGates and Mary C. Morgan, "The Perils of Special Revenue Sharing for Community Development," *Journal of the American Institute of Planners*, July, 1973, pp. 254-264.

³ *Ibid.* See also Sherry Arnstein, "A Ladder of Citizen Participation," *Journal of the American Institute of Planners*, July, 1969, p. 216.

⁴Lawrence M. Friedman, *Government and Slum Housing* (Chicago: Rand McNally and Co., 1968), pp. 159, 166.

Index

Current Situation

Bond delay due to less risk. All EIR will be approv
no danger of suits. Interest rate will be les
Get bids in for total plan & no total cost.

Ground breaking

Construction —